Women in Nigeria Today

These proceedings were prepared for publication by
the Editorial Committee Women in Nigeria:

S. Bappa
J. Ibrahim
A.M. Imam
F.J.A. Kamara
H. Mahdi
M.A. Modibbo
A.S. Mohammed
H. Mohammed
A.R. Mustapha
N. Perchonock
R.I. Pittin

Editorial Consultant:

D.L. Badejo

Cover Concept:

A.M. Imam
H. Mohammed
N. Perchonock
R.I. Pittin

Women in Nigeria Today

Zed Books Ltd.

Women in Nigeria Today was first published by Zed Books
Ltd., 57 Caledonian Road, London N1 9BU, in 1985.

Cover designed by Andrew Corbett.
Cover symbol by Tyrone Geter.

Printed by The Bath Press, Avon.

British Library Cataloguing in Publication Data

Women in Nigeria today.
   1. Women — Nigeria — Social conditions
   I. Women in Nigeria
   305.4'2'09669   HQ1815.5
   ISBN 0-86232-447-5 ✓
   ISBN 0-86232-448-3 Pbk

US Distributor
Biblio Distribution Center, 81 Adams Drive,
Totowa, New Jersey 07512

Contents

Tables

Introduction

Genesis of the Seminar

The papers in this book comprise the proceedings of the first seminar on Women in Nigeria, held at Ahmadu Bello University, Zaria, on 27-28 May 1982. The initiative for the seminar arose from an on-going, somewhat acrimonious, debate among colleagues in the Faculty of Arts and Social Sciences at ABU on the nature of women's oppression. One side contended that women's oppression was an aspect of, and subordinate to, the issue of class oppression. Once class oppression disappeared, women's oppression would automatically be resolved. The other position held that oppression of women could not be reduced to class oppression, although the two forms of oppression interact to define the position of women in society. The struggle against women's oppression should be conducted in alliance with the struggle against class oppression, but at the same time, the particular ways in which women were oppressed need to be recognized and dealt with in specific ways.

As a result of this debate, and its important implications, it was decided to hold a seminar to discuss these issues more thoroughly and systematically. Participants came from all over Nigeria, and were drawn from teaching, the mass media, medical and other professions as well as students, housewives, and other interested individuals. One hundred and twenty participants registered, although actual attendance was much higher. Of this number, 75% were women, although men too made useful contributions. In fact, the positions taken on the various issues did not reflect sex lines — all sides of the argument had both men and women supporters.

The seminar consisted of two days of intensive discussion; there were eight sessions, during which twenty-five papers were presented. Discussions continued informally between sessions, during meal breaks, and in the evenings, often lasting into the early hours of the morning. By the end of the seminar, participants agreed that they had spent an exhausting but exhilarating time.

Problems of Terminology

One problem that arose early in the seminar discussions was the ambiguity in the usage of various terms and concepts among the participants. For instance, the phrase "working-class women" (or "working women", "women workers"), as used by many of the participants, reflects everyday Nigerian usage, which differs from the way the term is used elsewhere. In Nigerian usage (and particularly in the mass media), the term "working-class women" refers to women holding salaried employment, especially in white-collar occupations — eg. salesgirls, nurses, clerks, secretaries and civil servants, but also including lawyers, doctors, university lecturers, and senior civil servants. This usage, widespread as it is, nevertheless has the effect of blurring class distinctions. The seminar thus found it necessary to clarify in specific contexts exactly what "working class" referred to — either the popular notion as expressed above, or a more precise definition which distinguishes between workers (such as secretaries, clerks, saleswomen, nurses, etc) whose labour is exploited by others, and those (such as senior civil servants, big contractors, lawyers, etc) who are themselves in a position to exploit labour.

Perhaps the most confusing terminological problem arising in the seminar was the distinction between *sex* and *gender*. In the course of discussion, it was explained that sex refers to biological, physical characteristics of male and female. *Gender,* on the other hand, is the socially defined capacities and attributes assigned to persons on the basis of their alleged sexual characteristics. *Gender* is a *social* not a biological category. Thus, for example, in some cultures farming is men's work, and is associated with masculinity; in others, it is done by women, and has feminine connotations.

At the seminar, one commentator heatedly expressed the idea that women are emotional (and hysterical), while men are rational. This is a typical example of social stereotyping according to gender. However, this particular individual seemingly disproved his own thesis by violently storming out of the room to the amusement of the other participants.

What is crucial in the sex/gender distinction is that we must always differentiate between the actual biological differences between men and women (such as the differences in reproductive capacity), and the socially-defined roles ascribed to men and women supposedly on the basis of these differences. As one participant noted, it is not breasts or vaginas that women use to wash dishes or clean the house — these roles are assigned to women by society, not by biology.

Views on the Question of the Position of Women

Four major ways of understanding the position of women in Nigeria emerged in the presentation of papers and discussion during the conference. One position which was brought up during the discussion was the idea that women have different capacities from men. The structural position of women in society is a reflection of these different biological attributes, and does not constitute the subordination of women to men. Most of the participants, however, were opposed to this. Several papers illustrated specific instances of women's oppression. Bukola Aluko and Mary Alfa's paper, for instance, illustrated the fact that even where both husband and wife engage in work outside the home, women are responsible for all work within the home, thus carrying a double workload. Aluko and Alfa, as well as Norma Perchonock, pointed out the unequal nature of women's rights of inheritance, especially with regard to land (most important in a predominantly agricultural country like Nigeria).

After agreeing that an examination of women's position in Nigeria demonstrates their subordination, the seminar moved to explanations of this situation. Aluko and Alfa argue that "the exploitation of women is not a class phenomenon but a gender phenomenon...subjugation and exploitation is gender based", since all women are defined by their roles in reproduction and have to take responsibility for domestic work — cooking, cleaning and childcare. Similarly, Therese Nweke refers to women as a colonized group. She remarks that

> colonial situations are generally marked by a number of variables, such as the majority group being regarded as the minority, the colonized having no say in the decision-making process, their forming a cheap pool of labour, and the visible, normally physical, sign of differences between the colonizers and the colonized. This differentiation forms the basis for discrimination, segregation, and humiliation.

She illustrates how all of these points can be applied to the situation of women. Thus, for example, in the common use of the dismissive phrase..

> "she's only a woman", the idea is to humour, to tolerate, and not to take seriously, not to behave as if both parties have equal rights, since one is (seen as) inherently inferior.

She argues, therefore, that for women, position and status are irrelevancies and class lines are blurred.

This approach was characterized in another paper, however, as falling into "vagueness and wanton generalization". Sule Bello sees women as being oppressed and exploited only as members of their historical social class. He points out that women clearly had, and continue to have,

3

different class interests. Thus,

> if we take a look at the history of Borno, Benin and Zaria, we see that at
> certain times women occupied high, if not the highest, positions as
> members of the dominant classes. Yet women in the lower classes, together
> with other members, resolutely opposed and overthrew them.

He argues therefore that feminism "obscures the essential struggle"
and is a "petit-bourgeois" movement which results from "the psycho-
social problems of certain classes of women". Rather than espousing
feminist positions, he felt that women should concern themselves solely
with class struggle.

The majority of the seminar's participants saw both these approaches
as inadequate to a full understanding of women's position, and
presented evidence that both gender subordination and class oppression
work to define women's situations. Both Ayesha Imam and Bene
Madunagu consider the experience of socialist countries, where the
ending of capitalist class relations has not necessarily meant the ending
of women's subordination.

Several papers consider the ways in which class exploitation differentially affects men and women. Norma Perchonock shows how the
same political authorities deprive peasant men and women of land in
Kaduna State, but that peasant women are exploited both qualitatively
more, and in a qualitatively different way — often by male members of
their own families. A.B. Zack-Williams, looking at women labourers in
the construction industry in Jos, concluded that they play an important
role in petit-bourgeois accumulation in Nigeria, relatively more than
men in similar positions, because the socially inferior position of women
makes it possible for their employers to pay them even lower wages than
male workers.

Caroline Knowles' paper pointed out that women's position cannot be
"read off", or deduced from class relations. Her study of an agricultural
development project in Borno State showed that while peasant farmers
as a category were being excluded from the control of production,
women were even further marginalized by being considered simply as
extensions of (male) farmers, despite the fact that they play a significant
part in the local economy through participation in the agricultural
labour force.

'Molara Ogundipe-Leslie points out that Nigeria is a third world,
neo-colonial nation and that "the reactions of the women differ from
class to class". Nonetheless, she goes on to note that certain features of
Nigerian society apply to all women irrespective of class such as the
insecurity of polygynous marriage, the social compulsion to have
children, the denial of safe, legal contraceptives and abortion, the load
of domestic work, and so on. As Hauwa Sani Dangogo put it, while the
system of class relations, of the masses as opposed to the bourgeoisie, is an

appropriate way of classifying our society, I find it difficult to identify with the view, and see the subjugation or exploitation of women in this country, and in the world as a whole, as the handiwork of people bent on fuelling class divisions.

To sum up, the four positions presented are as follows: The first was that women's and men's biological differences are reflected in the organization of society, and thus society treats women as subordinate to men. Second, that all women are oppressed because they are women. Third, that women are oppressed, but not all women, only those who are members of oppressed classes. And finally, that women are oppressed both as members of subordinate classes and as members of a socially inferior gender group. The majority of participants agreed that the last position was most appropriate to the understanding of women's positions in Nigeria, ie, that class exploitation and gender subordination interact with each other to define women's position.

Women's Liberation in Nigeria

The women's liberation movement as it has emerged in Western society, and as it has been presented in the Nigerian media, seems to be concerned mainly with the problems of educated, middle class and elite women, as Elizabeth Obadina points out in her paper. In the Western world, women's liberation has been organized around primarily legalistic issues (equal pay for equal work, equality of job opportunities for men and women, etc), or the question of the division of labour in the family, especially who is going to do the housework. While these concerns are important for all women, and pertinent to the condition of women in Nigeria, some other strands of the Western women's liberation movement are less so. For instance, as Obadina notes, the most vocal section of the Western movement, the radical feminists,

> focus increasingly on female sexuality and female separateness. Most of the women who organize themselves in the mainstream Women's Liberation Movement in the West seek to live quite apart from men, seeking emotional, sexual and domestic satisfaction from other women.

But even the legalistic and economic concerns of the Western women's movement seem to be lost on the Nigerian mass media, who tend, in their presentation of women's issues, to emphasize the exotic or frivolous issues at the expense of the substantial ones. In the Nigerian media, especially the newspapers, the women's page usually discusses such matters as "how to catch (or keep) a husband", the "other woman", "how to be attractive to men", etc — all of which discuss and perpetuate a stereotyped notion of women's roles, and the idea that women only exist in relation to men. (This stereotype, moreover, has been borrowed

5

from Western "romantic literature" in the pre-liberation movement days, and is in contradiction to the traditional economic and emotional independence of women in Nigerian society.)

In addition, wide media coverage is given to elite women's organizations (such as the National Council of Women's Societies), which are engaged either in philanthropic activities, (emphasizing the "nurturing" gender stereotype of women, or which are organized primarily as support groups for their husbands' activities (such as the Inner Wheel, made up of wives and widows of members of the Rotary Club, or the Legislators' Wives' Association, etc). Coverage of women in political life is usually limited to interviews with a few prominent women (ministers, commissioners, permanent secretaries). Such interviews generally focus on the question of how these women manage to play a double role — as a wife and mother, and as a public figure. In response, these successful women invariably reply "my husband is very understanding". (They never mention the army of household servants, their relatives, or others whose support makes their "success" possible.)

Many of the issues of the Western liberation movement, and virtually all of the problems discussed on the women's pages of the Nigerian media are of little relevance to the average woman in Nigeria. Over 70% of Nigerian women are part of peasant farming families. They must work with their husbands on the farm, trade in the market place, or involve themselves in some other economic activity (crafts, food processing, etc) in order to provide for themselves, their children, their other relations. Both they and their menfolk must work long hours, at gruelling tasks, just to be able to survive at the barest level of existence. The concerns of these peasant women are not whether their husband spends too much time at the club (see the paper by Aluko and Alfa), but whether the family can keep their farmland in the face of pressure from big farmers and feudal functionaries who want to appropriate it, whether the family can afford to dispense with their children's labour while they are away at school, whether the family can avoid the predations of middlemen and money-lenders whose activities threaten the very survival of the peasant family as a viable economic unit.

In addition to these problems which affect both men and women in rural communities, the women have additional concerns — the insecurity of polygynous marriages (discussed by Bene Madunagu and 'Molara Ogundipe-Leslie in their contributions); local medical practices (such as *gishiri* cuts in Hausa-speaking areas) which may render women incapacitated for the rest of their lives (as discussed by Mairo Alti-Mu'azu in her paper); the lack of inheritance rights in many communities (as discussed by Aluko and Alfa and other contributors); and of course the double burden of taking care of the home and children while at the same time pursuing a full time economic activity.

In the urban centres too the situation is similar. Many women work in factories, in petty commodity production and petty trade (the "informal sector" of the economy), in addition to their child-rearing and housework. A large number of women live alone, bearing the economic and emotional burden of rearing children by themselves, often without the support of the extended family system prevalent in rural communities but less common in town. In the case of those women living with their husbands who might be factory workers, petty traders, poorly paid civil servants or teachers, the family would likely still be living barely on the edge of subsistence. Their worries are not "how to stay beautiful", or "problems of being a female permanent secretary", but how to keep their children fed and clothed, how to find money for school books and uniforms, how to cope with the lack of basic health facilities, how to make ends meet when the money does not stretch to even the basic essentials. Compared to the problems of the poor majority in Nigeria, the concerns of elite women, as reflected in the media, seem frivolous indeed.

Although elite women, like women everywhere, are in need of liberation from gender sterotyped roles, from male chauvinism and patriarchal attitudes, the majority of Nigerian women are in need of this and much more besides — they are in need of liberation from a social and economic system which exploits the labour of the many for the benefit of the few. In this system, women and men both are exploited as members of oppressed groups. Within the system of class oppression, however, women suffer particular forms of exploitation as documented by many of the papers in this volume; thus they are subjected to a system of double oppression.

But the class system which divides society also divides women. While elite and privileged women suffer from gender based oppression at the hands of men, at the same time these women are in a position to exploit others, including other women (as underpaid household servants, as employees in business enterprises, as customers in the market). It is thus clear that a purely feminist movement which does not take into consideration these fundamental class distinctions cannot solve the problems of most women in Nigeria.

On the other hand, most radical social movements have ignored or denied the specific difficulties tht women face.

What is to be done?

Given the theoretical perspectives on the problems of women's oppression in Nigeria, as discussed above, and given the concrete situation of class and gender oppression to which the majority of Nigerian women are subjected, the question that must be asked is: **What is to be done?** At the conference, Renée Pittin, R. Mustapha and indeed all the participants, argued that a pre-requisite for a solution to the problems facing women in Nigeria is that women must organize themselves to fight

7

against the oppressive conditions which deprive them of their basic human rights. The fight against women's oppression must be carried on in alliance with other groups and forces which are struggling against all forms of exploitation in society. At the same time, the specific nature of women's oppression needs to be acknowledged by all participants in the struggle against injustice and social exploitation.

As a result of the agreed need for women to organize to promote their liberation, the conference participants decided on the formation of an organization to pursue the following aims and objectives:

1. Preamble

We believe: That the majority of women, like the majority of men, suffer from the exploitative and oppressive character of Nigerian society.

That, however, women suffer additional forms of oppression and exploitation.

Women, therefore, suffer double opression and exploitation — as members of subordinate classes and as women.

2. Our organisation will engage in research, policy-making, dissemination of information, and action aimed at improving the conditions of women.

3. The Organisation will act:

1. To promote the study of conditions of Women in Nigeria, with the aim of combating discriminatory and sexist practices in the family, in the work-place, and in the wider society;
2. To defend the rights of women under the Nigerian Constitution and the United Nations Human Rights Convention;
3. To provide non-sexist alternatives to government and institutional policies;
4. To fight against the harassment and sexual abuse of females in the family and elsewhere;
5. To promote an equitable distribution of domestic work in the family;
6. To provide a forum for women to express themselves;
7. To ensure for women equal access to equal education;
8. To combat sexist stereotypes in literature, the media, and educational materials;
9. To provide the means of educating women on relevant issues;
10. To form links and work with other organisations and groups fighting sex and class oppression;
11. To fight for social justice.

Women in Nigeria produces regular newsletters, holds annual conferences to discuss different aspects of the conditions of women, and takes action aimed at ending all forms of women's oppression in Nigeria. Group and individuals interested in participating or in knowing more about the activities of this organisation can write to:

Women in Nigeria
P.O. Box 253
Samaru, Zaria, Nigeria.

Acknowledgements

The holding of the first conference on **Women in Nigeria**, and the publication of the proceedings in this volume could not have been carried out without the help of many groups and individuals who gave so generously of their time, their energy, and their funds. For support in organizing the seminar, we would like to thank the following: first, to Professor Ango Abdullahi, Vice-Chancellor of Ahmadu Bello University for a contribution of N2,000, and for delivering the Opening Address which showed an acute awareness of the problems facing women in Nigeria; to the Ag. Head of the Department of Sociology, Dr. Patrick Wilmot, for the departmental donation of N1,000 plus paper and secretarial services; to all of the staff in the Sociology Department Office for their cooperation, especially Caleb Madaki and John Oduh; to the staff of ABU Bindery Unit for printing of posters; and lastly, to all the contributors and participants, colleagues, friends and well-wishers in Zaria and elsewhere who helped in various aspects of the seminar organization.

For help rendered in the publication of this book, we would like to thank: Dee Badejo, for undertaking the tedious and painstaking work of editing and giving advice on production; the New Nigerian Development Corporation, for its generous donation of N5,000 towards publication costs; the Kaduna State Government, for its donation of N1,000; Triumph Publishing Company, Kano, for donation towards costs of editing and typesetting; and to all the members of Women in Nigeria, for their comments and their support.

Ayesha M. Imam
Norma Perchonock
Zaria, November 1982

Special Thanks
I would like to take this opportunity on behalf of all the participants to express their sincere gratitude to Ms. Ayesha Imam, who virtually single-handedly organized the seminar, and worked tirelessly through its successful conclusion. There is no doubt that without her vision and her energy the seminar would not have been held.

Norma Perchonock.

PART I
Theoretical Perspectives

Towards an Adequate Analysis of The Position of Women in Society

Ayesha M. Imam

Most analyses of the position of women in society are essentially a variation or combination of one of the following:

(i)   women's position is a result of the natural division of labour based on biology. Hence women are neither oppressed nor exploited.

(ii)   women are subordinate through some form of universal sex oppression. Hence women are oppressed and/or exploited by men.

(iii) women's position is derivable from class relations in society. Thus women's oppression is at the hands of the ruling class.

While these forms of explanation can produce some useful insights (or the latter two at least), they are all inadequate — even at the most general level of understanding, much less in terms of devising strategies to alter concrete situations. This paper demonstrates their inadequacy and those based on any combination of them. Suggestions towards a more adequate framework may then be made.

It may seem redundant to have to start by criticizing explanations based on "nature" by now. However this is not so. Not only do more sophisticated forms continue to emerge, such as sociobiology, but the assumptions behind it continue to crop up in discussion of kinship, division of labour and so on. Secondly, at the level of popular consciousness, especially in Nigeria, it continues to be the dominant paradigm for perceiving the position of women in society. Men use it to justify their behaviour; and women, although they may feel oppressed, experience a sense of apathy or helplessness since the situation is apparently natural and therefore immutable. Thus the debunking of the "nature" myth is particularly important.

At a general (and possibly even polemic) level, I have criticized biologically based explanations of women in society elsewhere[1] — so I will confine myself here mainly to the intellectual concerns raised by the sociobiology theorists, such as Desmond Morris, Robin Fox and E.O. Wilson. Their main thesis is that human social organization corresponds on a parallel with innate human needs and drives which are biological in nature.

Thus innate male aggression explains war, territoriality and domination over women. Polygyny and male promiscuity are expressions of a bi-sexual species of which the males have a particularly strong sex drive. A long period of infant dependency results in universal norms of motherhood, and to a lesser extent, fatherhood. Men's dominant position in society, and women's submission is hence a natural expression of male and female biological capacities. As such it is neither oppressive to women nor changeable. Marshall Sahlins summarizes the position in his critique as follows:

> Social organisation is rather, and nothing more than, the behavioral outcome of the interaction of organisms having biologically fixed inclinations... (The idea) is one of isomorphism between biological properties and social properties.[2]

Leaving aside for the moment the debate over how much males are innately aggressive or females innately submissive and how much is due to socialization, I will just remind you that, as Clifford Geertz points out, culture preceded the human species as we know it by approximately over two million years. People act as social beings and not biological individuals. Sahlins sees the central problem of the sociobiological thesis as denying the autonomy of culture. He makes the point that while biology may be essential for human society it is not a sufficient condition for it. The mediation of culture interrupts biological determinations. Sahlins focuses his critique at the level of kinship — being a feature central to both anthropology and sociobiology.

For socio-biology the object of human society is the reproduction of the species, the unit of genetic response to environmental circumstances being the population of inter-breeding organisms. But it is through the individual that reproduction and change take place. Logically the survival of the individual should take precedence over that of the group. This however raises the paradox of why altrustic behaviour is transformed into genetic egotism. Thus, an organism's death may nonetheless benefit that organism to the extent that it enables particular proportions of other organisms sharing genes to survive. On the basis of this, socio-biology can then posit group relations and all apparently altruistic behaviour as the results of a process of biological natural selection and genealogical relationships.

However Sahlins and others demonstrate that in none of the bewildering diversity of kinship systems that exist in various societies do the principles of who are and are not defined as kin follow the principles of genealogical relationship. Sociobiology is therefore forced to resort to a secret wisdom of the genes which orders human society regardless of that society's conscious interpretation or self-mystifications of the situation. Wilson, for instance, refers to the human mind's "intuitive calculus of blood ties".[3]

This proposition of the genes' unconscious knowledge is ridiculous in itself. Sahlins proceeds to argue however that not only are actual kinship systems not comfortable to biological co-efficients of relationship but that these various concepts of kinship are the true models of and for social action in those societies. Sahlins' critique gives no space to the determinations of the various forms of kinship systems which could give the (misleading) impression that they are arbitrary. The matter at issue here, however, is the point that culture is a mediation which interrupts any strictly biological causation.

Symbolization is a distinctive feature of human society. Language and culture are not expressions of biology but order what biological imperatives there are. Saussure (Volosinov, Eco and others) have pointed out the arbitrary character of the sign. It does not naturally represent objects but generates meaning, i.e., it enables things to mean within a system of differentially related other meanings. This point holds in parallel, not simply for the nature of the sign as a word, but also as myth in symbolic systems (following Barthes' usage) or as inscribed in social practices (following Althusser).

Individuals are born into a society of pre-formed symbolic constructions and social practices which mediate relations in society, such that social organization cannot be reduced to biological determination. Neither kinship systems in general, nor the subordination of women to men in particular, can be explained by reference to innate genotypical capacities.

This point must be related not only to the sociobiological thesis but also to certain theorizations of the concept of the division of labour which appear in writers who reject biological determinism. Maxine Molyneux points out in her critique of androcentric bias in Marxist anthropology that many writers fail to analyse the concept of the sexual division of labour. The term is used with the underlying assumptions that it is technical and/or natural. Engels, and many Marxists follow him in this, wrote:

> The division of labour was a pure and simple outgrowth of nature: it existed only between two sexes. The men went to war, hunted fish, provided the raw materials for food and the tools necessary for these pursuits. The women cared for the house and prepared food and clothing. They cooked, weaved, sewed. Each was master of his or her own field of activity.[4]

However, this formulation suffers from the same faults as the sociobiological thesis. Firstly, sexual divisions of labour are maintained by determinate social-cultural practices, such as, in primitive societies, kinship and mythology. How can they then be natural? Secondly, it will not account for the variations in which agents are allocated along sexual lines in different societies. Thirdly, in many societies the sexual division of labour has not simply been technical in the sense of allocating agents to equivalent places in social production. It has been a gender hierarchy as well as gender differentiation. To refer to sexual division of labour as technical obscures this area of the social determination of women's subordination. Rather, sexual division of labour must be seen as a socially mediated product which is linked to biology but not determined by it. As Molyneux puts it:

> The sexual division of labour is linked to biology, but it is not founded on it; instead it must be conceived as a relation mediated through complex social processes and subject to sometimes contradictory determinations.[5]

This section has attempted to show the inadequacy of theoretical frameworks which base themselves on representing social relations as expressions of nature or biology. Female subordination to males in societies cannot, therefore, be explained as natural or inevitable precisely because they are socially constructed relations. However, one must then consider the bases of female subordination and the mechanisms whereby it is maintained.

This section considers the theories which attempt to explain female subordination as a result of universal systems of sex oppression. Theorists along this line point out that sex oppression neither began with capitalism (or class relations) nor does it automatically disappear in socialist societies. This is not an unimportant insight but nonetheless these analyses have serious drawbacks for providing an adequate explanation of the position of females in societies and thus for strategies which change this situation. Shulamith Firestone, for instance, argues that the biological family inherently represents a universal sex/class system mediated through power psychology. She states that the biological family of male, female and infant throughout time and space has been characterized by female dependence on males because of their biology, infant dependency, mother-child interdependency and a division of labour based on natural reproductive differences. Firestone's position is similar to that of the sociobiological thesis. Therefore the same criticisms on the "natural" division of labour can be made in respect of her.

She differs however in two respects. Firstly, what is "natural" may nonetheless be oppressive. Secondly, what is natural is not immutable.

Issue can, however, be taken with her contention that "even in matriarchies where women's fertility is worshipped, and the fathers' role is unknown or unimportant, if not perhaps on the genetic father, there is still some dependence of the female and infants on the males." Firstly, as writers like Kathleen Gough, Eleanor Leacock and John Moore point out, there is no evidence of matriarchal societies (as opposed to matrilineal). More importantly, Sally Slocum argues that the earliest societies were not characterized by "man the hunter" with dependent women and children. Rather the bulk of subsistence needs were provided by gathering — an activity which need not be interrupted by pregnancy, childbirth or lactation. Female dependence on males is not a universal constant. Judith Van Allen, in fact, argues that Igbo women became more economically dependent on males (and not simply during periods of pregnancy and childbirth), during colonialism and the development of capitalism, despite the fact that pre-colonial Igbo society was predominantly patrilineal.

Christine Delphy's position is very similar to Firestone's; but it is based on social relations within the family rather than biology. Delphy argues that women form a distinct class as the subordinate group in what she terms the domestic mode of production. Within this, men form a ruling class who appropriate the labour of their wives, whether in serving them and their children or in producing goods which may have exchange-value as well as use-value. In return, women get what men deem necessary for female subsistence. This domestic mode of production exists with other modes of production, within which men form a ruling class who appropriate the labour of their wives whether capitalist, feudalist or socialist. For Delphy, women are outside the class relations of social production except in as much as they themselves directly engage in work outside of the domestic. In this case they have two class positions. Though women may have different social situations, this is by virtue of the common fact of marriage — through which they are subjugated in the domestic mode of production. Hence "the main enemy" for Delphy is the patriarchal relations of the domestic mode of production. Women need to unite to fight this.

Both Delphy and Firestone claim to be applying Marxist method (i.e. historical materialism) properly in their analyses. However, while it is agreed that, hitherto at least, much Marxist analysis has had distinct gaps in the treatment of women, neither Delphy nor Firestone have used this method. For Firestone, after the biological determinations in her work have been criticized, there is no other form of determination to sustain the claim of materialism. One is left with an idealist (i.e. power-psychology) explanation.

The main criticism of both these theorists however is that, as with other theorists positing universal systems of sex oppression, they are ahistorical. They cannot account for the differences between, for instance, working class and bourgeois women within capitalism, or changes in the position of women from one dominant mode of production in a social formation to another, or for variations in women's situations from one society to another, such as the different situations of women in Nigeria under purdah in dependent capitalism and white women in the USA under mature capitalism. As Sartre says (of "Vulgar Marxist" economic determinists), it is "an inflexible refusal to differentiate", "a bath of sulphuric acid" in which everything is attributed to an abstract patriarchy and any qualitative differences are soaked away. In fact these analyses more nearly resemble Durkheimian method than Marxist. A basic unit (the horde, the biological family, or the domestic mode of production) is isolated and all human societies in time and space are nothing but variations of combinations of these with no essential difference.

The theories which posit a universal system of sex oppression to understands the position of women all suggest that to eradicate women's subordination all females must come together autonomously. They may or may not ally with other oppressed groups but there is explicitly no theoretical basis to do so. But, it is difficult to see how, for instance, the wives of the Emir of Kano and of the departmental cleaner can come together in any sustained mobilization, or even that the differences in their situation will not outweigh the common factors.

The third main framework of analysis which attempts to provide an understanding of the position of women in society is orthodox Marxist. It restores to an explanation of women's position the historical and concrete dimension which theories of universal sex oppression ignore but it too is problematic for a full understanding of women's situation.

Orthodox Marxist analysis of women is based mainly on Engels' work in *The Origin of the Family, Private Property, and the State*. The biological determinism of one of his assumptions has already been mentioned above. The trend of the argument however is as follows. In the early stages of society, productive resources were appropriated communally. The division of labour was technical and in the genes both men and women had public rights. With the development of productive resources, came the production of surplus and the extension of the ownership of personal effects to private property-holding. Production for exchange began to eclipse production for use. As this occurred, the significance of women's work began to decline into a necessary but socially subordinate part of production. Women's status declined from that of adult members of society into wards, wives and daughters — social dependents.

Families began to be perpetuated through time via the inheritance of property. This required a control not only of women's productive labour but of reproductive labour also. Some men began to gain control, through their control of property, over other men and women. Thus the social subordination of women, the control of women's labour and sexuality are all related to the development of productive forces and the institutions of private property and the state — in sum, women's subordination is derivable from the development of class relations. Women's subordination thus benefits the ruling class in any social formation but is a "secondary contradiction" of the main struggle which is that of class.

This line of analysis grounds women's oppression in material circumstances and goes some way to explaining historically concrete circumstances and the different situations of women within the same socio-economic formation. However many anthropologists and ethnographers (such as Moore, Gough, Godelier, Terray) have pointed out that in the absence of a redefinition of the Marxist concept of class, historically gender hierarchies preceded class relations and that there are non-class societies which operate female oppression. On the basis of this ethnographic material women's subordination cannot be derived from the development of private property and class relations. Though it should be noted that this is not the same thing as arguing that there has always been male domination or that all societies have been sexually inegalitarian.

Since the analysis presents women's subordination as not only secondary to but also attributable to class relations it would imply that if exploitative class relations are transcended so too will be women's oppression. This has clearly not been the case. In China, Cuba, the USSR and so on, women have continued to undertake the responsibility for domestic work as well as socially productive labour. If Marxist analysis is not to lay itself open to the charge of idealism (i.e. there are mental attitudes towards women, which though no longer supported materially, continue to hover in the air) then it needs to come to terms with the specification of gender hierarchies.

In addition this line of analysis does not account for those aspects of women's specific oppression as women regardless of class situation. Heliath Saffiotti's formulation that the division of labour within a class is merely technical is subject to the same criticisms advanced earlier in relation to biological determination and sexual division of labour. Maureen MacIntosh's analysis argues that women's subordination is embodied in a division of labour relatively favourable to men even within the same class. Thus feminist struggle is not divisive. Since the working class or peasantry is already materially divided this must be recognized and also fought.

The position in this paper has been to argue that the three main frameworks which attempt to explain women's position in society are inadequate. The first posits an isomorphism between biology and society which does not exist. The second is over-general and ahistorical. While the third neglects the specificities of women's subordination. What is required is an analysis which can reproduce the insights of the latter two forms of explanation. That is it must account for gender hierarchies and class relations at a theoretically related level which is at the same time historically and concretely specific. The work that MacIntosh and Mina Caulfield are doing (to name but two) at the moment are steps in this direction but as yet they are only the beginnings of such an analysis.

The development of this analysis is required because any strategy for changing society must be based on an adequate understanding — and this includes strategies for the eradication of women's subordination. Hence, the strategies which follow from the theories discussed are all inadequate. Women's oppression will not be removed by doing nothing, a completely isolated women's movement, or a movement which is only a secondary adjunct to class struggle. I suggest that what is required is a women's movement prepared to tackle the specificities of gender inequality but imbued with a historically concrete understanding of class relations, working to develop theoretical and practical links with other oppressed groups.

References

Caulfield, M.D., 1977 "Universal Sex Oppression?" *Catalyst,* Nos. 10-11, pp60-77.

Delphy, C., 1977 *The Main Enemy,* Women's Research and Resources Centre Publications, London.

Firestone, S., 1971 *The Dialectic of Sex,* Bantam, U.S.A.

Godelier, M., "Sex and Power", *New Left Review,* 127.

Gough, K., 1975 "The Origin of the Family", in Reiter, R., (ed), *Towards an Anthropology of Women,* Monthly Review Press, U.S.A., pp51-76.

Leacock, E., 1977 "Women in Egalitarian Societies", in Bridenthal, R., (ed), *Becoming Visible: Women in European History,* Houghton Miffin, U.S.A., pp11-33.

MacIntosh, M., 1981 "Gender and Economics", in Young, K., McCullagh, R., and Wolkowitz, C., (eds), *Of Marriage and the Market,* CSE Books, U.K., pp1-15.

Moore, J., "The Exploitation of Women in Evolutionary Perspective", *Critique of Anthropology,* Vol.3 Nos.9/10, pp83-100.

Oakley, A., 1972 *Sex, Gender and Society,* Temple Smith, London.

Rosaldo, M., 1974 "Woman, Culture and Society", in Rosaldo, M., and Lamphere, L., (eds), *Woman, Culture and Society,* Stanford University Press, U.S.A., pp17-42.

Sacks, K., 1975 "Engels Revisited", in *Towards an Anthropology...,* pp211-235.

Saffiotti, H., 1976 *Women in Class Society,* Monthly Review Press, U.S.A.

Scott, H., 1975 *Does Socialism Liberate Women?* Beacon Press, U.S.A.

Slocum, S., 1975 "Woman the Gatherer", in *Towards an Anthropology...,* pp36-50.

Van Allen, J., 1976 "Aba Riots or the Igbo Women's War?", in Hafkin, N.J., and Bay, E.G., (eds), *Women in Africa,* Stanford University Press, U.S.A., pp59-85.

Problems of Theory and Practice in Women's Liberation Movements

Sule Bello

It is under difficult circumstances that I have undertaken to write this paper. This undertaking, despite other pressing problems, I have done because I consider a clarification of the "Women Question" at the present stage of Nigeria's political-economic development very important and quite decisive. I will therefore in this paper largely be concerned with raising questions about what exactly is the "position of women" and what role women are destined to play in the political-economic development of the country.

Furthermore, I feel highly obliged to present a position on the "position of women" because in the last two years we have had a series of controversies with a number of my female colleagues on this issue. In fact, it was after one of such debates that we thought it would be worthwhile to call for a seminar and at least begin a more systematic debate on the issue. In view of this, I will set forth what the notice of the seminar has identified as the major issue to be discussed. The notice states that the seminar

> will consider the position of women and whether women's exploitation/ subjugation is as members of a class or sex group or the inter-relationship of the two. The specific conditions and experiences of women in society generally and various spheres (e.g. industry/agriculture/marriage...) will be analysed and strategies suggested for changing the situation will be suggested.

I will come back to this at the end of this article. For the meantime, however, it helps us focus the debate on whether the oppression of women is related to their class position or is generally and simply due to their being women per se.

It seems to me that there are three dominant tendencies within the women's liberation movement. The first is that which is posited by radical feminists to the effect that the domination of women is principally due to their being women irrespective of the social system. The specific nature of female oppression in this case is variously given as their reproductive biology, emotional relations to men and domestic work.

The second general position is that of feminists who tend to identify the "political system" as the major factor in the oppression of women. There are different versions of this. Two tend to stand out as principal. The first is that of women who see the problem as lack of opportunities within the capitalist system and therefore struggle for women's rights. The second, of socialists, argues that the solution to the problem of women is an integral part of the solution of the working class oppression and thus directs their activity towards otherthrowing the capitalist system as part of the working class. Lastly, a tendency, of recent, has arisen. This had to do with the eclectic proposition that the oppression of women is due to the fact that they are both women as well as members of a particular class.

One of the first observations I have to make relates to the general theoretical weakness of these movements with the sole exception of socialist feminists who see the struggle as an integral part of the working class movement. To start with, to identify "women's oppression" with their biology leads us into two major problems. The first is that women, irrespective of the society or their class, are oppressed because they are women. This certainly lacks any political-economic precision or historicity. Secondly, to attempt to explain a historical phenomenon on the basis of biological make-up is at best mystificatory. This problem also bedevils women who try to marry this biological (or gender) standpoint with property, or class relations. Thus the singular question "how are women oppressed as women" defies explanation. For example, the most specific example generally common to these is the issue of household work. But is household production itself not part of, and largely determined by the prevalent system of production? Or still let us take yet another example which is very general, i.e., that women, as women, have been oppressed throughout history. The question then arises "is it not a fact that history is in fact a succession of class oppression and revolution?" Are women not an integral part of these classes? Has there been no qualitative change in the position of classes in general and women (as members of classes) in particular?

Let us now look more closely at the historical character of the women's liberation movements we are considering. We see that they tend to abstract and isolate women and the specific injustices they suffer from given societies and social relations of production. Certainly, since in a discourse of this nature it is not enough to identify what particular conceptions or framework inform specific brands of feminist or women's liberation movements. Above all, it is most important that this position be explained in relation to the general aspiration of all oppressed classes in society. To fight for "equal rights" might sound radical but too, in the process, legitimate and sanction neo-colonial oppressive relations, which is the main cause of inequality, is certain retrogressive. But what does an abstraction from the general mode of production and specific class relations amount to if not to a tacit denial of them. In sum, these movements largely confirm themselves as nothing but other versions of petit-bourgeois movements. Which women do they fight for — the professional women? the peasant women? the working women? or even the declasse women? Vagueness and wanton generalization is what we fall into if we resort to biology rather than the definite composition of classes and the general characteristic of the state. Let me call Dorothy E. Smith, a woman who has spent most of her life in the women's liberation movement, to my aid.

> Social democrats [petit-bourgeois reformists] take the view that the state is independent and capable of working on the side of the oppressed and the exploited. It does not recognize the state in capitalist society as the political means by which the ruling class controls the society in its interests. By putting forth the view that the state is neutral and independent of particular classes, social democrats assume that it can be used by people to remedy injustices. This way of working in the movement at first produced some results — day care facilities were expanded, abortion law reforms seemed possible, the Equal Rights Amendment in the U.S. was ratified in many states. But now these possibilities of reform and gains already made, are being cut back. Women's oppression is intensified as a result of economic crisis and the relief and support that the state could make available isn't forthcoming. The state itself undermines the illusion that it is on our side.

Yet, even if we accept that the struggle for various rights, etc., is a necessary part of the struggle to overthrow oppressive relations in general, would it not be naive to limit, truncate and reduce it to the psycho-social problems of certain classes of women?

Let us now try to illustrate what we have said with reference to Nigerian women. The position so far is that feminism as a biological phenomenon, like blackism and youth movements, obscures the essential struggle and lumps together, under a banal banner, interests which might even be practically opposed. The various professional bodies of women and those which are versions of all the political parties in Nigeria today largely operate to further consolidate a system which opposes the interests of workers and peasants (men and women alike). They also work principally to advance their own corporate interests and not that of women in general and in abstraction.

Similarly if we look at the colonial period, we see that despite the fact that in a number of cases we had exclusive women's organizations, they however fought for their specific interests and for or against colonial subjugation. The Aba Women's Riot and the activities of the Market Women's Association readily come to mind. If we however turn to the pre-colonial period, we also see that women operated, variously, as members of specific classes and acted accordingly for the preservation of or destruction of that system. This they did with or without their knowing it, consciously or unconsciously and willingly or unwillingly. If we take a look at the history of Borno, Benin, and Zaria, we see that at certain times women occupied high, if not the highest, positions as members of the dominant classes. Yet women in the lower classes, together with other members, resolutely opposed and overthrew them. So much for the General Women — the women outside history, society and class struggle.

I would like to address myself to the "position of women in Nigeria", as posited in the notice to the Seminar, which I have already quoted. This I do in order to make my position clearer. I have three observations to make in this:

1. The notice, by implying that the fundamental problem of oppression is general to women as women and not say as working women, peasant women, or even the family as an economic (productive, reproductive and consumptive) or social unit has set the problem upside down and blanketed it as a sexual problem.
2. Similarly this oppression cannot be both because they are members of a class as well as the fact that they are women. The latter implies this cannot change unless they cease being women and as women it has been with them throughout history. Thus this combination seems to me to be both a tautology and a composite error: Women are oppressed as a class because they are women and not due to the prevalent character of property relations.
3. Finally if we accept that after identifying the conditions of women in various production relations such as manufacture and agriculture etc., we will suggest strategies for "changing the situation". What does it imply: reforming their conditions of work or working towards changing it and thus the system?

In conclusion, it seems to me that women who are really concerned with oppression should address themselves to oppressive relations. That is to say that they will ally with the oppressed classes in opposition to an oppressive system. It is only when women are freed from the current property relations that they can be said to be fully liberated. For other injustices which are largely psychological and social such as humiliation, overlordship, etc., are founded on this basis.

I will end by quoting at length another female activist.

> it is crucial to the organization of women for their liberation to understand that it is the family as an economic unit, at the heart of a class society that is basic to their subjugation. Such understanding makes clear that child-bearing itself is not responsible for the low status of women, as has been the contention of some radical women's groups. And more important, it indicates the way in which working class women, not only in their obviously basic fight on the job but also their seemingly more conservative battle for their families around schools, housing and welfare, are actually posing a

more basic challenge than that of the radicals. By demanding that society assume responsibility for their children, they are attacking the nature of the family as an economic unit, the basis of their own oppression, and a central buttress of class exploitation. Therefore, while some activities of the middle class radical women's groups can be linked with the struggles of working class women, such as the fight for legalized abortion, others are so psychologically-oriented as to be confusing and diversionary.

Even if we consider the position of many women outside the family such as purely working class women, destitute women or women who have to sell their flesh for a livelihood can we still abstract from the system?

Rapporteur's Report:

S.M. Bappa

The papers presented in this session dealt with the theoretical framework of the Seminar and the discussions that followed were centred on ideology, class struggle, and women's liberation. While some participants accused advocates of women's liberation of being insensitive to the on-going class struggle, others responded by pointing out that class struggle should not be blind to the needs of women's liberation. Both sides, however, seemed to agree that the two could be placed side by side, i.e., placing women's liberation within the context of the working class struggle.

The discussion on Marxist theory was a prolonged and heated affair. Some participants saw sexual oppression as having originated in conditions specific to pre-capitalist modes of production, while others suggested that sexual oppression existed even in pre-class societies. According to these discussions, capitalism has created new forms of oppression which affect women and has also created the material conditions for the abolition of much of the pre-capitalist forms of sexual oppression. Socialism, on the other hand, has further expanded the scope for elimination of sexual oppression. Some participants pointed to what they claim to be an insufficient understanding of Marxism in terms of women, economic formation, and mode of production. They insisted that women must be seen as part of a social organization, that they are affected by this social organization and come to terms with how this determines their position. It was also noted that in socialist countries steps have been taken to tackle the position of women in society. These steps have been taken precisely because these societies are socialist, e.g. Mozambique, USSR, and Cuba.

Some participants, however, insisted that engaging in class struggle does not automatically guarantee liberation for women. Examples were cited to back up this argument, e.g. Mozambique, where, according to these participants, class struggle has made tremendous gains, but women are still relegated to domestic labour.

Other interesting highlights in the discussion included a lively debate on "gender hierarchy", which was defined as socially-constructed perceptions, capacities and roles which are ranked and which are based on alleged sexual superiority. A commentator suggested that women should be moral leaders of society, and not concern themselves with the issue of women's liberation. However, many participants rejected this on the grounds that it fits into the case of ideals which cannot be realized unless the social structure is changed.

A discussant referred to Islam as a liberating force in 7th century Arabia with regards to the position of women. He called for the recognition of Islamic norms which affect the position of women in an Islamic society which, he said, need not be based on property relations. This discussant called for a concerted effort to demystify issues which have imposed limits on women, such as the vague Islamic ideology and "kulle" (purdah) system. Only then can we talk of the relevance and significance of property relations within the totality of the mode of production.

Some time was also spent discussing the possibility of developing an understanding of social science which takes into consideration female values, experiences, and status. It was agreed that from this, new concepts and frameworks could be developed which would alter or enhance the position of women in society.

The general agreement at this session was that we cannot deny the importance of class struggle but that finding solutions to sexual oppression will require additional effort in backing up progressive legislation and practical efforts within the struggle.

Conceptual Framework and Methodology: Marxism and the Question of Women's Liberation

Edwin and Bene Madunagu

Prologue: The End of a Debate

It is not logical to assume that sexism, which has flourished throughout most of human history and long before the rise of capitalism, will be eliminated merely by equitable distribution of material wealth and the abolition of reactionary laws. Sexism has survived through the ages because it embodies privileges that men are unwilling to surrender. These privileges are not only material, but sexual and psychological. The willingness of women to believe that men will repudiate all dominance over us in the name of socialism — or any other — without a fight, is putting the ultimate victory of feminism in danger... Under a socialist system, sexism will not die out unless people are conditioned and propagandized from childhood into antisexism just as surely as the present system and previous generations were indoctrinated with sexism. Once the material conditions of sexism are eliminated, its psychological and sexual privileges must be made as immoral and horrible to a new generation as Satan was ever made in the eyes of any Puritan child.

Angela Denis Powell: *Socialism and the Fight for Women's Rights* (1976)

Men lean on their sexist attitudes and sense of superiority like a crutch to help hold them under the weight of a society that strips them of real opportunities for self-fulfillment. But these very male attitudes that oppress women also dehumanise men and confine them in narrow sex stereotypes as well. When the material basis for narrow sexual definitions of male and female roles is eliminated and all human beings are given new opportunities to develop their potential, men will not need to bolster their egos at the expense of women.. This is not to say that men will automatically come to support the women's liberation struggle; it is the mobilisation of women themselves that helps educate men about the fact their real interests lie in supporting equal rights for all... Women must build a massive movement of women to fight sexism... We should unite with men in a revolutionary socialist party to fight capitalism.

Linda Jenness: *Socialism and the Fight for Women's Rights* (1976)

Presentation of the Question

Two preliminary, but essential, points must be made.

First, it is often forgotten that the word "oppression", just like "exploitation", is a relationship: it is a relationship between *unequal* human beings or *unequal* groups of human beings. To say that someone is oppressed is to say that he is oppressed by someone else, for an isolated individual — a Robinson Crusoe — can never be oppressed. When we say, for instance, that workers in a capitalist society are oppressed by capital we mean that capital is a "carrier" of social relationship (as a social product) which, to workers, is a relation of oppression. In short, people are not oppressed "in general" (that is by everything or by nothing) — although they can be oppressed by *something* in a general way (the way capital oppresses) — nor are people oppressed by a thing, considered merely as an inanimate object.

Secondly, oppression — when conceived on a level above that of everyday *casual* relationship — is an institutionalized relationship. (It is in this context that oppression acquires the qualification "social".) The continual reproduction and perpetuation of certain forms of oppression are made possible by the fact that they are socialized or institutionalized, and to abolish a certain form of social oppression is to change the institution within which it is reproduced. For instance, if women are oppressed in the family, then to abolish this oppression is to abolish the institution of family — as we know it.

What then do we mean by "women's" oppression? To answer this question we have to consider the various relationships into which women enter, either as individuals, or as members or strata (i.e. as "social agents") of the female sex — or indeed as both. We identify three spheres of life where women's oppression takes place: the family, the society, considered as a class society, and the society at large.

Women as members of the nuclear family

The nuclear family is today not only the basic economic unit of society, but also the primary institution for the reproduction of the human race. Within this institution women appear as wives, mothers, children, maids, servants, etc. But when women's oppression in the nuclear family is discussed attention is normally focused entirely on women as wives and mothers. We shall adopt this focus simply because we intend to deal with the question of children, maids, servants, etc., more generally later and not because the oppression of these other categories of people is less severe or that they are less human, or that all these forms of oppression can really be separated — except for the purposes of analysis.

The oppression of women in the family is located in (the character of) their roles:

(a) The woman, as housewife, "looks after" the family — giving it that primary nourishment which is necessary for the members of the family to fill their places and perform their roles in the society at large. But this socially *necessary* labour (of housewife) takes the form of an *unpaid* "private service".[1] Because she spends most of her time as an unpaid servant, she and her children become dependent on an individual man — who is the "breadwinner".

(b) The woman, as mother, provides "the reproduction of the labour force".[2] But according to Eleanor Burke Leacock: "In some ways it is the ultimate alienation in our society that the ability to give birth has been transformed into a liability."[3] That is to say that the role of the woman as child bearer is exploited to perpetuate her social inequality with men.

Women as members of "the Society", considered as a class society.
If the present-day society is a class society, then women (either as individuals or as a group) cannot be above or below class divisions — if these divisions are real. The man-woman, husband-wife, father-mother dichotomy which exists in the nuclear family dissolves in the sphere of class society since class divisions cut across women as a group, just as they cut across men. Whether a housewife belongs to the same social class as her husband — together with the rest of the family, or belongs to a social class independent of her husband by virtue of the place she occupies in a "historically determined system of social production",[4] the fact remains that women, like men, are found on opposite sides of class divisions. This means that whereas some women *suffer* class oppression (maids and servants come in here) other women *perpetrate* it.

Women as members of "the society at large"
In this sphere of life, "sex" oppression merges with class oppression. A housewife performs unpaid service at home; and precisely on account of this, the totality of her labour power is less valued than that of her male counterpart:

Women have less valuable labour-power to sell and consequently get a bad bargain even if they put in forty hours a week at a factory. Employers are quick to point out that, given the degree of exhaustion produced by a woman's two jobs, a woman's paid work cannot be as productive as a man's. The woman's labour time, for this reason alone, is less valuable and must be sold cheaply.[5]

Since class determination, and hence class oppression, are not only economic, but also political, social and ideological at times, this merger of "sex" and class oppression is at once economic, political, social, cultural, ideological, etc. We may cite a few elements of this merger.

(a) *State laws (Political):* There is a law in Nigeria which requires a married woman to obtain the permission of her husband before application for a passport can be approved. This is a perfection and extension of women's dependence in the family. Of course the two forms of dependence ideologically support and reinforce each other.

(b) *Social:* The right to maternity leave has just been extended to unmarried working mothers in Nigeria; but then it is without pay. This means that a woman is liable to punishment for getting pregnant outside the "normal" institution. On the other hand, since abortion is illegal, she is also liable to punishment if she does away with "abnormal" pregnancy. In short, a woman is tacitly asked to abstain from sex, but no similar requirement extends to men.

(c) *Ideological:* There is a countless number of social taboos meant to regulate the conduct of women both in private and in public. Female children should help their mothers in the house, thereby preparing themselves for their future role as housewives and mothers; women should be faithful and obedient to their husbands; women should not be promiscuous; women must be accompanied to public places (stadia, restaurants, hotels, etc.) if they are not to lose their dignity...

These are the sources and forms of women's oppression: sources and forms that are continually fed and reproduced. We shall now proceed to consider Marxist responses to them: responses to oppression which is so historical as well as profound, so real but often denied. As Juliet Mitchell boldly asserts:

> No women's liberation movement that denies the class struggle, and no class struggle that underplays the oppression of women, can be a fully revolutionary force. No analysis that ignores the basis of women's specific oppression is a revolutionary analysis.[6]

Classical Marxist Formulations

Marx and Engels were not the first critics or socialists to denounce the age-long degradation of women which reached its culmination in bourgeois society. Indeed, on this particular subject, Marx and Engels frequently quoted Charles Fourier (1772-1837), a leading French socialist of his time:

> The change in a historical epoch can always be determined by women's progress towards freedom, because here, in the relation of woman to man, of the weak to the strong, the victory of human nature over brutality is most evident. The degree of emancipation of woman is the natural measure of general emancipation.[1]

To Fourier as well as to other so-called utopian socialists, there could not be significant progress towards the liberation of working people from capitalist oppression in the absence of an equally determined attempt to abolish the specific oppression of women; how can the society be said to be free when half of it is in bondage (except socialism is just another form of exploitative society). But, just as on the question of capitalist oppression in general, utopian socialists could not go beyond general denunciation on the question of women's specific oppression: they had very little or nothing to say as regards what constituted the preconditions for the liberation of women or how these preconditions could be created.

One of the very first of the very few serious analyses of "the women's question" from the scientific socialist point of view came from August Bebel (1840-1913), a German socialist leader of international reputation. In this work, *Women Under Socialism,* Bebel drew attention to the two-fold character of women's oppression:

> The mass of the female sex suffers in two respects: On the one side, woman suffers from economic and social dependence upon men. True enough, this dependence may be alleviated by formally placing her upon the equality before the law, and in points of rights; but the dependence is not removed. On the other side, woman suffers from the economic dependence that woman in general, the working-woman in particular, finds herself in, along with the working man.[8]

Bebel saw the two sides (class and individual) of the women's question as linked, indicating a single process of solution, whose essence could only be the unfolding of a woman's powers and faculties in all directions, to the end that she becomes "a complete and useful member of human society, enjoying equal rights with all".[9] The women's question is therefore a part — a specific part — of the social question; and if socialism is a solution to the social question, it must, in particular, be a solution to the women's question. This immediately led Bebel to a political conclusion: women's participation in the revolutionary movement enables

> more favourable relations between husband and wife to spring up in the ranks of the working class in the measure that both realise they are tugging the same rope, and there is but one means towards satisfactory conditions for themselves and their family — the radical reformation of society that shall make human beings of them all.[10]

The *classical* Marxist formulations of the question of women's oppression are derived essentially from Engels' *The Origin of the Family, Private Property and the State*. Engels located the origin of women's oppression in the emergence of monogamy (for the woman and not the man!) as a form of family. In contrast to earlier forms of marriage (pairing, group and polyandrous marriages), where the economic and social unit of society was the clan, monogamous marriage transformed the nuclear family into the basic economic unit of society, within which a woman and her children became dependent upon an individual man.[11] Engels further argued that the social relations of women to men — which monogamy transformed into relations of dependence — "deteriorated with the advent of class society".[12]

Just as the historical emergence of the capitalist mode of production — together with the development of large-scale industry and general rise in the productivity of labour — was seen by Marx and Engels as creating, for the first time in human history, the material *conditions* for the liberation of mankind from want, exploitation and oppression, so did it create the *conditions* for the liberation of women. Marx had already noticed the tendency of capitalism to draw women and children more and more into social production (production outside the family) since private service within the family, though socially necessary, does not have a place in capitalist calculation. Engels believed that this tendency was creating the conditions for the liberation of women:

> ...the peculiar character of the supremacy of the husband over the wife in the modern family, the necessity of creating real social equality between them and the way to do it, will only be seen in the clear light of day when both possess legally complete equality of rights. Then it will be plain that the first condition for the liberation of the wife is to bring the whole female sex back into public industry, and that this monogamous family as the economic unit of society be abolished.[13]

The charge of "economic determinism" cannot be made against Engels for he was talking about *the conditions for the liberation* of women and not *the liberation of women:* only with their *full* and equal entry into social production,[14] that is, only with the achievement of equal social rights for men and women, will the conditions be created for the liberation of women from "their status of *unpaid servant* in the house".[15]

Let us briefly consider the implications of Engels' formulation. Since, as we have earlier noted, a woman's status of *unpaid servant* is linked with the discrimination she suffers as regards pay and work opportunities (the exhaustion she carries over from her "other job" counts much against her) and since oppression of women is much older than capitalism (in the sense that women's oppression is *not* a mere outgrowth of capitalism), Engels' thesis can, in fact, be reversed. A new thesis then appears: Women cannot enter fully and equally into social production until they cease to be unpaid servants in the house, that is, until they are liberated.

We do not advance the new thesis to contradict Engels' thesis — which remains true. We merely intend to show that neither the women's question nor its solution can be conceived mechanically: when this is done, that will follow! No. The oppression of women is too profound for a mechanical solution to be prescribed. As we have earlier said, it is at once economic, political, social, cultural and ideological: it merges in various spheres of life with class and ethnic oppressions; it exists in *all* countries of the world in various forms and in varying degrees of intensity. According to Fourier, "the humiliation of the female sex is an essential feature of civilisation as well as of barbarism. The only difference is that the civilised system raises every vice that barbarism practises in a simple form to a compound, ambiguous, hypocritical mode of existence..."[16] (We may add, however, that the seriousness and determination with which solutions are sought to the social oppression of women vary from country to country.)

Engels had thought that the drawing of ever greater numbers of women into industrial production would, with time, start to undermine the basis of the nuclear family — since the husband would then cease to be the sole "breadwinner" of the family, and, in any case, an erstwhile full-time housewife would be left with little time to perform her unpaid service at home. The liberation of women from unpaid service and the consequent destruction of the nuclear family — together with women's *equal* and *full* participation in social production — would mean the liberation of women! This was indeed an over-optimistic expectation.

But the world is not faced with a new tendency: the degree of women's involvement in social production has not been matched by the degree of their liberation from unpaid labour and other forms of social degradation. In the advanced capitalist countries where more and more housewives are daily being drawn into wage and salaried labour as well as other types of self-employment, the dominant tendency is that most of these housewives now carry a *greater* burden by having to combine their labour outside of their homes with private service at home. The story is essentially the same in the Third World — the only difference being that here, unlike in the advanced capitalist countries, women are mainly engaged in petty-commodity production and trade.

The nuclear family, as the basic economic unit of society and where women suffer the primary and crudest forms of degradation, remains unthreatened socially — at least not in the manner Engels envisaged. The question of women's oppression has to be reformulated.

The Women's Question 'After Marx and Engels'

As we have said earlier, just as women's oppression is older than capitalism, so is the general denunciation of this specific oppression older than socialism and Marxism. But a general denunciation of an evil can only assist people to become aware of its existence: it is not a substitute for a solution. In a sense, generations of post-Marx Marxists have continued the tradition of general denunciation: and the development of Marxist theory and political practice has, admittedly, been very slow in the area of women's oppression.

But it is wrong to claim — as many "critical" or "humanist" Marxists and feminists do — either that the women's question has never been seriously treated by Marxists, or has been abandoned, or has never constituted a subject for serious Marxist discussion or debate.

Marxists have always insisted that a distinction should be drawn between *formal* rights and *real* rights, that is between the formal equality of all ("equality before the law, the equality of the well-fed and the hungry man, of the man of property")[17] and the real inequality existing between individuals, groups and social classes. This distinction is very crucial when dealing with the women's question, for the mere proclamation of equality of men and women will not do away with the existing social inequality between them. It will be naive, for example, to assume that a mere proclamation of social, legal, and political equality of men and women will liberate women from the degradation they suffer at home and in society in general, for as Trotsky pointed out, "as long as woman is chained to her house work, the care of the family, the cooking and sewing, all her chances of participation in social and political life are cut down in the extreme".[18]

This again brings us back to the question of the condition for the liberation of women — a condition which, as we have seen, was located in the expansion of capitalist production. According to Lenin:

> The chief task of the working women's movement is to fight for economic and social equality, and not only formal equality, for women. The chief thing is to get women to take part in socially productive labour, to liberate them from domestic slavery, to free them their stupefying and humiliating subjugation to the eternal drudgery of the kitchen and the nursery.[19]

But Lenin was not an utopian socialist. He realized that the task of liberating women from their oppression is an arduous one which cannot be accomplished by mere exhortation. "The struggle", according to him, "will be a long one, and it demands a radical reconstruction both of social technique and of morals. But it will end in the complete triumph of communism."[20]

Marxists have always believed that all forms of social and domestic oppression — including the specific oppression of women — would end with the attainment of communism, a social order which Marx characterized in his *Critique of the Gotha Programme* as follows:–

> In a higher phase of communist society, after the *enslaving subordination of the individual to the division of labour,* and herewith also the antithesis between mental and physical labour, has fanished; after labour has become not only a means of life but life's prime want; after the productive forces have also increased with the all-around development of the individual, and

37

all the springs of cooperative wealth flow more abundantly — only then can the narrow horizon of bourgeois right be cross in its entirety and society inscribe on its banners: "From each according to his ability, to each according to his needs!"[21]

But faith in the power of communism — the realm of freedom — does not mean that the struggle for the emancipation of women will have to be put off to a distant future. For, in the first place, the precondition for the emergence of communism will have to be struggled for, and created; and in the second place, women — who constitute half of mankind — will have to be involved in this struggle — not as an appendage, but as a social group who have a specific wrong to put right. The question then arises: what should be done now?

Trotsky took up the question and suggested the *socialization of domestic labour* as a necessary complement to the effort "to get women to take part in socially productive labour". By socialization of domestic labour Trotsky meant the creation of *public institutions* to undertake the care of children, collective cafeteria services, collective laundry services, etc. To the extent that these institutions are developed and their services expanded, to that extent will housewives be freed to take part fully in "socially productive labour"; and to the extent that they take part in social production under these conditions, to that extent will it be difficult to return to the old regime of unpaid domestic labour.

Trotsky's idea of what he called "collective family housekeeping units representing the first, still very incomplete, approximations to a communist way of life"[22] is a realistic refinement of Engels' prescription, for it does not envisage the inevitable destruction of the nuclear family: it rather envisages the purging of the nuclear family of its oppressive character by the gradual socialization of the tasks hitherto heaped on housewives without pay.

It goes without saying that only a revolutionary government committed to the construction of socialism and communism can undertake such a gigantic task, which demands, among other things, a massive redeployment and reallocation of society's resources (human and material) and energy. The task even goes beyond mere political will:

> a radical reform of the family and, more generally, of the whole order of domestic life requires a great conscious effort on the part of the whole mass of the working class, and presumes the existence in the class itself of a powerful molecular force of inner desire for culture and progress.[23]

Women's Liberation and the Struggle for Socialism

History has taught us:

(a) that just as the socialization of the means of production creates the foundation for *real* democratization of all aspects of social life, so does it create the *condition* for the liberation of women from their specific oppression;

(b) that a socialist revolution does not automatically resolve the question of women's oppression — which can, indeed, continue in new forms;

(c) that a socialist revolution is incomplete which leaves half of mankind under specific oppression;

(d) that the inclination, capacity and will of a revolutionary socialist movement to resolve "the women's question" — or any specific social question, for that matter — are reflected in its character, programme and organizational structure. (For instance, a socialist movement which does not struggle against male chauvinism within its ranks cannot be serious about women's liberation!)

These lessons must inform every genuine socialist movement. Indeed, the greater the ability of a socialist movement to formulate an all-embracing revolutionary programme, and mobilize the people for struggles against all forms of social oppression, the greater its *authenticity* and *relevance*. This is a vital political lesson which no serious socialist movement can afford to ignore.

The implication of these lessons is that a specific programme of struggle for women's liberation must be integrated into the general programme of struggle for socialism. This does not mean that a socialist movement should merely include a commitment to the liberation of women in its charter and voice this commitment from time to time as occasion demands. It rather means that a revolutionary socialist movement must extend *critical* support to feminist organizations and struggles — *whether these organizations are allied to the movement or not and whether the struggles are led by the movement or not.* Although a genuine revolutionary socialist movement must aim at integrating all revolutionary organizations under the banner of socialist revolution, this integration must not be a condition for its support for struggles against specific forms of social oppression.

We use the term *critical support* because a revolutionary socialist movement must not appropriate or endorse the illusions associated with the struggle against ethnic oppression. While supporting all struggles against the specific oppression of women, a socialist movement must always make it clear that all victories scored by oppressed people will always remain partial and unstable "unless and until the two ruling groups — the foreign and domestic capitalists — are forced to give up their power, property and privileges".[24] This is the condition for a permanent and total solution of "women's question".

As we have earlier said, it will be wrong for a revolutionary socialist movement to assign *primary* importance to socialist revolution and only *secondary* importance to the liberation of women, or — what is the same thing — to say that the struggle for women's liberation must await the realization of socialism. This is a wrong political strategy for at least two reasons:

(1) The *critical* promotion of feminist agitation helps to radicalize women against the status quo. It also helps to reveal to feminists that the capitalist structure imposes an absolute limit on their freedom.

(2) Just as partial victories (called reforms) can be exacted by the oppressed classes under capitalism so can partial victories be scored by women through feminist agitations. For example, as Juliet Mitchell has said:

> equal pay and equal work opportunities are crucial anti-capitalist reforms, not just for abstract limited notions of justice, as we commonly think, but because they make the capitalist pay more for getting less. Even indirectly, they can help to make private capital pay for what happens to women at home.[25]

This is all we can say as regards the duty of a revolutionary socialist movement in the sphere of women's liberation. The debate as to whether women's oppression can survive socialist revolution or not is idle outside revolutionary struggle. To those whose only contribution to revolutionary struggle is this endless debate, we say: "The philosophers have only interpreted the world, in various ways; the point however, is to change it."[26]

Notes

1. Eleanor Burke Leacock, Introduction to Engels' *Origin of the Family, Private Property and the State* (International Publishers, N.Y., 1975), p.41.
2. Bhikhu Perekh, *The Concept of Socialism* (Croom Helm, London, 1975), p.223.
3. Eleanor Burke Leacock, p.40.
4. V.I. Lenin, *Selected Works In Three Volumes,* Vol. Three (Progress Publishers, Moscow, 1975), p.172.
5. Bhikhu Parekh, p.225.
6. Bhikhu Parekh, p.230.
7. This passage, attributed to Charles Fourier, was cited by Marx and Engels in their joint work *The Holy Family* (Progress Publishers, Moscow 1975), p.230.
8. *Monthly Review,* N.Y. Volume 31, No.2, June 1979, p.42.
9. *Monthly Review,* p.42.
10. *Monthly Review,* pp.42-43.
11. Eleanor Burke Leacock, p.29.
12. Eleanor Burke Leacock, p.30.
13. Frederick Engels, *The Origin of the Family, Private Property and the State* (International Publishers, N.Y., 1975), pp.137-138.
14. Bhikhu Parekh, p.222.
15. Bhikhu Parekh, p.222.

16. Marx and Engels, *The Holy Family,* p.230.
17. V.I. Lenin, *On the Emancipation of Women* (Progress Publishers, Moscow, 1972), p.80.
18. Leon Trotsky, *Problems of Everyday Life and other Writings on Culture and Science* (Monad Press, N.Y., 1973, p.38.
19. V.I. Lenin, *Emancipation,* p.81.
20. V.I. Lenin, *Emancipation,* p.81.
21. Marx and Engels, *Selected Works in Three Volumes,* Vol.3 (Progress Publishers, Moscow, 1970), p.19.
22. Leon Trotsky, *Problems of Everyday Life..,* p.43.
23. Leon Trotsky, *Problems of Everyday Life..,* p.37.
24. Leo Huberman and Paul M. Sweezy, *Socialism in Cuba* (Monthly Review Press, N.Y., 1979), p.19.
25. Bhikhu Parekh, p.225.
26. Marx and Engels, *Selected Works in Three Volumes,* Vol.1 (Progress Publishers, Moscow, 1973), p.15.

PART II
Women in Nigerian History

Women in Nigerian History: Examples from Borno Empire, Nupeland and Igboland

Halima D. Mohammed

As we headed towards Sabon Gari in the Volkswagen car, a man with his three male children cut across us on his bike. He wanted to cross over to the other side to the mosque. It was Friday. The man driving our car commented that the man's house would be helpless, or even useless if all the men (the childen and the man) on the bike were suddenly run over by our car. I usually don't allow such comments like this (which naturally come from the man) to pass without making men realize the roles of women, and their ability to do as men can do, especially having regard to what they have done in our history. And in most cases, the men agree with me, but they point out that the patrilineal nature of our society always makes men (and even some women) regard women as inferior but this has not historically been the case. I shall take examples of women in Nigerian history to point out clearly what I mean. These examples are from the Borno Empire, where women are known to have organized the internal structures of the palace and its connection with the state organization; from Hausaland, where a woman, Queen Amina, is known to have had considerable success in wars; from Igboland and Nupeland, where women are known to have had important roles in the political lives of their communities despite the patrilineal system of those societies.

Women in Borno History

"The harem organization and its connection with the other state organization".[1]

> It was said that in the Amir's household there were seven ladies and 60 men, of the seven ladies the first was the Gumsu... The courtiers of the Gumsu were 60 men of noble ranks. There were 40 slaves who worked for her and 20 men at-arms who went out to fight and who maintained Gumsu's authority. Each of these 20 men commanded a thousand slaves which shows us how the harem organization could be the microcosm of the state as a whole.[2]

The office of the *magira* links the harem with the outside world (in the kingdom) along clear lines of political control over territories and authoritative decision-making and action.[3] In addition to the role of the *magira* in the palace (as the head of the palace women) and consequently the head of womenfolk throughout the state, we can see that there exist links between the harem organization and the general state organization, as was the case with the *Gumsu*. The *magira* was also one of the principal fief-holders in the state and she possessed a full complement of administrative staff including men-at-arms through whom she imposed her political authority.[4] Under the *magira* were her assistants, the *magiram* and *Dogoma*, who decided and judged cases among the harem women, but when the case proved too difficult for them to decide, they took it to the *magira* and when she proved legally incompetent to decide, the case was referred to the Alkali (chief judge) who decided according to the *sunna*.

> And to each one of them, there is land apportioned on which they levy the Kharaj (of the land) and the Zakat (of the inhabitants). These lands freed the *magira* from the necessity of oppressing anyone in order to obtain her sustenance. And each one of them has an Alkali who is knowledgeable in the book of *sunna*, who adjudicates on her behalf in all legal matters that occur and he keeps records of all these matters.[5]

Queen Amina of Zazzau

Amina's history is dismissed as legend, or folktale, obviously by historians who are in most cases men. They couldn't believe her remarkable success in wars. But we find mention of her in Sultan Bello's *Infaq al-maisuri* and the *Kano Chronicle*. In *Infaq al-maisuri*, Amina is said to have "waged wars in the Hausaland and took them all, so that the men of Katsina and the men of Kano brought her tribute. She made war in Bauchi and against other towns in the south and the west, so that her possessions stretched down to the shores of the sea".[6] And the *Kano Chronicle* records that

> at this time, Zaria, under Amina, conquered all the towns as far as Kwararafa and Nupe. Every town paid tribute to her. The Sarkin Nupe sent 40 eunuchs and 10,000 kolanuts to her. She first had eunuchs and kolanuts in Hausaland. In her time, all the products of the west were brought to Hausaland. Her conquests extended over 34 years.[7]

In Daura, the legendary ancestor of the Hausa people, Bayajida, was said to have married the Queen of Daura-Daurama who was the ruler of Daura. I think it is after Bayajida's establishment of a political structure over Hausaland, that the male dominance as rulers in Hausaland began. But the title *magajiya* is given as the senior title in Daura. Titles such as *Iya, Saraki-Gabsai, Makama* etc., are female titles of Daura which date from earliest times and are still maintained.[8]

Among the women of royal blood in pre-Fulani Nupe, three women of rank existed: *Ninwoye, Sagi,* and *Wogbo.* At the court of ancient Nupe, the titles were bestowed by the king on his mother or father's sister, elder sister, or daughter, that is, a woman of about 40-50 years. She is to be unmarried, or else her marriage would be formally dissolved on her appointment to the rank, and she would forthwith be regarded as unmarried. The Fulani adopted the first two ranks, abandoning, however, the condition of celibacy or nominal celibacy, and made the two daughters of the first Etsu, *Sagi* and *Nimaraye.* The two ranks have remained in the royal house of Nupe since then.[9]

Among the Bida women, those not from the royal house, we find another women's rank, *Sonya.*

She is, as the Nupe put it the *"sagi* of the poor"; what the royal princesses do for the women of the nobility the *Sonya* does for the women of her class:

She advises them, and arbitrates in their quarrels, taking however, the more serious cases to the *sagi.* The *Sonya* might also be called a female officer of state. All large-scale women's work that is done in Bida by the order of the king is organized and supervised by her — for example, the beating of the floors in the houses of the king and the royal nobility. The *Sonya* is, above all, entrusted with the supervision of the market. "She is elected by the Bida women who are regular traders on the market, another rank is confirmed by the *Etsu.*"[11]

At the village level, we also find a titled, "head of the women", called *Sagi,* like the royal princess in Bida. She is usually a woman about or over 50. She is elected by the married women of the village and her appointment is confirmed by the chief... like the *Sonya* in Bida, the Village *Sagi* advises the women, organizes women's work, arbitrates between them, and receives small presents from every business transaction which they carry through.[12]

These ranks and offices represent forms of status which the women acquire in their own right, on the grounds of descent, or personal ability, or both independent of their status as wives of men who occupy this or that social position.[13] The status by descent of the Nupe women is not affected by marriage. If it is affected, some of "low" birth who marry above their status into the aristocracy can claim the status of their husbands, and women who marry beneath their station do not lose their status but raise their husbands to their own level. The men will be allowed to share most of the social and political privileges of the class into which they marry.[14] In cases where the man is not

fully admitted into the titled class, his children would always acquire the status of their mother. Daughters may thus inherit the status of their fathers, and both sons and daughters, that of their mothers... This social regulation may seem surprising in an otherwise strongly patrilineal society, but this one-sided interpretation of the change of status that goes with marriage is not an expression of matrilineal kinship tendencies... rather it expresses political interest, deep-seated class sentiments, which cannot admit of a lowering of status in any one high-born.[15]

In Yorubaland, we learn that women contributed to the economy by engaging in petty trading (foodstuffs and other articles of small value) which was largely in their hands. Women traders travelled considerable distances. Clapperton found women from Oyo trading at Kulfo in northern Nupe in the 1820's.

Igbo Women

In traditional Igbo society, women did not have a political role equal to that of men. But they did have a role — more accurately, a series of roles — in the political life of their communities despite the patrilineal organization of Igbo society.

> In this society, political power is diffuse, and leadership was fluid and informal. Community decisions were made and disputes settled in a variety of gatherings — village-wide assemblies, women's meetings, age grades, secret and title societies... Decisions were made by discussions until mutual agreement was reached. Any adult present who had something to say on the matter under discussion was entitled to speak — as long as he or she said something that others considered worth listening to; as the Igbo say, "A case forbids no one". Leaders were those who had "mouth". Age was respected, but did not confer leadership unless accompanied by wisdom and the ability to speak well.[16]

There are thus no distinctions between what we call executive, legislative and judicial activities, and no political authority to issue commands... Only within a family compound could an individual demand obedience to order. There, the compound head offered guidance and protection to members of his family, and in return, received respect, obedience, and material tokens of good will. Neither were there any distinctions between the religious and the political. Rituals and any political discussions were interwoven in patterns of action to promote the good of the community. These rituals, too, were performed by various groups of women, men, and women and men together.[17]

"Women as well as men thus had access to political participation; for women as well as for men, public status was to a great extent achieved, not ascribed. A woman's status was determined more by her own achievements than by the achievements of her husband."[18] In traditional

Igbo society, women have political institutions. These institutions express women's disapproval and secure their demands by collective public demonstration and through group strikes. The gatherings that appear to have performed the major role in self-rule among women and that articulated women's interests, as opposed to those of men, were the lineage-wide or village-wide gatherings of all wives, the *Inyemedi*, which came to be called *Mikiri* or *Mitiri*. *Mikiri* were multi-purpose women's associations. They provided women with a forum in which to develop their political talents, and a means for protecting their interests as traders, farmers, wives, and mothers through collective action — against individual women, individual men, and men as a group... In *Mikiri*, women made rules about markets, crops and livestock that applied to men as well as women, and exerted pressure to maintain moral norms among women. They heard complaints from wives about mistreatment by individual husbands, and discussed how to deal with problems they were having with the men as a whole.[19]

The British tried to introduce ideas of "native administration" into this system of diffuse authority, fluid and informal leadership, shared rights of enforcement, and a more or less stable balance of male and female power.[20] The British did not take into consideration that the appointment of one man to represent the village was an abrogation of Igbo concepts. And under the arbitrary rule of the warrant chiefs (as the representatives of the British were called) women suffered most.

> In November of 1929 in Calabar and Owerri provinces, thousands of women converged on the native administration centres. The women chanted, danced, sang songs of ridicule and demanded the caps of office (official insignia) of the warrant chiefs... prisons were broken into and prisoners released at a few locations. Attacks were made on 16 Native Courts, and most of them were broken up or burned. The 'disturbed area' covered about 6,000 sq.miles and contained about two million people. It is not known how many women were involved, but the figure was in tens of thousands. On two occasions when British District Officers had called in police and troops, the women were fired upon, leaving 50 women dead and another 50 wounded.[21]

Reforms were made in 1933, but women's traditional political role was ignored. Reforms were introduced to adjust traditional Igbo male and male-dominated political roles to correspond with those of the Europeans. The British felt or assumed that girls and boys, women and men should be treated and should behave as people supposedly did in "civilized" England. Not only was strong domination introduced into Igbo society indirectly by new economic structures; it was also directly imposed by the recruitment of only men as part of the native administration. These new economic and political structures were supported by the inculcation of ideology in the mission schools.[22]

Conclusion

From the few examples considered so far, it is clear that women, if and when given the chance, can play crucial roles and excel in them. Queen Amina for instance controlled a large extensive area within her 34 years of conquest. The men would no doubt call her a man-woman (half man-half woman) not a true woman: that is, if they ever believed her existence in history without dismissing it as legend or folktale.

However, the cases of Borno and Hausaland show that the class structure was a significant factor affecting the degree of freedom enjoyed by women. Thus only women belonging to the aristocracy have been able to rise to greatness either in politics, administration or education. Ordinary women were too busy raising children, cooking and going to the farm or the market to make a name in life. For upper class women, the possession of slaves freed them of these labours (except reproduction). In Nupeland, because of class differentiation, upper class women who married commoners in fact raised the status of their husbands!

Among the Igbo, the social system gave importance to achievement and participation so that women enjoyed certain institutionalized roles and privileges. They were generally freer than their counterparts in the rigid and hierarchial social systems of the Kanuri, Hausa, Yoruba and Nupe. Perhaps, this was partly why they were in the forefront of the nationalist struggle in Igboland. They resisted the warrant chiefs and took up arms against the native administration introduced by colonialism, while the men silently accepted what was imposed.

It is clear, therefore, that women are not inferior to men. The truth is that they were not given the chance to prove their abilities. Also as we have seen the class or social structure further reduced the woman in most cases to a secondary role. Even among the aristocracy, not all women enjoyed the same degree of privilege or freedom.

Notes

1. This is the title of the article by Moh'd Yanbue which was translated by Kyari Tijani in *Al-Idara fi Kizain al-mamlaka*.
2. Kyari Tijani (trans), *Al-Idara fi Kizain al-mamlaka*, p.17.
3. Ibid p.19. The title of *magira* is given to the Queen Mother of every Mai during the Saifawa dynastic rule of every Shehu of the present el-Kanemi dynasty. It came into being around 1569. It was said that the *magira* Aisha kili bint Dunoma acted as regent for the young Mai Idris B. Ali, having earlier saved him from threats of his life by both her father and her brother Abdullah. She perhaps even recalled him at the critical time for his succession. Thus, every Queen Mother is bestowed with this title up to present day. (From the *Groundwork of Nigerian History*, Heinemann Educational Books, Ibadan 1980, edited by O. Ikime). The title of the *Gumsu* is often given to the senior wife of the Emir.
4. Ibid p.19.

5. Ibid p.20. The *Kharaj* is tax levied on people who inhabit the land of authority. The *Zakat* is one of the compulsory pillars of Islam, where every Muslim is to give out to the poor some measure of what he has accumulated. In this case, the *magira* who was the principal fief holder levied the *Kharaj* and the *Zakat,* she doesn't see it as oppressing anyone, and the people who give out the *Kharaj* don't feel they are oppressed. After all, she owns the land, doesn't she?

6. Muh'd Bello Ibn Uthman, *Infaq al-maisuri,* translated and paraphrased by E.J. Arnett as *The Rise of the Sokoto Fulani,* Kano 1922.

7. Palmer, H.R. *Sudanese Memoirs,* Vol.1, Government Printer, Lagos, 1926.

8. Ibid p.8.

9. Nadel, S.F., *A Black Byzantium: The Kingdom of Nupe in Nigeria,* Oxford University Press, London 1969, p.147.

10. Ibid p.147.

11. Ibid pp.147 & 148.

12. Ibid p.149.

13. Ibid p.149.

14. Ibid pp.149 & 150.

15. Robin Law, *The Oyo Empire c1600-c1836: A West African Imperialism in the Era of the Atlantic Slave Trade,* Clarendon Press, Oxford, 1977, ch.10.

16. Judith Van Allen, *Aba Riots or the Igbo Woman's War? Ideology Stratification and the Invisibility of Women* in Hafkin and Bay, (eds), *Women in Africa,* Stanford University Press, U.S.A., 1976, pp.59-85.

17. Ibid pp.16 & 17.

18. Ibid p.17.

19. Ibid p.17.

20. Ibid p.20.

21. Ibid p.12.

22. Ibid p.27.

Women in Pre-capitalist Socio-economic Formations in Nigeria

Gloria Thomas Emeagwali

The Woman Question in the Context of Pre-capitalist Socio-economic Formations: Some Comments

The woman question should be seen as fundamentally related to the infrastructural conditions and environment at specific periods in the transformation of the production process. In the course of this paper, a few observations vis-a-vis historiography and the period in question will be made and some specific comments would be given on the issue of the activities of women in pre-capitalist socio-economic formations such as existed in Nigeria before the nineteenth century. A great part of the paper is conjectural for reasons discussed in the initial part of the paper.

Historiography and the Woman Question

When we examine the historical works which deal with the period in question, it becomes noticeable that the specific roles contributions and general activities of women is a neglected theme relatively speaking. We are, in fact, dealing with gross sins of omission in terms of historical reconstruction. In the first place the sources in themselves, for reasons which are yet to be fully explored, are essentially man-centred. The so-called "bare facts" seem to deal with phenomena which focus very little on women's activities. There are some explanations for this tendency. In the first place it should be stressed that *facts* are in themselves the product of multiple forces and influences. They are in themselves theoretical constructs.[1] A specific world-view which relegates women to the background would therefore have specific implications for documentation at the level of the primary sources and the interpretation of such documents.

Another possible reason for the paucity of sources and the poverty of information on the subject of women may also be cited. This is the specific nature of the activities of women in pre-capitalist formations in agrarian-based economies.[2] This will be discussed later in the paper. Furthermore the types of questions asked by the historian indeed influence the focus. It is an observation that is valid for the reconstruction of pre-capitalist formations in general and the issue has been touched on in my recent analysis of the *Groundwork of Nigerian History*.[3] Furthermore, the historian who sees the historical process in terms of leading personalities coming from the dominant ruling group is more apt to neglect the activities of women as members of the producer class. His focus on women would therefore be limited to a few hand-picked individuals which the man-centred sources may have thrown up. Women personalities such as Queen Amina of Zaria for example and other forces of oppression would be highlighted in so far as they are members of the ruling class but in terms of the generality of women producers, the analysis would be silent. Historical methodology which sees the historical process within a wider framework is more capable of focusing on the activities of women in general.[4]

Aspects of Pre-capitalist Formations

It has been suggested earlier in the paper that aspects of pre-capitalist formations have in fact influenced the specific activities of women and the ways in which they have been represented, or, indeed not represented. The fact is that in the era before the expropriation process takes place and before labour becomes a commodity, in the period before industrial capitalism, we are indeed dealing with a situation where there is a concentration of resources and activities in the agrarian sector. The application of technology to production is minimal. Power is generated primarily by non-mechanical devices. The application of mechanical and chemical principles of production has not taken place to any significant level. Power is therefore essentially generated by human or animal forces. The development of the means of production is relatively minimal compared to later phases when production for exchange value becomes generalized. It is at this point in time that control of the means of *reproduction* becomes particularly crucial. It is in this context that we should understand the ways in which dominant groups feature. It is in this context that we can examine the role of the elders for example in pairing, marriage, and bride-wealth acquisition, and other issues related to the reproduction of society in forms of social relations and more so in terms of the biological.[5]

It might be revealed that a great deal of what passes for sentimentality and sanctified laws indeed are justification for the control over subsistence and labour power, inclusive of female labour power.[6] In such a situation where human labour is a driving force in production and where the consolidation of such labour power would enhance the possibilities for material wealth and the possibilities for surplus appropriation, it becomes an issue of noticeable importance. The control of the means of *reproduction* and the control over women as producers is indeed an avenue to the consolidation of power which has material wealth at its base.[7] Given the fact that one woman may in the long run be the source of multiple hands on the farm, we may conjecture that the female producer is an asset. Is this then one of the reasons why women are hardly seen or heard of in the texts? Is it possible that by virtue of her central importance to production and reproduction she is particularly made part and parcel of dependent relations and becomes more a victim of oppression than her male-producer counterpart? The issue is intricate and complex and it is for the historian to try to unravel the apparent mysteries and puzzles. This is not to suggest that the woman question must now be the dominant theme in historical reconstruction and this is not to say that the woman question must not be seen in the context of the class question and class analysis, but in as much as we have identified serious gaps in knowledge of this area, it is necessary to bridge them. Furthermore the clarification of the issue is essentially to be seen within a materialist perspective.[8]

Finally, it should be noted that in the case of Nigeria, in the pre-capitalist context, we are dealing with the articulation of different modes of production and that even within this period there might be noticeable distinctive phases. In the earlier periods of historical development there is less surplus production. We continue to get evidence from the archaeologists of the way in which there has been transformation in the design and nature of tools and equipment for production, items which along with labour are vital for production and productivity.[9] They determine to a large extent the degree of surplus production.

Now the question is whether this general change over time has had significant repercussions with respect to the role of women. Do women enjoy a distinctively different position in the earlier phases? What essentially is the role of women when production for use-value is still dominant? In what ways are there changes when production for exchange takes place and when these take place as a consolidation of the agrarian features mentioned earlier? Are there noticeable changes in superstructural forms such as law, cultural manifestations such as literature or ideological norms such as religion? Furthermore we may well ask for some analysis of the nature of the interaction between man and woman in the family unit itself, and the extent to which the development of labour over time affects the relationship. Is the relegation of woman to a subservient role to be seen as simultaneous with her loss of control over the means of production on the micro level?[10] At what time does the woman become dependent and when does she become exploited within the family itself? These are some of the questions that historians of Nigerian pre-capitalist formation must address themselves to. Even when the answers seem elusive, the questions should still be asked so as to constantly remind us of our ignorance on this important subject and so that we pursue historical reconstruction with specific objectives and as well try to develop the ways and means to cope with the unsolved problems.

Notes

1. The issue has been dealt with recently in A. Temu/B. Swai in *Historians and Africanist History: A critique* (Zed Press 1981). A pioneer work on the issue is found in E.H. Carr, *What is History?* (Penguin, 1961). Carr stresses the point that the facts are not like "fish on the fishmonger's slab". They are "like fish swimming about in a vast and sometimes inaccessible ocean". p.23. I have also attempted to look at the issue in the context of *explanation* (see G. Thomas Emeagwali, "Explanation in African History", Silver Jubilee issue, *Journal of the Historical Society of Nigeria* (forthcoming).

2. To speak of *pre-capitalist formations* is to speak of the sum total of the specific combination of productive forces and production relations at a specific period in historical development. The latter are central to the economic base of the formation, and as pointed out elsewhere, "the dialectics of productive forces and production relations is the motive force behind social development". See for example Marx/Engels, *Pre-capitalist Socioeconomic Formations* (Progress, 1979). The focus in the paper is on the period before the transition to industrial Capitalism/dependent capitalism. In this period the means of production are relatively undeveloped and the surplus is appropriated from activities which are largely agricultural.

3. See for example G. Thomas, "Political Institutions in Pre-Nineteenth Century Nigeria: Some observations on the Groundwork of Nigerian History", Paper presented at the 27th Annual Congress, *Historical Society of Nigeria,* Port Harcourt, 13-17 April 1982.

4. The materialist model, which focuses on the totality of production relations, productive forces and superstructural forms, is specifically referred to here.

5. Insight into the issue has been gained from Meillassoux's analysis of the social organization of the peasantry. See the relevant article in D. Seddon (ed), *Relations of Production* (Cass, 1978).

6. The reference here is to elements of the "ideological formation" which simply justify and reflect the prevailing conditions.

7. Here *means of reproduction* should be seen as distinct from *means of production.* The emphasis is on the biological in the case of the former.

8. See note 4.

9. When we refer to the productive forces, it is essentially to the means of production such as tools, and equipment and land etc., in addition to labour power.

10. The focus here is primarily on the production activities taking place in the family compound.

Rapporteur's Report:

Ahmed Modibbo

It was noted that there is a dearth of information on the role of women generally in Nigerian history before the twentieth century. The question was raised as to how one is to discover the role of ordinary women, as well as of aristocratic women, during this period. A paper contended that in the Nupe court, when the king appoints a female relation to a title, she either remains unmarried, or has her marriage dissolved. This contention needs to be established.

Another paper noted that the need of women's labour in the pre-capitalist social formations encouraged polygynous practices in Nigeria. But was this experience ever noticed in pre-capitalist Western Europe? Another conclusion was that if and when they are given the chance, women can be "successful". This was challenged and the meaning of "success" was questioned as was the contention that the Nigerian man is successful. In reaction to the points raised on women in history, it was suggested that looking at women as a separate factor in history is diversionary. Rather they should be seen as part and parcel of social units in relations of production. However, gender relations are one of the determinants affecting the role of women in history.

The observation was made that in the process of collecting data for research purposes, women in certain parts of Nigeria decline to talk about their experiences, particularly as related to political and economic issues, except in the presence of their husbands. Another question was raised which sought clarification in connection with the widely-held presumption that Islam holds that a woman's "paradise" is in the hands of her husband. A participant replied that this is tied to the Hadith — but in the wider context of obedience to "constituted authority".

Finally, an observation was made on the question of the position of women as it relates to the whole system of inheritance. There is a deliberate attempt to deny women access to the means of production and control of political power. Also it was observed that in the context of class relationships women are usually left out.

Part III
Women in Production

Female Labour and Exploitation within African Social Formations

A.B. Zack-Williams

Introduction

This paper seeks to highlight some examples of "over-exploitation" of female labour within African social formations. According to Claude Meillassoux, over-exploitation exists, "when the remuneration for labour is less than the cost of the reproduction of labour power".[1] Two arguments being developed in this presentation are the following:

(1) Over-exploitation of female labour is part of a general process of over-exploitation of African labour
(2) The process of over-exploitation of African labour is only possible because of the articulation of capitalist and pre-capitalist modes within the social formation.

The rest of the presentation is divided into four sub-sections. In the first section certain theoretical issues are discussed; the concepts of exploitation and over-exploitation are discussed. The following section contains some examples of over-exploitation of female labour in a number of African societies. The final section consists of the conclusion.

Theoretical Issues

Meillassoux has noted that: "the study of exploitation and over-exploitation brings together problems of the reproduction of labour power — and of reproduction".[2]

In short, a study embracing the above approach must be able to locate the specific nature of production within the social formation. In another work,[3] I have argued that Third World social formations epitomize an articulation of modes of production. To argue that African social formations constitute a variegated articulation of modes of production is to pose the question: why has capitalism failed to destroy the pre-existing modes of production with which it had long been in contact? In order to answer this question, we have to look at the nature of reproduction[4] of the capitalist mode, and the role which the pre-capitalist modes play in

61

aiding the reproduction of capitalism. Herein lies the origin of over-exploitation of female labour in Africa.

Various reasons have been given for the failure of capitalism to destroy pre-capitalist modes. These include: the nature of the pre-capitalist modes which in some cases show strong resistance to change;[5] and the form which capitalism assumes within the peripheral social formation. Taylor, with whom this argument is associated, has produced a periodization of the penetration of capitalism into Third World social formations. The first period he refers to as "penetration under the dominance of merchant capital". This process tends to reinforce the unity of the direct producer to his means of production. The second period is characterized by "penetration under the dominance of commodity export". Whilst this form of penetration tends to strengthen production for exchange, it also begins to break down pre-capitalist modes. The third and final stage is that of penetration under the export of capital.[6] According to Taylor, it is at this stage that the direct producers are separated from the means of production and this marks the beginning of the destruction of the pre-capitalist mode. This stage is possible because capital affects the very means by which the pre-capitalist mode is reproduced, i.e. "by undermining the reproduction of its determinate relation of production".[7]

A more significant reason (from our point of view) for the conservation of pre-capitalist modes is the role that they play in the reproduction of capitalism. Meillassoux has argued not only that "agricultural self-sustaining formations" fulfil roles which complementary to the reproduction of capitalism in the formations of the centre, but that these roles are ones which capitalism prefers not to take up on its own. He notes that:

> the agricultural self-sustaining communities, because of their comprehensiveness and their raison d'être, are able to fulfil functions that capitalism prefers not to assume in underdeveloped countries: functions of social security. The cheap cost of labour in these countries comes from the super-exploitation, not only of the labour from the wage-earner himself but also of the labour of his kin-group.[8]

Exploitation and Over-exploitation

Within the capitalist mode, exploitation refers to the appropriation of surplus value (or to surplus labour under the pre-capitalist modes). Labourers who are totally dispossessed of the means of production are forced to sell their labour power to the capitalists, the owners of the means of production. From the total value produced by labour, capital has to reward the latter wages for the sale of labour power. The remainder (i.e. surplus value) is the property of the capitalist class and is appropriated as it wishes. The difference between total value and surplus value defines the rate of exploitation under capitalism.

For the working class to continue to produce itself, direct (hourly) wages must be supplemented by indirect wages. This indirect wage, in bourgeois sociology, is usually discussed under the rubric of "social security". It includes such items as: family allowance, old age pension, sickness and unemployment benefits, and maternity benefits. This indirect wage which is usually calculated "on the precise needs of up-keep and reproduction",[9] is realized only in the developed capitalist centre, but lost to those who work in the periphery. It has been estimated that in the developed countries, indirect wages account for some 40% of socially necessary labour time.[10]

In African societies, it is widely known that a large number of workers are not completely integrated into the wage labour economy.[11] Even those who are tied to the hourly wage system are not divorced from production systems outside of the capitalist mode. Many of these are migrant workers (seasonal and "target" workers) who migrate to the rural areas at the end of their "contract". This process of rural-urban migration aids the process of primitive accumulation and contributes to capital, by augmenting surplus value, due to the failure of capitalists to pay indirect wages. This indirect deduction is usually referred to by Marxists as "labour rent". The extraction of labour rent is what in this paper we refer to as "over-exploitation".

Empirical Questions

Whilst it is beyond the scope of this paper to calculate African women's contribution towards labour rent, yet there are certain indicators which lead us to conclude that such a contribution must be very high.

Firstly, a study by E.B. Simmons has shown that there is considerable social pressure on all women to engage in a social occupation.[12] Similarly, Polly Hill has noted that in Katsina, "virtually all women have some economic acitivty other than farming".[13] Furthermore, in the case of women in *Kulle* (seclusion), Shea has noted that even though they are excluded from agricultural work, yet they are able to take up craft work (such as spinning and weaving of cotton cloth), preparation and sale of cooked food.[14] Women in other parts of Africa are also involved in this so-called informal sector.[15] In the urban areas of Africa, many women work as petty commodity producers and petty traders. In the case of the former, they produce soap and textile materials as well as providing cheap cooked food for the urban proletariat. The provision of these commodities at prices which are below what capitalist enterprise would have offered, means that women's labour helps to provide a subsidy to the wage of the capitalist class. This is because the provision of these cheap articles for mass consumption helps to maintain low wage rates[16] and hence intensifies the level of exploitation of the wage-earner.

Secondly, a recent study by Anna Conti on an agricultural project scheme in Upper Volta has shown how international merchant capital and finance capital have succeeded in organizing Voltarian rural women in order to produce a wide range of crops which are bought by merchant capital for sale in the European market.[17] The scheme, which is meant to ensure the best returns to finance capital, is premised not on wage labour, but on "nuclear family structure". In order to achieve this task, Conti has argued that capital assumed a syncretic form:

> To carry out this strategy, capital...cannot act as pure mercantile, productive or finance capital in their distinctive forms but as a combination of all three. Second, due to a need for stable, skilled, but non-wage labour, capital reorganizes kinship in smaller units (i.e. nuclear families) which dictate both production and reproduction relations.[18]

Conti goes on to argue that this organization of reproduction resulted in "a loss of economic independence for women and an increase in their work load as producers and reproducers". This is due to the fact that merchant capital failed to invest in physical infrastructure such as good roads and transportation facilities. For example, transportation of cotton and other crops was "done by women on their heads". Finally Conti notes that the profitability of the project was "based not only on the means of production being 'self-financed' but on the high contribution of female labour, (with) women bearing the burden of reproduction without being included in the costs of capital. This 'subsidization' of capital represents one of the main sources of capitalist accumulation".[19]

Thirdly, in another study, Deborah Bryceson has argued that whilst proletarianization can objectively free women from male control,[20] in practice, women may continue to experience male domination in certain crucial matters, such as: time that a woman can commence work, how her wage is spent, cooking and child-care. Even when women are "liberated" by their engagement in wage labour, this does not mean that they have a decisive say in matters of fertility and sexuality. Furthermore, Bryceson points out that because the proletarianization of women is always incomplete, this means that women have to continue to play a role in food production, which as we have seen acts as a wage supplement and as a means of lowering the wages of female and male workers alike. Finally, Bryceson notes that often women have to work in such low paid jobs that their incomes have to be supplemented by the sale of their sexuality in addition to their labour power.

Fourthly, it is now acknowledged by such international organizations as the United Nations and the International Labour Organization (ILO), that quite a significant part of women's work remains "uncounted and ignored because so much of it is unmonetized".[21] Unrecorded female employment in Africa is far more extensive than is usually realized. For example, a correspondent for the weekly *West Africa* observes:

Unrecorded female employment may include unpaid labour on the farm or other family enterprise; work performed within the confines of the home; "occupational multiplicity", involving many different kinds of work, and therefore difficult to record, and patron/client relationships, with poor women assisting better-off women, and receiving payment in meals.[22]

Fifthly, African women tend to be "over-employed with pitifully low returns".[23] Using figures provided by the ILO, Erumsele noted that "Africa has by far the highest proportion of economically active women" in the labour force in 1970. Of the 10 African countries studied by the ILO over 45% of the women are in the labour force. This is close to male participation in Africa, which varies from 46%-62%. The figures also show that over 80% of women in the age group 25-44 are economically active.[24] Even the few African women who survive into old age continue to work after this period.[25]

Finally, we have argued above that the capitalist mode is able to avoid the payment of indirect wages (in the form of social security benefit) and is obliged to pay only the immediate sustenance of the labourer. The main reason why capitalism is able to pay for labour power below its cost of reproduction is the existence of a supply of labour power which is produced and reproduced outside the capitalist mode. Much of this supply of labour power is represented by female labour. As we have noted earlier, female labour is utilized in agriculture, petty commodity sector and in the home. Female labour plays a crucial role as a source of social security. This is largely due to the fact that as child bearers, women are reproducers of the direct producers, and are responsible for the old, the sick, the infirm and the young. These are functions which remain unremunerated by capitalism.

Conclusion

In this paper I have briefly looked at some examples of over-exploitation of female labour. Whilst I will not suggest that these are the only instances, yet they are enough to show the importance of female labour in the reproduction of capitalism within African social formations. Since much of this labour is external to the capitalist mode, it means that it goes unremunerated by capitalism, thus justifying the claim of the over-exploitation of female labour within African social formations.

Notes

1. Meillassoux, Claude, "Historical Modalities of the Exploitation and over-exploitation of labour", in *Critique of Anthropology,* Vol.4, No.13 & 14, Summer, 1979, p.7.
2. Ibid.
3. Zack-Williams, A.B., *"Underdevelopment and The Diamond Industry in Sierra Leone",* Unpublished, Ph.D. Thesis, Sheffield University.
4. The term reproduction as used in this paper has nothing to do with the functionalist interpretation of repetition and perpetuation of social systems. Indeed as Terray has noted: "what is being reproduced above all else is a contradiction." Thus in this paper reproduction refers not to the resolution of contradictions, but to the renewal of "the fundamental relation of production". See E. Terray, "On Exploitation: Elements of An Autocritique" in *Critique of Anthropology,* Vol.4, No.13 & 14, pp.29-39.
5. B. Bradby, "The Destruction of Natural Economy," in *Economy and Society,* Vol.4, No.2, May 1975; J.G. Taylor, *From Modernisation To Modes of Production,* Macmillan, 1979.
6. Taylor.
7. Taylor, p.219.
8. C. Meillassoux, "From Reproduction to production," *Economy and Society,* Vol.1, No.1, 1972, p.102.
9. C. Meillassoux, "Historical Modalities", p.15.
10. A.M.M. Hoogvelt "A Re-examination of the Concept of Exploitation: the Articulation of Modes of Production", Mimeo, n.d.
11. Hence the need to theorize an articulation of modes of production.
12. E.B. Simmons "Some Notes on the Economic Roles of Women in Northern Zaria Province", Rural Research Unit, Social Science Seminar, Institute of Agricultural Research, A.B.U. Zaria, Oct. 1970, Mimeo, quoted in P.J. Shea, *The Development of An Export-Oriented Dyed Cloth Industry in Kano Emirate,* Unpublished Ph.D. Thesis, University of Wisconsin, 1975.
13. P. Hill, "The Myth of the Amorphous Peasantry: A Northern Nigerian Case Study", NISER Reprint Series, No.53, *Nigerian Journal of Economic and Social Studies,* XV, 2, 1968, p.244, quoted in Shea, p.70.
14. P.J. Shea, pp.69-71.
15. For the case of Sierra Leone, see this author's "Underdevelopment... in Sierra Leone".
16. C. Gerry, *Petty Production and Capitalist Production in Dakar: The Crisis of The Self-Employed,* Conference on the Urban Informal Sector, SOAS, 1977, p.10.
17. A. Conti, "Capitalist Organisation of Production Through Non-Capitalist Relations: Women's Role in a Pilot Resettlement in Upper Volta". *Review of African Political Economy,* Nos. 15 & 16, May-Dec. 1979, p.75-92.
18. Conti, pp.75.
19. Conti, pp.75-6.
20. D. Bryceson, "The Proletarianisation of Women in Tanzania", *R.A.P.E.,* No.17, Jan.-April 1980, pp4-27. She goes on to argue that male dominance over female is due to the latter's "Potentiality as Child-bearers".
21. B. Cole, "Women of the World Unite", *West Africa,* No.3288, 28 July 1980, p.1377.

22. A.A. Erumsele, "Women's Part in Rural Development", *West Africa,* No.3291, 18 August, 1980, p.1540.
23. Erumsele.
24. Erumsele.
25. In 18 African Countries surveyed by the ILO over 30% of women remain economically active after the age of 65. The figure varies, with Lesotho recording the highest, almost 76% (see Erumsele).

Women Under Development: Some Preliminary Remarks

Caroline Knowles

Introduction

It is the intention of this paper to offer some tentative remarks about the concept "development" in the context of an irrigation scheme in northern Nigeria, and to document the construction of gender roles for women living within the scheme. I hope to establish that the category "women" has a specificity which cannot be reduced to the relation women have to the mode of production, as is suggested by many Marxist analyses, but that their coherence as a category is established through a discursive construction of the common position occupied by women in the social formation.

My study, which is in its infancy, is located in a settlement which is part of an irrigation scheme peopled by the Kanuri. My remarks are not, however, intended to give a sociological account of these people, or to assert their unity and coherence as a "people". But rather to simply document elements of their construction of femininity. Whilst I do not want to sociologize the notion of a tribe as a unified and coherent group, to challenge the concept of ethnicity is beyond the scope of this paper.

It is also the intention of this paper to distance itself from the sociology of development.[1] There are numerous accounts of development which deal with the generalized set of relations which come into play with the impact of technologically sophisticated modes of production, whether in agriculture or industry, on the third world. Instead, my emphasis will be to examine the concrete details of an agricultural development project, as this provides a focus for an interrogation of the concept "development" as a set of practices and ideologies with an administrative structure. This examination can be achieved through a "reading" of the feasibility studies which set out the details of the scheme and its implications. In this way, it should be possible to avoid reducing the concept "development" to a confrontation between capital and traditional modes of production.[2]

It is not intended that this paper should offer any conclusions either about development or the role of women under its impact, but rather that it should assess the extent to which the method of discourse analysis[3]

68

can be used to investigate specific objects, in this case "women" and "development", and make a small contribution to the study of the position of women in a specific settlement in northern Nigeria. Indeed, I am trying to assess what discourse analysis has to offer in an understanding of the social construction of feminity. As such this paper will raise more questions than it will resolve in its attempts at conceptualizing men in the context of "developing" Nigeria.

Conceptualizing Women: Some Theoretical Considerations

Engels' *Origin of the Family, Private Property and the State* indicated the interdependence of class and gender oppression. In the final analysis, however, Engels was unable to do more than suggest the entry of women into the labour force where they would be exposed to the same relations of exploitation as men. The search, through anthropological discourses, continues in a quest for the origins of female oppression, yet the evidence points increasingly to the fact that women have, since the dawn of time, taken part in productive labour of some kind.[4] Yet participation in the productive relations of a social formation does not specify anything unique about the position of women in relation to men. The early formulations of Marxism/feminism got round this by specifying the position of women in terms of their dual productive relation, inside and outside of the home. Their arguments suggested that women were unique in that they were the only group to assume this dual responsibility. A much more rigorous analysis may be achieved by deflecting from the central importance of the mode of production in the establishment of gender categories. Whilst it is not the intention of this paper to deny the importance of the mode of production pertinent to each social formation, it is my intention to challenge those interpretations which see all other relations in the social formation, in which the oppression of women is inscribed, as ultimately reducible to the mode of production. This kind of essentialism and reductionism is unhelpful in developing an understanding of the theoretical position of women and the strategies appropriate to challenging their oppression.

In presenting a challenge to theories which locate the peculiar position of women in a biological determinism, Marxism has both neglected the organization of sexual difference and reduced it to a material base in the set of economic relations which characterize the mode of production. Cousins (1979) has pointed out that the elements of a theory of a mode of production do not require a sexual division of labour, but a class division of society. Thus the concept of a mode of production presents a level of abstraction and generality in which gender divisions are not pertinent. Indeed the relations of capital and labour are abstract and indifferent to sexual differences.

Similar conceptual problems are encountered in locating the specificity of gender divisions in a theory of patriarchy. Along with mode of production, the relations of a patriarchal society, which locate the oppression of women in authoritarian male structures, have been identified as the other material basis for female oppression. This, too, involves a reduction of female oppression to an essence, in this case male authority. Whether female oppression is located in the structures of capitalism or of patriarchy, the effect is the same. All effects are ultimately "read off" from a central cause. In both of these modes of analysis, the problem of women's oppression is posed as a unitary field of effects with a unitary cause, capital or men. Women should not be conceptualized as an unproblematic totality, encompassing a unitary field of objects, but must be conceptualized according to the discourses in which they are constructed.[5] In this way it is possible to conceptualize women as oppressed by the effects of ideologies which are located in a multiplicity of discourses and practices rather than through certain economic functions necessary to capitalist relations of production.

The construction of women as a category for analysis, however, must proceed from scratch. To treat women as a naturally occurring category of the human population does not help the analysis at all. If gender is treated as "given" then we return to biological determinism. To assert that women have a biological specificity is banal and unhelpful in the task of analysing their position in different, historically specific social formations. Feuchtwang (1980) points out that the problem is not the term "gender" but its grounding in an origin. Thus men and women are not once and for all "given" categories, but their respective positions must be defined in certain societies at specific historico-political conjunctures.

In order to further develop the analysis facilitating the construction of gender categories, I shall develop the notion of a constraint in the production of discourses. A constraint functions to compel. It imposes a direction on statements which cannot be ignored. Whilst not actually producing statements directly, constraints produce the conditions in which statements are made and practices followed. In the course of the analysis, I shall attempt to identify some of the constraints which are responsible for the construction of sexual difference in the context of the development scheme.[6]

If we were to project the analysis further and comment on the kinds of struggles women might engage in, then it would be possible to develop the analytical framework to include a discussion of their constituencies (what they might be demanding in the process of struggle) and their communities (who they might be representing in their struggles). But to attribute certain kinds of struggles to them at this stage would be presumptuous. These can only be determined in the process of developing an on-going dialogue with them and determining what they see as the issues.

Conceptualizing Development

Development has been differently defined by different agencies in different conjunctures. In the process of decolonization, development was broadly a political concept in that it referred to the establishment of liberal democratic forms of administration in the political community. The only form in which independence was ever conceded by Britain was in the form of a federation set up along Western lines, though usually with a limited franchise and consequently a limited political community. Industrial and agricultural development were seen as infrastructural elements in the overall development of a former dependency towards nationhood. The input of British "aid" in the period which followed independence for former colonies operated a bias which indicated British conceptions of development. In the case of India (the first black country to gain independence), development was defined totally in terms of industrialization and urbanization, and consequently the transformation of the peasantry into an urban proletariat. By the time that African independence came on to the political agenda, there was a recognition that development could embrace rural areas also. The statement which follows is an example of the way development is currently defined by an aid-administering institution.

> Development assistance is the term used to describe the flow of financial and other resources to the developing countries to help them raise their living standards, through, for example, improved agricultural methods, better public health, the spread of education and new industries.

The statement then went on to outline the kind of "aid" Britain was prepared to offer to African countries.

The project with which this paper is concerned has partly subscribed to this definition of "aid" and its institutional arrangements by employing British technical assistance to assess the feasibility of the project, and by employing British consultants and foreign contractors to execute the construction of the scheme. This should be borne in mind as the conceptualizations of development employed in the development scheme are outlined.

Rather than assert a definition of development, it is necessary to examine the manner in which development was perceived and construed in a specific relation to the irrigation project. This is done through an examination of the feasibility studies and the actual agricultural practices related to the scheme. It is not the intention of this paper to assert the general applicability of the development concept which can be "read" from this scheme, as the idea of development may well be constructed differently in each scheme.

The decision to irrigate 41,830 acres of Borno State was taken in respect of the need to feed a rapidly growing population at the same time as reducing Nigeria's food import bill. The considerations upon which the decision to irrigate was based are set out in the feasibility study. These act as a constraint on the scheme in that they define the range of possible options open to an irrigation scheme. They define what could be grown and how it could be done. Consequently these considerations constrained the conceptions of development of which the scheme was an expression.

The irrigation scheme was primarily constrained by the rationale of economic orthodoxy. In the feasibility study, there was an emphasis on the need to ensure that the financial returns of the project represent an adequate return to the capital invested. This was to be recovered from the farmers who were the beneficiaries of the scheme by their handing over a proportion of their crops to the authority. This, incidentally, has been a focus for much local resentment on the part of the farmers. The project's concern with financial returns is discussed under the heading of "Returns to the Government". The feasibility study stated that:

> ...returns over the first twenty years of the scheme to the government (will be made up of) ...staff income tax payments, the produce tax on cotton, duties paid by the project and estimated tax from indirect income... In the tenth cropping year (1985), the estimated receipts to the North East State should amount to 36% of estimated local revenue in the 1971-2 financial year. These total receipts would represent a 3.9% rate of return on capital invested in the North East State.
>
> (1973 *Feasibility Study*)

In examining the definition of development being offered in the feasibility study so far, it has become clear that what is intended by development is a fairly conventional capitalist investment programme. One or two things need to be said about this. In the first place, it is obvious that the social and economic well-being of the local people is not highly placed in this definition of development. (But it is not ignored as I shall indicate later.) Secondly it is necessary to see the statement just outlined in the context of the purpose for which it is intended. A feasibility study as a text and site of enunciation is required to set out the range of options open to the client who commissioned the study. Its task is to point out the advantages to be gained from the scheme, but it need not do this in terms of financial reward. There are, indeed, a range of options open in defining development, for example improvements in health services and amenities or the spread of educational services. To present financial returns as an important factor represents a choice which indicates a set of assumed priorities on the part of the audience by those who commissioned the study.

A second, but related, financial constraint underlying the thinking behind the scheme, concerns the economic viability of growing crops under irrigated conditions at all. As most of the crops to be grown in the scheme could be grown in other areas of Nigeria under rain-fed conditions at a lower unit cost, it was recommended that production under irrigated conditions should only take place if an "effective demand" could be established for the crops. Effective demand in this context means demand which could not be met by expanding existing production under rain-fed conditions. The report also stipulated that marketing outlets should be established before the scheme was set up.

The two constraints just outlined are based on national rather than regional criteria. Development was, therefore, largely constructed in terms of a set of economic priorities relating to the economy as a whole. The third constraint set out by the study was neither national nor based on the constraints of economic orthodoxy. It concerned the need for calculations to be made in terms of rather more social considerations.

> However, it is thought that returns to capital will not be the major criteria considered when the decision on implementation is taken. Other factors such as the savings on foreign exchange, particularly on wheat, is a major consideration in agricultural development policy. The immediate need to boost food production together with the social need to produce employment and development opportunities in an area which has been neglected in the past, will also be major considerations along with the returns to capital.
>
> (1973 *Feasibility Study*)

Whilst social rather than economic considerations were presented as a matter of importance in this statement, the bulk of the feasibility study deals with statistics concerning crop yields and price estimates which indicate the rate at which the farmer would be able to repay the authority its investment in the project.

The project has had a number of effects on the lives of the people in the area. The constraints outlined above are responsible for these. One of the changes brought about by the project was the change in the farmer's relationship to the land. A tenancy agreement was brought into effect with the project, replacing customary rights to land, whereby the farmer no longer held the land under whatever traditional arrangement had persisted before. After irrigation work was completed, the irrigated land was returned to the farmer in proportion to the amount held before the scheme, with the difference that the farmer entered into a landlord-tenant relationship with the authority. Under the conditions of this tenancy, the relationship between landlord and tenant could be terminated by twelve months' notice given by either party. This is a condition which threatens the farmer's security to some extent.

A further stipulation of the tenancy agreement insists that the tenant has to agree to allow the authority to prepare the land in the interests of:

> ...good husbandry practice and fulfillment of the prevailing agricultural policy of the authority.
>
> (*Feasibility Study* 1973)

The interests of good husbandry were defined by the authority, so that in practice the farmer had little to say in what should be grown or the method of cultivation.

The constraints of economic orthodoxy, including the need for a return on capital investment, removed from the farmer the right to grow the traditional crops of the area and the right to use traditional techniques of cultivation. Development in this context meant enforcing highly productive cultivation techniques and strictly enforcing which crops should be grown. The scheme was to be managed by the authority, and the farmers lost control over the labour process in return for an increase in their incomes.

Farmers in the area had traditionally grown guinea corn on a single season mono-crop basis. In future crop rotation was to be practised and there was to be a change in the kinds of crops grown. The cost and conditions estimates of the feasibility reports indicated that rice, wheat and seed cotton were to be grown for local use. Plans were also laid to grow high value crops, tomatoes for sale and processing and onions for export. In addition to this, the Commonwealth Development Corporation was to have 10,000 acres for commercial wheat production. Not only did the scheme institute important changes in the labour process, it also involved a complete change in which crops were to be produced. Mechanization replaced traditional methods of work and farmers were told when and how to irrigate their land. The management of the scheme has been a problem for the authority as the controls they need to exercise in order to fulfil their financial constraints have to some extent been resisted by the farmers.

Another effect of the development process in this area has been an increase in local incomes. The feasibility study estimated that the scheme would lead to an increase in income of up to four times the previous level. In one particular area it was estimated that the project would generate a disposable consumer income of around N2 million. It was thought that this would lead to an increase in trading and service industries as well as grain marketing and processing. Indeed, considerable infrastructural changes in the area were envisaged. Development in this context was being defined to include a general movement towards a cash economy, rather than an economy based on subsistence, and the development of consumption.[7]

It should also be noted that a further effect of the irrigation scheme was to disrupt farming whilst the work of preparing the land was in progress. Because of this, it was suggested by the feasibility study that whilst the work was in progress, the displaced (male) labour force should be employed in construction. This is a considerable imposition on those who have traditionally been occupied on the land, and offers no opportunities for women.

The definition of development offered in the feasibility study is, however, being contested by those for whom it was intended. The construction of alternative definitions of development by the men and women living under the scheme requires further research. But it should be noted that the concerns of the men in the area were for the installation of a water supply and the development of health facilities.

Women and the Development Concept

Discussions of the role which women were to play in the irrigation scheme were absent from the feasibility study and the considerations of the development authority. If women had been included in their considerations, it would have been possible to comment on the role which they were assigned. But because they do not feature, it is only possible to comment on the significance of their absence from the discourse. In discussing human resources in the area, the feasibility study uses two categories, "adult males" and "families". Women do not feature, except implicitly as part of the family unit. They do not feature either as a part of the potential labour force or as a force to be consulted in the development process. Whilst the authority took great care with its public relations policy in the irrigated area, it did not appear to consider it necessary to consult the women. A later feasibility study relating to the extension of the irrigated area mentioned that women had been absent from its considerations, but did not attempt to rectify this situation. The study recognized that women played an important part in the village economy but chose not to document the extent of their productive activities.

The absence of women from the study's considerations indicates their marginality to the development process. They are not considered as a possible or actual labour force in their own right, but simply as an extension of the farmer. As such they are not considered to have the right of disposal over their own labour power. The discourse on the scheme, in so far as it was concerned with securing the cooperation of the local population, spoke only in terms of the farmer. Farmer, in the locality, is not a title which is applied to women. Women in the area do not consider themselves to be farmers even though many of them put in as much agricultural labour as men. This point is supported by the results of interviews conducted with the women. When asked about their work activities they described their activities on the compound. It wasonly through direct probing that it was possible to get them to describe their contribution to farming activities. The title "farmer" is therefore commonly understood to indicate a set of activities conducted by men. The women's identification of farming as tangential to their sphere of activity, which they define as the compound, indicates the extent to which gender categories are occupationally structured. This thinking obscures the large contribution women in the settlement make in the field of agriculture.

The above observation, based on speculation about the absence of women from the discourse, makes possible another. It is likely that not only are women not considered a labour force outside of their relation to men, but they are also only defined as members of the community through their relation to men. This is supported by the observation that at all times in their lives women are under the authority of men as fathers, husbands, and sons when a woman reaches old age. Thus, at all times in her life she is defined as someone's daughter, wife or mother. These definitions have a particular institutional form which is inscribed in family and marriage patterns. It is unlikely that women were considered irrelevant to the process of development, but rather they were considered to have no relation to the development process in their own right. Therefore, their constitutional equality as citizens belies the fact that they are less than full members of the political community.

The specificity of women as a gender category in this particular Kanuri settlement may be tentatively suggested from an analysis of their position.[8] Their position is defined through their discursive construction in certain institutions and practices which relate to the process of development.

The specificity of women in the settlement examined is partly constructed through a division of labour. The labour process is premised on the existence of definite tasks being appropriate to women, though these do not appear to be premised on assumptions about physical strength as is the case in many Western societies. As far as the labour process is concerned, the irrigation scheme has affected the role of both men and women, in that the inappropriateness of traditional techniques to the conception of development imposed by the economic rationale of the scheme, has removed a certain amount of autonomy from both sexes. But within this set-up, women do not have a direct relation to the processes of change, but rather have a relation which is mediated through men. It is likely that as far as the women in the scheme are concerned, one authority has simply been replaced by another. The authority of the males through whom they are defined is replaced by the authority of the scheme's managers to which women do not have direct access. For this reason, the scheme has had a greater impact on the position of men rather than women.

The division of labour in this particular settlement was such that women were solely responsible for the tasks on the compound, with the exception of hut building and repair which was carried out by men. In addition to their domestic compound duties, some women engaged in petty commodity production in the form of small-scale craft activities, primarily embroidery. In addition to this, some women engaged in agricultural labour. The participation of women in agricultural labour appears, as many writers have suggested, to be a function of the husband's wealth.[9] The women spoken to confirmed that their husbands did not like them farming but had no choice being unable to employ workers. Many of the women also suggested that they agreed with the view that they should not be required to work on the farms.

The participation of women in agriculture was spread over three months of the year and occurred at planting and harvest time. Men, on the other hand, worked for four months of the year. Because men and women work alongside each other, there is no sense in which there can be a pretence about the need to exclude women who have to work in agriculture. Like men, women worked in the fields from around nine until two, though unlike men they then had to return to the compound and deal with their domestic duties. Unlike Western societies, the participation of women in the labour force does not appear to be structured by their child care duties, as women of working age (puberty until around fifty) are not necessarily defined as central to this activity as they are in most Western societies.

At harvest time the women work on the threshing of wheat, which is a physically demanding activity, whilst men transport the threshed wheat back to the village on donkeys. During the planting season, the men do the hoeing whilst women remove the hoed weeds and serve food to the men prepared in the village.

From this rather brief and superficial example, it can be seen that women play a significant part in the local economy through their participation as an agricultural labour force, and that the division of labour in this settlement played a considerable part in the construction of gender categories.

One or two comments are necessary on those women who do not form part of a labour force which is active outside the compound.[10] Adult women are the only category who have the "right" not to participate in productive labour. The women, however, do not control this "right". Of the women interviewed, those whose husbands were local government officials and teachers said that they were not allowed to work, or indeed leave the compound at all except for festivals, weddings and funerals. The restriction of the personal freedom of the women to move from the compound is an important element in defining their specificity as a category. Their confinement was, of course, under the control of men. Some of the women spoken to accepted that this was correct behaviour for women, but others expressed a desire to work outside of the compound, though not in farming[11] and cited their husbands as the factor restricting them from doing this. In challenging the right of men to confine them, the women were offering an alternative construction of femininity.

On the question of seclusion, the irrigation project is likely to have serious effects for the women. Jackson (1978) has suggested that increases in wealth in Islamic communities has tended to lead to the increased seclusion of women. Her observations are based on the wives of Hausa farmers in the Kano River Project. If the calculations of the development authority in Borno are correct and local incomes rise substantially, then it is possible that there will be an increase in the seclusion of women in line with Islamic orthodoxy. It is also possible that the increased mechanization of agriculture will also contribute to the exclusion of women from the agricultural labour force. In this respect, women experience the development process in a way which is radically different from that of men.

As well as leading to the increased seclusion of women, it is also possible that certain kinds of agricultural development, notably those which lead to the use of land for private commercial ventures, will lead to poorer women being given employment opportunities which did not previously exist. In the case of the Kano River Project, the operations of a Belgian holding company growing vegetables for the European markets, exploited the position of a potential female labour force by paying very low wages to women for the work they did. Whilst it is true that a successful strike by the women led to an increase in their wages, there was still a large discrepancy between the male and female wage in the scheme. Thus a private company was able to exploit the specific position of women in Hausa societies by paying them much less than the cost of their reproduction as a labour force because of the structures of male authority in which women are not necessarily responsible for their reproduction as a labour force.

At this point, it is possible to suggest that the penetration of capitalist relations integral to the development concept has, or is capable of, changing the position of women in certain societies, whilst maintaining their specificity as a category. The transformation of traditional modes of production has not changed the position of women in respect of male structures of authority, though it is capable of redefining their specific position as a group. The impact of development on women leaves a curious mixture of traditional and modern elements in defining their position as a group the essence of which cannot be ascertained from an analysis of the relations or production.

In further specifying women as a category, whether they are active in productive labour or not, it is necessary to mention that Kanuri women are virtually excluded from occupying any political or public office. This is partly related to their educational position. Many women who marry at puberty do not continue their education to a level which would make the assumption of public office possible. But quite apart from educational qualification, women do not become village elders or headmen. This exclusion of women from public and political office was not always the case. Lawal (1981) pointed out that in Borno State, prior to the 1804 Jihad, aristocratic women at least held some influential political positions. Titled women held fiefs, although their role in politics was largely confined to the harem and the palace. The *Gumsu*, the elder wife of the *Mai*, looked after the affairs of women. The *Magira* or Queen Mother was in charge of the palace women and there were three other titles for women, the *Arena,* the *Mawlat* and the *Kafir.* These looked after the *Mai's* concubines.

Ordinary village women did not, it appears, hold offices of authority, although Lawal points out that they did engage in craft activities such as spinning, weaving, pottery and petty commodity production as well as agricultural labour. So their contribution to the local economy was far from insignificant despite their exclusion from political and public functions.

It has been demonstrated that sexual difference in the settlement in question is inscribed in a number of discourses and practices. Women are constructed through the sexual division of labour, through their exclusion from public and political office, through their indirect relation to the production process which is mediated through men, and finally through their conjugal role, underwritten by the Koran which defines specifically the nature of conjugal relations which should persist between men and women. The nature of the conjugal role, the result of a particular historical development, has instituted a set of practices in which women are defined as the property of men throughout their lives, in which they do not have the right of disposal over their physical movements, their own bodies or their offspring which are by custom the property of men. The construction of women in the context of the irrigation project does not challenge this definition, neither does it have the right to.

Conclusions and Observations

It remains only to suggest that women, as discursively organized in the development scheme examined, occupy a position which is both radically different from men and not reducible to a set of class relations. This is also the point at which it is possible to speculate on some of the constraints operating in the construction of women outlined in this paper.

The first constraint to be considered is an institutional one and refers to the set of conjugal and family practices which severely limit the role which women may play in the community. No one, male or female, lives outside the family structure. But for women this means not being able to live outside of their socially defined relations to men in the community. This, in combination with their seclusion, points to a perception of women as the property of men along with other material artifacts.

The second constraint is closely connected to the first. It concerns a set of ideologies relating to the constructed, as opposed to the formal, rights of women. Because women do not have a relation to production, development, or even in some cases the world outside of the compound, except through men, it is possible to suggest that in a formal sense, they do not actually exist as social beings in their own right. I am not attempting to suggest that this is the result of a conspiracy on the part of men, as this position accorded women is socially constructed; that is, by men and women. Indeed it could be suggested that men, and the community in general, are also victims of this particular construction of femininity which leads to the denial of the human potential of half of the Nigerian population. Neither can the position of women be attributed to a conspiracy of the part of capital as the exploitation of women does not require the particular construction outlined.

In essence, women in the community examined are not even second-class citizens. They are not citizens at all except in the formal juridical sense, as citizenship carries with it the right to relate to the political community as an individual, something which is denied women. If this situation is ever to change, it will do so as the result of the struggles of the women involved to redefine femininity in line with the ways in which they want to live.

Notes

1. See for example the work of Gunder Frank, "Sociology of Development".
2. I would argue that to see all "underdevelopment" in terms of the penetration of capital into pre-capitalist modes of production is to see all history as the history of capital.
3. By discourse in this context, I mean a set of things spoken about. Discourse can be in verbal or written form and concerns an arrangement of objects and concepts in a presentation of "reality". Discourse analysis is a method outlined by M. Foucault (*The Archeology of Knowledge,* 1977) for the reading of statements (the units of discourse) around a particular set of objects and concepts. In the discourses examined in this paper, "women" and "development" are key objects and concepts.
4. See N.M. Tanner, A.L. Zihman and F. Dalberg.
5. In the context of the research conducted, discourse refers to the statements of the feasibility study and the verbal statements collected in interviews.
6. Constraints may take a number of forms. They can be a set of circumstances, ideologies or official declarations.
7. The establishment of capitalism in agriculture requires the generation of consumption.
8. Position in this context relates to a place defined in the process of discourse rather than a fixed place in relation to men. This position will be differently constructed in different discourses in different contexts. Therefore I am suggesting not that women have a fixed position which can be defined once and for all, or that they are always disadvantaged in relation to men.
9. See Jackson (1978); Smith (1961) and Yeld (1960).
10. Participation in small-scale commodity production is not incompatible with seclusion as long as the women do not themselves market their products.
11. Marketing was the activity preferred by confined women.

References

Aaby, P. (1977) "Engels and Women", *Critique of Anthropology,* Vol.3.

Adams, P. & Minson, J. (1979) "The 'Subject' of Feminism", M/F.

Adlam, D. (1979) "The Case Against Capitalist Patriachy", M/F No.3.

Agarwala, A.N. & Singh, S.P. (1968) *The Economics of Underdevelopment.*

Barrett, M. (1980) *Women's Oppression Today.*

Central Office of Information (1977) *Britain and the Developing Countries. Africa.*

Central Office of Information (1975) *Overseas Aid: A Brief Survey.*

Cousins, M. (1979) "Material Arguments and Feminism". M/F.

Edholm, F., Harris, O. & Young, K. (1977) "Conceptualizing Women", *Critique of Anthropology,* Vol.3.

Feasibility Report (1973).

Feuchtwang, S. (1980) "Socialist, Feminist and Anti Racist Struggles". M/F.

Foucault, M. (1977) *The Archeology of Knowledge.*

Frank, A.G., *The Sociology of Development.*

Hunter, G. (1969) *Modernising Peasant Societies.*

Hirst, P. & Hindess, B. (1975) *Pre-Capitalist Modes of Production.*

Jackson, S. (1978) "Hausa Women on Strike", *Review of African Political Economy,* No.13.

Lawal, S.U. (1981) "Women and the 1804 Jihad". Unpublished seminar paper.

Reiter, R.R. (1977) "The Search for Origins: Unravelling the Threads of Gender Hierarchy", *Critique of Anthropology,* No.3.

Smith, M.G. (1961) "Kebbi & Hausa Stratification", *British Journal of Sociology.*

Williams, S.K.T. (1978) *Rural Development in Nigeria.*

Yeld, E.R. (1960) *Islam and Social Stratification in Northern Nigeria.*

Double Oppression: Women and Land Matters in Kaduna State

Norma Perchonock

The particular forms of oppression of women in any society occur within the context of class oppression in that society. Women are, along with men, oppressed by particular types of class structures and forms of exploitation. In addition, there are often certain forms of oppression in society which are applied to women as a group, as distinct from those institutions which also oppress men. This phenomenon is usually referred to as the "double oppression" of women — i.e., women suffer oppression by virtue of their class position in society, and also by virtue of their sex.

This paper looks at this double oppression experienced by peasant women in Kaduna State. Our aim is to understand the specific ways and the institutional mechanisms which operate to prevent these peasant women — as members of a particular class, and of a specific sex-defined group — from obtaining their fundamental human rights, and from realizing their fullest potential as human beings.

We intend to focus on the double oppression of women in relation to the question of land and land ownership. In any predominantly rural society — which Nigeria is at present — where the majority of the population belongs to farming families, it is obvious that the question of access to land as a basic means of production is very fundamental. The ability of families, (as the basic production units in this society), to feed themselves and to obtain the basic requirements of existence, will depend on their access to land to pursue farming activities.

We will discuss this question of double oppression of women in two parts. First, we will look at the class context of women's oppression, and the situation in which peasant women suffer from specifically class-based forms of exploitation. In the second part, we will look at some instances in which women seem to be exploited simply because they are women. As women, certain basic rights are denied them, and they lack the power to defend themselves against certain institutionalized forms of authority within the family, the courts, or the political system. By looking at the problem in this way, we hope to show the inter-relationships between class and sexual oppression as it operates in this situation.

We are particularly fortunate, in Kaduna State, to have at our disposal a wealth of detailed material related to the issue of land, in the form of the *Report* of the Land Investigation Commission.[1] As this report will provide us with the data on which our analysis and conclusions are based, we need to briefly discuss how the report came to be written, and the nature of the data it contains.

The PRP Government of Kaduna State had made the issue of reform of land administration in the state one of its basic programs. In pursuit of this, a Land Investigation Commission was established on 6 December 1979.[2] Soon after, the Commission began its work, starting with public sittings in Zaria on 17 December 1979. The Commission spent 10-14 days in each of the Local Government Areas of the state, listening to complaints from the public. "During the sittings, the Commission invites the complainants to state their cases in front of the respondents or their representatives as the case may be. Both parties are given full rights to express themselves and bring forward any documents or witnesses to support their case."[3] In addition, the Commission conducted on-site visits to disputed areas, requisitioned official and private documents, and took other measures to insure that full information was made available to them.

In all, 20,875 cases were filed with the Commission.[4] However, this figure of over 20,000 complaints actually does not reflect the number of individuals involved in these cases, because in many of these situations, whole communities are represented by a single complainant — in the case where their collective interests had been affected, such as the construction of dams, acquisition of land for forest or grazing reserves, road construction, rural and urban layouts, large-scale private acquisition or cases of political victimization. The total number of individuals involved in the various cases reported therefore constitutes a much higher number than the actual number of cases.

Of course it was impossible for the committee to hear all cases in each Local Government Area. A system of random selection was utilized, and the Commission feels that "the cases heard are highly representative of all the other cases outstanding".[5] According to my own calculations, the Commission actually heard publicly a total of 1489 cases in its sittings in the 14 Local Government Areas of the state. Out of this number, the complaints brought by women numbered only 120, or about 8% of all the cases heard. In addition, as the following table indicates, the cases brought by women were not randomly distributed among all the Local Government Areas, but seem to be more concentrated in some than in others:

Local Government Area	Total Cases	Women's Cases	Percentage
Funtua	184	9	4%
Malumfashi	158	19	12%
Dutsin-Ma	94	27	28.7%
Kankia	165	17	10.3%
Jema'a	122	3	2.7%
Saminaka	63	2	3.1%
Katsina	137	9	6.6%
Mani	93	6	6.5%
Daura	102	4	3.9%
Zaria	182	13	7.1%
Ikara	68	2	2.9%
Kaduna	98	7	7.1%
Birnin Gwari	33	3	9.1%

In discussions with the Chairman of the Commission, Mallam Yahaya Abdullahi, of the IAR, I tried to ascertain the reasons for this skew in the data on women. He explained that in the early sittings, where large crowds pushed forward to present complaints, the women tended to be in the background, and hence tended not to be called for presentation. Later on, the Commission realized that there were actually many women who wished to come forward and present their cases, and the Commission made a particular effort to ensure that some of these were actually heard. In addition, it was Mallam Yahaya's impression that in some areas, such as Dutsin-Ma, the actual number of women wishing to present cases was higher than in some other areas.

These factors, combined with the social obstacles that would normally discourage women from coming forward and making complaints in a public setting, leads us to the conclusion that this relatively small number of 120 complaints actually represents the tip of an iceberg. I believe we can infer from the information available that there are actually a very large number of peasant women in Kaduna State who have been affected by maladministration and oppression in the matter of land. And judging from the nature of the complaints heard, I believe we can assume that the cases the Commission did hear from women are quite representative of the types of situations that women find themselves in.

We should also note that, as previously mentioned, many of the complaints brought forward, and presented by men, also involve women either directly or indirectly, as members of the affected communities. Examples of this are shown in the following two cases, showing respectively (a) an instance of large-scale private acquisition of land and, (b) a case of political victimization:

(a) Bara community — represented by Joseh Baballe — Jema'a LGA[6]
He complained that their farmlands were seized by the Emir of

Jema'a near Unguwan Chori and given to Dr. Christopher Abashiya to make a farm. The acquisition was made last year. They further said that these farmlands which were given to Dr. Abashiya belong to nine families. They said that they do not know Dr. Abasihiya and they were not consulted or paid any compensation and even their village heads were not contacted before the acquisition was made.

The Commission found that Dr. Abashiya obtained the land from the Hakimin Kagoma and Sarkin Jema'a who also signed a paper to the effect that the land had no owner on the basis of which Dr. Abashiya got the C of O which he applied for in April 1979 and obtained in July of the same year.

The Sarkin Jema'a and Hakimin Kagoma when contacted actually admitted to not knowing the real owners of the farmland. Therefore we feel that Dr. Abashiya was given a C of O as a result of this lapse and misinformation on the part of the District Head and the Emir of Jema'a who made no efforts to ascertain the ownership of the land.

We recommend that the C of O be revoked and the farmlands returned to their actual owners and that Dr. Abashiya be made to negotiate with the people directly. (112-113)

(b) The People of Rafin Gora — represented by Boyi Rafin Gora na Alhaji — Funtua LGA

The people of Rafin Gora brought a complaint before the Commission that the Magajin Tandama and Alhaji Tukur Bakori (the then representative of the District Head of Bakori), were the brains behind the destruction by burning of their village, Rafin Gora, 14 years ago. They further alleged that a total of 70 houses were burnt and both Alhaji Tukur Bakori and Magajin Tandama were present on the two days of combined police and army operation, and in fact the two were directing the operation. The people further complained that as a result of this, they lost their houses, their properties and according to them there were losses of lives. With no place to stay, the people were dispersed from the village and a lot of them were sent on a diaspora from which many never came back...

(Although both named individuals denied involvement), the Commission in the course of its investigation found that the operation mounted against the people of Rafin Gora was an act of political victimization carried out during the first civilian regime with the knowledge and consent of the then Regional and Federal Governments.

The whole issue really revolves around the fact that the people of Rafin Gora at that time were overwhelmingly supporters of the defunct NEPU and the actions taken against them were directed by the NPC controlled regional and Federal Governments. (45-47).

85

Obviously in cases like these, men's and women's interests are both involved as members of the affected communities, so even where the data does not specifically mention women we should keep in mind that they are often affected directly by the cases presented to the commission.

In order to understand how women are oppressed as members of a particular class (the peasantry), we need to look at the structure of the society in which this oppression operates. We can best do this by taking an historical perspective, because many of the institutions which operate today as instruments of class oppression are relics of an earlier historical era, which have been taken over and adapted to fit the requirements of new systems of exploitation.

The Nineteenth Century

At the beginning of the 19th century, most of the village communities in what is now Kaduna State were integrated into the new emirates founded as a result of the Jihad of Usman dan Fodio. Previously existing state structures were also absorbed; and it is likely that the resulting emirates were more highly centralized in terms of administration and political power than the previous Hausa states had been. The vast majority of the inhabitants of these emirates were farmers, organizing production in extended family units called *gandu* (p. *gandaye*).[7] Since agriculture formed the most important productive activity, peasant farmers were the basic producing class in the society. In addition, most of these farmers had additional occupations — in crafts, manufacturing, trading, etc. — which they pursued either during the long dry season or simultaneously with farming.

The agricultural communities were thus the source of foodstuffs to feed themselves and the non-agricultural producers, the source of agricultural raw materials for manufacturing (cotton, indigo, hides and skins, etc.) as well as the source of some of the manufactured goods; others were produced by urban-based craftsmen.

These peasant farming communities were part of the wider political system of the emirates and ultimately of the Caliphate, and in their productive activities were very much subject to the demands of the feudal emirate structure. They were forced to turn over a portion of their agricultural or craft production, in the form of taxes, paid to the village or hamlet head (or guild head, in the case of some crafts), who kept part of it, and sent on the rest to his superiors — the fief-holders (titled officials) who resided in the capital, and thence to the Emir and the Sultan of Sokoto. In addition to taxes, however, perhaps an even more important aspect of surplus appropriation was through the control of labour. The peasant farmers were required to work on the estate *(gandun sarki)* of the officials of the emirate, the village head, and the *gandu* of any of the fief-holders who held such lands in their area. In this type of corvee labour (called *aikin gayya*), the peasants worked alongside the slaves and clients of the officials involved.

Within the village communities themselves, it seems that most families had access to land, although the distribution of such holdings was far from equitable. Buying and selling of land was practised, as well as the sale of labour for wages. Land was also acquired through *jingina* (pledge or mortgage), which was an important way whereby the richer individuals in the community were able to acquire the land of the poorer ones. Land was also lent (*aro*) either free or for a nominal fee. The most important way in which individuals obtained land, however, was through inheritance. In addition to peasant smallholdings, and the estates of feudal officials, many urban-based wealthy businessmen owned large farms in rural communities, which were cultivated by a combination of slave, client, and possibly wage labour.

The local officials of the emirate structure, particularly the village head acting as agent of the fief-holder, had power to allocate uncultivated land (either bush land, or land which had not been farmed for a number of years) to new immigrants, and had many other powers over land transactions. In addition, they organized the *aikin gayya* on their own estates and those of the fief-holder.

The role of women in this system in the 19th century needs much more research and investigation. At the moment, many important questions must remain unanswered due to lack of information. The system of Islamic law allows women to inherit farms, as well as other forms of property, but we do not know the extent to which women actually did own farmland in this period, since customarily (in the pre-Islamic period, and, it seems, in non-Islamic communities) women did not inherit farmland, although they participated in farm labour.

We need to know more about the degree of women's involvement in agricultural labour. It seems that the practice of wife seclusion (*kulle*) was not widely practised except among the wealthy of the urban areas, and it is probable that women were involved in agricultural production to a much greater extent than they are today. Since taxes were paid by the family head on behalf of the family unit, it seems that women did not pay farm taxes as individuals. We do not know, however, whether for example women grain sellers paid any form of market tax, or whether craftswomen such as weavers, potters, etc., paid taxes through the guild structure. Were women part of the labour force recruited for *aikin gayya*? What were the specific contributions from women towards appropriated surplus production? These and other questions must await further research before we can satisfactorily answer them.

The Colonial Era and the First Republic — c. 1900-1966

Colonialism fundamentally altered the basic social and economic as well as political relationships of the communities of this region. Agricultural production was directed towards producing commodities for export (cotton, groundnuts, etc.) and the peasants were coerced (directly, or indirectly through taxation policy) into growing these crops, often at the expense of foodstuffs. The indigenous system of crafts and manufacturing which had provided the tools, clothing and other requirements of the community was likewise decimated through deliberate colonial policies designed to eliminate local industries and hence create a market for British exports. The organic links between urban and rural areas, based on regional trade in foodstuffs and raw materials for industry, were broken, and the urban areas lost their former role as centres of production, and instead became collecting points for channelling agricultural products to Lagos and then overseas. As a new class of middlemen (the buying agents, and factors for expatriate trading companies) arose, linking the peasantry to the foreign firms who purchased their produce and sold them imported manufactured goods.

This period saw the intensification of capitalist relations of production in agriculture. Labour, previously sold on a small scale, became a more generalized commodity, aided by forced labour policies of the colonial administration — to construct the railways, roads, prisons, etc.[8] Labour migration — a common phenomenon in the pre-colonial era *(cinrani)* — was channelled particularly into the export crop-producing areas as well as mining centres like the Jos Plateau. Along with the increasing commercialization and individualization of labour came the breakdown of large family farming units, the *gandaye,* and production came more and more to be on an individual basis.

This period also witnessed the growing importance of wife seclusion, now practised by many wealthy individuals even in rural areas, and the consequent withdrawal of women from a good deal of farm work. In poor families, or those with few children, women's labour was still required, as it is today. In other families, married women withdrew into the compound, and practised other occupations like craftwork, preparation of cooked foods, snacks, etc. It would be interesting to have information on the changing occupational division of labour among women during this period. We need to know how the decline of the *gandu* system of production affected women's productive roles, and the division of labour within the family unit. But at the moment, our information on these matters is either scanty or non-existent.

The colonial transformation perhaps moved more slowly in matters of land than it did with labour. In urban areas, it is true that the new class of middlemen and speculators invested heavily in urban real estate, and urban land came to be a highly valuable commodity. In agriculture, however, the policy pursued by the British and their immediate successors emphasized peasant commodity production, rather than large-scale capitalist agriculture. Although the members of the old feudal class continued to use their prerogatives to accumulate wealth based on agricultural production (through continued use of forced labour, seizure of land, and appropriation of taxes), in general there was not a serious trend towards capitalist investment in agricultural production.

Politically, colonialism also altered many relationships. The Caliphate, as well as all other societies in Nigeria, lost their fundamental sovereignty. Members of the ruling class who refused to co-operate with the British were killed or deposed. The remainder were co-opted to become agents of colonialism.[9] The British consolidated the previously fragmented fiefs into districts, and compelled the fief-holder to reside in his area of jurisdiction, thus creating what we now call district heads. But perhaps more importantly, the British deliberately placed the so called "traditional" rulers between themselves and the peasantry, thus leaving these institutions (although very much altered) to function as a cushion to absorb and contain potential peasant protest, and as an instrument of coercion to carry out the new oppressive policies aimed at the peasantry. Thus were the remnants of the feudal system co-opted by the colonialists and given a new role to play as the hand-maiden of new types of capitalist exploitation. We will see shortly the importance of these structures in the continued exploitation of the peasantry.

1966-Present

The period after the fall of the First Republic saw many fundamental changes in the Nigerian economy. The Civil War, the "oil boom", and concomitant changes in the international economy coincided with a drastic decline in peasant commodity production. At the same time, government policy towards agriculture, encouraged by the World Bank and other international agencies, was moving towards large-scale, capital-intensive agriculture, both private and state-sponsored. In the private sector, civil servants, army officers, and businessmen sought to acquire large areas of land for farming. This trend has intensified throughout the post-civil war period, and it is certainly continuing to do so today. This, of course, has resulted in increasing alienation of land from peasant producers; as we will see, the feudal functionaries play a key role in this process. On the one hand, by virtue of their age-old feudal rights over peasants in their community, they seize land on various pretexts. On the other hand, as the servants of the new bourgeoisie, they sell this land to the businessmen, retired army officers and civil servants who want it for commercial farming, or just for speculation.

The continued control of local political authority relationships by the old feudal class, and the fundamental lack of democratization of local political institutions up to the Second Republic has, of course, affected all peasant farmers in these rural communities. But, as we shall see, it has had a particularly devastating effect on women. This is because these local functionaries, particularly the village heads, have a great deal of power in personal and legal matters, such as in cases of divorce (where often village heads must act as witnesses, or are called in to settle disputes), or in cases of inheritance of land and houses. These officials generally take advantage of the socially and legally diminished position of women to seize their rightful inheritance, or otherwise prevent them from acquiring what is justifiably theirs. It is even not unheard of for village heads to seize the women themselves in the course of acting as mediator between husband and wife. The courts also are institutions which actively participate to deprive individuals of their rights, as the data will show, particularly in the case of women.

The recent period has also been characterized by such trends as urban expansion, in the course of which many farmers lose their land, and increased construction of schools, roads, and other public projects like dams, etc. It is perhaps inevitable that farmers will have to be displaced as a result of such projects. However, here too we see opportunities to exploit the peasants, primarily through the process of payment of compensation. This compensation is paid through the local government and/or traditional authorities. The rate of compensation is itself grossly inadequate, but even these meagre sums hardly reach the peasants. Usually the compensation is appropriated by the officials whose duty it is to effect the payment. As the *Report* of the Commission clearly shows, inequitable payment, and general corruption in the system of payment, were among the commonest complaints received by the Land Commission. Bearing this historical background in mind, let us now turn to an examination of the data in the report, which will help us to understand the situation in a concrete way.

> As the Report points out, land acquisition and transfers in Kaduna State can be classified into two broad and related categories. The first is the class of lands acquired by government or Local Governments for various public projects including rural and urban layouts. The second is associated with land transfers, allocation, acquisitions and often seizures occasioned by the feudal arm of the land administration system. This is represented by the powers of the roles played by the "traditional" power structure in especially rural land transactions.[10] As can be seen from Table 1, over 89% of complaints identified the Government, the Local Government or the traditional authority functionaries as respondents... Moreover, in fact nearly 70% of the complaints received and analysed are over land acquisition for public projects where little or no compensation was offered.[11]

Table 1
Total complaints by respondents [12]

Respondents	Number	Percentage
Local Authority	5,589	26.8
Traditional Authority	5,383	25.8
Local Govt./Trad.Auth. (combined)	368	1.8
Government	6,743	32.3
Govt.+Trad.Auth.	508	2.4
Other Individuals	1,046	5.0
Other Combinations	1,238	5.2
Total	*20,875*	*100.00*

Table 2
Women's complaints by respondents [13]

Local Authority	3	2.5
Traditional Authority	78	65.0
Local Auth./Trad.Auth.	8	6.6
Government	14	11.7
Govt.+Trad. Auth.	1	8
Individuals (related)	10	8.3
Individuals (non-related)	6	5.0
Others	-	-
Total	*120*	*100.00*

When we compare the two tables, we notice some striking differences. Where in Table 1 (representing the total complaints filed with the Commission), the percentage of complaints against traditional authority is 25.8%, in Table 2 (complaints presented by women), it is 65%. In Table 1, the total complaints against individuals amount to 5%, in Table 2 this category (broken down in my analysis into relatives and non-relatives) totals 13.3%. Women also seem to have fewer complaints against Government (11.7%) than for the complainants as a whole (32.3%).

Certain patterns of exploitation of women with regard to land matters clearly emerge from a comparison of these two tables. A look at some of the concrete cases on which these tables are based may give us some insight into our problem of the double oppression of women.

Since the single largest category of complaints from women involves traditional authority, let us examine some of these cases:

(a) Case of Kadi ta Alhaji — Dutsin Ma LGA

She complained that they settled in the area of Magajin Babban Duhu who gave them a bush which they cleared. After her husband died he drove her away and seized the farm after they already planted their crops. The seizure took place only 6 years ago. She now lives in the village area of Gatari and her children have absolutely no farmlands.

The Magajin Babban Duhu said that when her husband came he gave him an *aro* (loan) of the farm, and his witness is Alhaji Labo, his Maiunguwa (wardhead). Her husband was using the farm for 7 years and when he died, he took his farm back.

She further said that she went to Katsina and she brought her witnesses and Sarkin Katsina gave her the farm back.

The commission is of the opinion that the Magajin Babban Duhu is a big feudal aristocrat with large holdings, most of which he acquired through several dubious means, especially seizing peoples' farmlands on the pretext that they migrated or died or that he gave them a bush to clear and when they migrated or died, he seized the farms. This we feel is actually oppressive with regards to the interest of the peasantry.

In fact, when people die, he seizes the farm despite the improvements they made on the farms irrespective of the fact that they leave a lot of children who were left farmless in this process.

Magajin Babban Duhu is not the only culprit in this, some other Maqqadai are also very callous in this regard.

We therefore recommend that Babban Duhu should hand over the farms to the complainant's children because we feel that he has no right to them. Because what he allocated was a bush and it is the father of the children who cleared it and died, so it is their inheritance. (42-43)

(b) Case of Rakiya ta Alhaji Usman Safana — Katsina LGA

She complained that she cultivated her farmland for 22 years and the Magajin Safana seized the farm 3 years ago. She said she complained in Katsina and the farm was returned to her but the Magaji seized it again. She went further to say that the farm is located just in front of her house and now it is Wakili Isa, the son of Safana, who is cultivating the place.

The commission recommends that the complainant should be given her farmland back. (41).

(c) Case of Amina Ta Gambo Hugaga — Kankia LGA

She complained that their father migrated and left them with a farm. They planted millet and the Magajin Fakuwa took over the farmland with their crops on it. She complained to him and he abused her 12 times. She said this happened 22 years ago.

The Magajin Fakuwa said that he was not around when this happened. He found his senior brother with the farm and he bought the farm from his senior brother and said that the farm is still with him. And he even admitted that his brother seized the farm from her.

Therefore we recommend that the Magajin Fakuwa should hand over the farm to her because this is a case of outright seizure. (106)

(d) Case of Indo Ta Mammen — Kankia LGA
She complained that she bought a farmland from one Ganga for N5.00. She said that she was cultivating the farm for 4 years and she was paying taxes on it for 4 years. Then 3 years ago she went to Katsina on *cin rani* to earn a living and when she came back she found that the Magajin Nassarawa has made layout on the farm.

The Magajin Nassarawa said that it was the Fulani who came and complained to him and the farmland was given to them to settle there. And that the names of these Fulanis have been recorded in the office of the District Head of Ingawa.

The commission observes that this woman is a very poor woman and often had to do physical labour or sell firewood to earn her living and her only farm was the one which was taken away from her during her absence. She is now quite old and her only son Ja'afaru has since left due to lack of farmland and she does not even know his whereabouts. The woman is now a domestic labourer.

We therefore recommend that she should be given an alternative farmland by the Magajin Nassawawa and the Hakimin Ingawa who were the people who took over her farmland and settled the Fulani inside and this should be done with immediate effect. (139-40)

The above cases are typical of the complaints the Commission received about abuses committed against peasants by traditional authorities. Although there might be some element in these cases of specific discrimination against women, in fact the types of seizures recorded here happen equally to men.

Now let us look at some cases of complaints against the Government:

(a) Case of Amina Geda Kofar Jatau, Hauwa Geda and Habiba Geda — Zaria LGA
They complained that they are all sisters and they have farmlands which they have inherited at Banzazzau. They said that they were initially approached by Alhaji Shehu Idris, the Emir of Zaria, when he was the District Head to sell the lands to him and they refused. But later on, the farms were acquired for the building of ABU Zaria — Advanced Teachers College. They were given no compensation at all after the acquisition. They complained to the Sarkin Ruwa who threatened Amina with imprisonment and she was even detained for one day.

Sarkin Ruwa on his part said that Alhaji Musa Gwarzo was the person who received the compensation. But Alhaji Musa Gwarzo who the complainants admitted is their uncle is now dead but they were sure that he did not receive anything.

The commission found that it is true that the complainants were not actually compensated. The commission further found that actually when the compensation was paid, the money meant for the complainants was embezzled by some officials.

And due to the absence of proper records it is impossible to determine who in fact it is who converted the compensation meant for the complainants to his own use. We therefore recommend that the local government should allocate a plot each to the complainants by way of compensating them for their losses. (25-26)

(b) Case of Hajia Raliatu — Dutsin Ma LGA
She complained that she bought from Shu'aibu Rabe Kadangaru a plot for N210.00 on which she intended to build a house. She travelled for a short time and came back to find that the Local Government had acquired the place for building a motor park. She was not paid any compensation, but she was promised an alternative plot which to date she was never given. (7-8)

(c) Case of Hajia Yarmallam Funtua — Funtu LGA
Her house was demolished on the authority of the local government through Sarkin Maska. She was paid only N150.00 for the house while she claimed to have purchased the plot itself for up to N250.00 from one Alhaji Tsoho Maikarfe. She had a receipt to butress her case. (7)

(d) Case of Diga Kaunar Alhaji Dan Durgu K/Namoda — Funtua LGA
That she came to Funtua and bought a plot on which she built a house. The house was demolished and she was not paid anything. She is now desitute and has nowhere to go. She now depends on the charity of Mallam Sule na Shata who now provides her with a place to sleep. (8)

While we do not have the space to document similar complaints from men, any one who reads the *Report* of the Land Commission can see that the above complaints are fairly typical of the types of complaints lodged against both traditional rulers, and the government and local authorities. In the cases cited above, the women involved are not being oppressed or discriminated against as women *per se* but rather as members, together with men, of a class of people who are poor and powerless. In these cases, we see that feudal functionaries utilize their own class position, and their political power, to effect control over the basic means of production in these communities — the land — and do so in their own interest, and in the interests of the group of people (the bourgeoisie) who are their masters.

Even in the case of government acquisition of land, clear class interests whose land is so acquired — compensation paid or not — are unlikely to be allocated a plot, or to be able to build a house to GRA specifications. The Government (or the State) after all, represents specific class interests. When we carry out our analysis we must be careful to see behind the facade of "public interest" to see actually whose interests are being served.

In addition to women being exploited by virtue of their being members of a class, as the above examples have shown, women are subjected to certain situations and circumstances which are unique to them as a sex-defined group. The Land Commission noted that it received a lot of complaints about women's inheritance rights.

> This is where women are often deprived of their right to inherit the lands of their fathers who had no other male heirs resident in the village. The viri-local nature of marriage means that often women marry and live outside the village area, so when their fathers die, the...Nomijidi[14] regulation is used to deprive them of the land without taking their special circumstances into consideration.[15]

In fact, aside from complaints against traditional rulers for outright seizure of their lands, women's complaints usually centred around the deprivation of their rights of inheritance. In these complaints, there seem to be three main agencies or institutions which women blame for their disinheritance: firstly, traditional rulers, secondly, the courts, and thirdly, their own relations. Often a combination of these operate to deprive women of their inheritance rights.

First, here are some cases of complaints against traditional authorities.

(a) Case of Habiba Mallam Dabo Gangarawa — Malumfashi LGA
She alleged that Sarkin Fulani seized her father's farmland. It was late Magajin Malumfashi who gave him the farm on *aro* basis because when her father died, the farm was left to her but she could not farm it because she has no male children, so she left it in the hands of late Magajin Malumfashi. In fact, late Magajin Malumfashi insisted before he died that he did not sell the farm or give it on *aro* basis to the Sarkin Fulani.

Sarkin Fulani on his part said that he does not know the complainant but he knew that the late Magajin gave him a farm and it was a bush which he had to clear himself. In fact, Sarkin Fulani has a writ of possession from the Funtua Area Court over the farm dated 13 April 1977 on case numbers 28/23/77. In fact he went to court with Garba Adamu Ruwan Sanyi and seven others against whom he won the case.

Garba Adamu on his part claimed that the farm actually belonged to him and not to the complainant or to Sarkin Fulani. But during the proceedings, one Mallam Yusufu Mohammad, Malumfashi, testified that the farm belonged to neither Sarkin Fulani nor Garba

Garba Adamu on his part claimed that the farm actually belonged to him and not to the complainant or to Sarkin Fulani. But during the proceedings, one Mallam Yusufu Mohammad, Malumfashi, testified that the farm belonged to neither Sarkin Fulani nor Garba Adamu. He said that he himself was staying at Rereji before he came to settle in Malumfashi. He said that the farm actually belonged to Habiba because he grew up and opened his eyes to find Habiba's father there. He said further that it was her father Goje who cleared the farm himself and that before going to his farmland he used to pass through that farm and find Habiba's father cultivating it.

He further said that it was the Magajin Borin Dawa who was then the Mai Unguwa (hamlet head) who sold the farm to Garba Adamu when the father of Habiba died. In fact, Habiba had no male children who could take over the farm when her father died.

The Magajin Borin Dawa testified that actually the farm belonged to the father of Habiba but he came to possess it, and he insists that the farm was neither sold nor was it given out by the traditional authorities.

…In the light of this new information we feel that Habiba should be given her farmland back…. But on a general note, this is what normally happens with regards to female inheritance on land especially when they do not have male siblings or children and the Commission has encountered several cases of similar nature. (133)

(b) Case of Tambaya Abdu Matar Duza — Kankia LGA
She complained that her father died and left a farm. She asked for the farm and the Magajin Yashe said that since she was a female, she could not inherit from her father. But she said that she is the only one from her father so as a result of this, she said that he drove her away from the village she was marrying, so she had to migrate to Tsa village area because if he sees her in the village area he will have her imprisoned.

One witness Mallam Isiya said that her father died and left a farm and it is the only farm the father had. And she paid *Ushira* on the farmland and was clearing the farm when the Magajin Yashe came and stopped her from working the farm. The witness further said that it is his senior brother Adamu and some other people who are now cultivating the farm and they all bought these from Yashe. Isiya is also living in Duza.

Yashe still did not agree despite overwhelming evidence that he seized the farmland, therefore we recommend that Magajin Yashe should give her farmland back and pay the people he sold the land to their money back. (96)

(c) Case of Hajia Hadiza Bukarawa — Dutsin Ma LGA
She complained that 12 years ago, the Magajin Babban Duhu seized her father's farmland at Bukarawa. The Maiunguwa testified that the farm is now in the hands of her former husband. He testified

that the farm is now in the hands of her former husband. He testified that it was the Magajin Babban Dubu who seized the place and gave it to her former husband saying that the woman should not own a farm since she does not pay taxes.

The commission observes that it was the Magajin who actually supported the former husband of the complainant, and gave the farm to him even though it was her own rightful inheritance. As such we recommend that her farm should be returned to her. (45)

(d) Case of Hadiza Juma Matar Iro — Dutsin Ma LGA

She alleged that her father's four farmlands were seized by Magajin Babban Duhu. She said that her father was imprisoned by the Magajin Babban Duhu and after he was discharged, he migrated to Gombe together with her senior brother 20 years ago. Her father left four farmlands out of which she was not given a single one even though she stayed behind because of marriage. Her father has already died, and her senior brother is still living in Gombe.

The Magajin Babban Duhu testified that he does not know the complainant, but later on it transpired that he knew of the case. Then he said that since it was himself that allocated the father of the complainant the farm, when he migrated he took over the farm and gave it to Gora.

But the complainant brought forward her witnesses who testified that it was not the Magaji who allocated her father the farms, but the father of the complainant bought the farms. These are Alhaji Dadi, who testified that the father of the complainant actually bought the farms from one Alhaji Garba.

But the Magajin Babban Duhu said that he did not know of the purchase of the farms. He said that it was the Mai Unguwa of Sabon Gari who informed him of her departure, and he gave out the farms.

The commission is of the opinion that this is normally what happens with regard to female inheritance, when the father migrates or dies and left some properties without any male heir around, the administrators of the estate normally neglect the interest of the deceased or the migrant's female children.

As such, we recommend that her farms should be returned to her if it is satisfied that she can effectively use them. If however, it is found that she cannot effectively utilize the farms, then the present occupants should give her adequate compensation for the lands. (34-35)

The above cases show that the village heads and other feudal functionaries take advantage of women's weak position in the community, and of the fact that they often marry away from their villages leaving their farms in the hands of others to look after for them, to interpret inheritance rules to suit themselves. The resulting situation generally deprives women of their rightful inheritance.

In addition to these local officials, the courts also collude in this process, as the following cases demonstrate:

(a) Case of Yashe Yakubu — Daura LGA

She complained that her mother gave her father's farm on *aro* basis to the Sarkin Fulani, and she went to Sarkin Fulani to claim the farmland and they went to court with the complainant 2 years ago. He said that he bought the farm from Alhaji Maikeke.

At this stage, one Mallam Musa, an old man, appeared and testified to the fact that it was the late Sarkin Fulani who borrowed the farm from the mother of the complainant. Alhaji Maikeke na Muduru at that time was a new migrant and the Sarkin Fulani gave him the farmland on *aro* basis. Later on, Alhaji Maikeke sold the farm to the present Sarkin Fulani after winning a court case against the complainant.

The commission is of the opinion that in spite of the court action and its judgement, the complainant actually is the rightful owner of the land... In fact, the commission found that the complainant lost the case because of female modesty and she refused to swear on oath. Her brother wanted to swear but he was disallowed because he was not the plaintiff.

The commission recommends that a legal way should be found so that this injustice should be corrected and the complainant given her farm back. (220)

(b) Case of Salame matar Mallam Alu dan Zaki — Dutsin Ma LGA

She complained that her husband went to Koranic school and left his farm in the hands of the late Magajin Gatari. He left her with a son and now the son has grown up and is asking constantly to give him his father's farmland.

She went to the present Gatari and she did not get the farmland, so she went from place to place up to Safana. She paid about N26.00 to several officials in order to obtain land but in the end she did not get it. The farm is now in the hands of one Iro na Hayi who was given the farm by the Magajin Gatari.

The Magajin Gatari on his part said that she came to him and asked for the farm which she kept in his father's trust, so they went to court with Iro na Hayi and the judge gave Iro na Hayi the farm.

The commission is of the opinion that Iro na Hayi was given the farm because of the influence of Magajin Gatari so we recommend that the Magajin Gatari should be made to give her an alternative farmland or in the alternative, give him his inherited farmland back. (49)

(c) Case of Aishatu Bazamfara-Kankara — Malumfashi LGA

She had a dispute over a piece of land with her husband with whom they have six children. She claimed that the farm belonged to her senior brother who is now dead. So her husband was cultivating the farm. After they divorced, she took her husband to court. The court, in its ruling on 12/1/78, decided that the farm should be the property of their children: Bashiro, Iro and Mu'azu. The court however gave her former husband the right of cultivation of the farm on behalf of their children. She in turn was given the right to the economic trees. She interpreted this ruling as conferring on her the whole title to the land. So she thought that since the farm was not returned to her, it was the District Head who prevented her from it. She claimed that she even went to the extent of bribing him to get the farm, and this he denied.

She was so frustrated that she went to cut down all the dorowa trees that were given to her, and again took the matter to the Governor who referred her to the Local Government. The Secretary inspected the place and found out what happened. He tried to placate her, but she did not agree. Her whole effort was directed at taking over the control of the whole farm.

It appears to the Commission that it was the court that brought the whole problem by the nature of its ruling. However, the Commission is of the opinion that the farms should remain the property of the children and once they grow up the access of her former husband to the farms should cease. Aishatu herself should be advised to keep calm and a farm, if available, should be allocated to her to placate her and help in the maintenance of peace. (181)

Of course the courts are not used to oppress only women — many of the complaints brought by men showed the courts to be instruments of oppression of the peasants in general. The *Report* of the Commission contains a wealth of material about the corruption of the legal process in dealing with land matters. As one would expect, those with wealth or influence usually are favoured by court decisions, regardless of the facts of the case. Neverthless, women seem to be at a special disadvantage in litigation. Many women are reluctant to go to court at all; if they do, as in case *(a)* above, they may be reluctant to swear or to accuse others in their testimony. Moreover, their lack of experience in public matters deprives them of the knowledge of how the system operates, who to "see" and how. As in the case of the administration of legal systems in so many societies, those in a disadvantaged position find it difficult (if not impossible) to obtain justice. Since in this situation women are at a special disadvantage (legally and socially), they find it especially difficult to gain their rights in the courts.

So far, the cases we have presented show the ways in which the system of political authority operates to oppress all members of peasant farming communities — men and women alike. We have also shown instances in which these same institutions, in addition, oppress women in particular ways which do not apply to men. Aside from oppression by feudal and governmental officials, however, women seem to have an additional source of complaint which is not common among the men who presented cases to the Commission — complaints against members of their own families. If we return to the tables on page 91, we will note the importance of women's complaints against individuals, and particularly complaints against their own relatives. Although I have not analysed the complaints from men on the same basis (i.e., dividing them into relatives and non-relatives), a reading of the Report indicates that it is extremely rare for complaints from men to be directed against their own relations. However, in the case of women this is quite common — 8.3% of all complaints, forming the third largest category after traditional authority (65%) and Government (11.7%).

Let us examine some typical cases of women's complaints in which their own relatives have, in collusion with the courts and traditional authorities, conspired to deprive women of their inheritance rights:

(a) Case of Guede yar Tanko — Malumfashi LGA
She alleged that Magajin Karfi seized their farmlands and sold them to three other people. She said that she was leaving and left the farmlands in the hands of her brother when Karfi seized the farm and sold them to Sulli, Kadi and Mari. In fact, according to her it was Haruna who is her brother who was left on the farm, but connived with Magajin Karfi Sule and sold the farms.

The Magajin Karfi Sule said that it was Haruna Bakin Gulbi Unguwar Wanzamai, her brother, who was kept in charge of the whole farms after their father migrated, as such the whole case is between Haruna and the Fulani to whom he sold the farms.

The Commission found out that it was actually her brother Haruna who sold the farms to other people and not the Magajin Karfi Sule. Therefore, we recommend that if she wants to obtain her full share of the farms, she should contact her brother, take him to court so that her share can be restored to her. (148).

(b) Case of Gambo Mamman Funtua — Kankia LGA
That she married in Funtua and she came back and asked for her father's farmland but the present Magajin Kakuwa told her that the former Magaji gave an *aro* of the farm of one Usman Soja.

Magajin Fakuwa said actually the farm belongs to the father of the complainant and it was his senior brother who gave Usman Soja the farm but he does not know whether Usman Soja bought it or he was given the farm free of charge.

We recommend that the farmland should be returned to the complainant and Usman Soja re-settled where possible. (106)

(c) Case of Takorau matar Dangwago Masari — Malumfashi LGA
She complained that her first cousin Akko pledged her farmland to one Hudu at Yar Kawuri, Masari. In fact, according to her, Akko refused to give her farmland back because according to him women have no inheritance.

The Commission observes that one of the ways in which systematic oppression of women manifests itself is through denying them their rights of inheritance, once their fathers died, leaving no male heirs. This system, we believe, should be rectified so that at least the children of the women would be able to inherit their property. (168)

Local Government and her junior brother, Maikano Na Riga, was given N1,600.00 compensation and he gave her only N200.00 out of the amount.
The commission checked this complaint and found the above to be largely true. Therefore, we recommend that the Local Government should take this up and try to see that Mairiga gets her rightful share of this compensation from her brother. (165)

The above cases indicate that in addition to suffering at the hands of the political system, women have another burden of oppression which men do not suffer from — the family system, where male relatives take advantage of women to seize their inheritance for themselves.

Conclusion: The Double Oppression of Women

In our presentation, we have tried to establish the class context of the oppression of women with regard to land matters in Kaduna State. We have documented the sources of the oppression of the peasantry — the feudal local officials, as well as government functionaries, acting in the interests of the ruling class in society, and against the interests of the peasantry. We have seen the mechanisms by which this system operates to deprive the poor and the powerless of access to their basic means of livelihood, i.e. the land. We have shown that all members of the peasant class — men and women alike — suffer from these institutional arrangements. These are the determining conditions which establish the context for the oppression of women.

We have also shown that women suffer specific forms of oppression which men are not subjected to. In the majority of cases, the same structures and institutions which oppress men (feudal office holders, government functionaries, the courts) are also the source of the particular forms of women's oppression. Thus we might say that in most instances, women suffer the same *type* of oppression as men, but to a more severe degree. In other words, the qualitative factors are the same for men and women, but quantatively (in terms of the degree of severity) women suffer comparatively more than men when placed in the same circumstances.

However, in certain instances, women also suffer from a *different kind* of oppression, that is oppression within the family system — an institution where men use their relatively greater power and authority to exploit their female relatives.

Women then, are doubly oppressed — oppressed first and more importantly by the system of political authority and economic class structure; secondly, by the system of authority within the family institution. These two types of oppression are closely related. We can understand that in a system where exploitation and individual gain are the basis of human relationships, and where women are already burdened by second-class status, women are bound to be exploited by their *relatively* more privileged male relations, who are themselves subjected to a condition of powerlessness and exploitation through the unjust economic system. While women need to organize to obtain their full rights within the family, it is obvious that this cannot be achieved without at the same time fighting against the total system of exploitative human relationships which characterizes the society as a whole. If the double oppression of women is to be overcome, the battle must be fought on two fronts.

Aside from documenting the nature of women's double oppression, the data in the *Report* of the Land Commission also gives us some important insights about the general nature of exploitation in different systems — namely feudalism and capitalism. While of course being aware that the remnants of the feudal system that operate today at the village level (and which are gradually being eradicated) are themselves dominated by the broader system of capitalism, we can see that they still tend to operate, in their relations with the peasantry, in essentially feudal ways. The essence of feudal relationships is the use of extra-economic relationships (political — legal authority relations) to dominate subject classes in society through the use of political coercion.[16] Typically, in a feudal situation, political authority is diffuse, and operates across a wide spectrum of social relations, including those within the family. We can see that this is still the case today in terms of the relationship between the peasantry and the local political structure. The authority of the village head extends to many aspects of life — from questions of land, of inheritance, of deciding who can migrate and settle in a community and who cannot, to questions of family disputes and quarrels between husband and wife. We have seen from that data, and especially from the tables on page 91, that women suffer from this sytem of feudal relationships *relatively* more than men. It is therefore in the interests of women in particular that the remnants of this system be eliminated — through a process of basic democratization of village level political structures, a process in which women must play a full part. It is obvious that the position of peasant women, within the class system and within the family, cannot be improved as long as these feudal institutions continue to exist.

Notes

1. I wish to express my gratitude to Mallam Yahaya Abdullahi, Chairman of the Lands Investigation Commission, for making his own copy of the *Report*

available to me, and for taking time to answer my questions and to discuss with me the special problems of women that the Commission has documented. Of course, the opinions expressed in this paper are my own responsibility. The *Report* of the Lands Commission is presenting being published by the Kaduna State Government. So far, Vol.1 (General findings and recommendations) has appeared, as well as the volumes on several of the Local Government areas. However, at the time this paper was being written, I only had access to the manuscript edition lent to me by M. Yahaya, so the page numbers referred to in this paper refer to this manuscript, rather than to the published volumes, except in the case of Vol.1, where the published edition is used.

2. The terms of reference of the Commission are as follows:

(i) To investigate and ascertain the validity of all cases of complaint over the acquisition of land by either individuals or corporate groups and make appropriate recommendations.

(ii) To investigate and ascertain the validity of all cases of complaint over the allocation of urban and rural plots for both private, commercial and residential purposes and make appropriate recommendations.

(iv) To examine the present system of plot allocation in both urban and rural areas with a view to identifying areas where malpractices have occurred and recommending appropriate measures.

(v) To recommend to the Government an efficient system of land administration in the State. Such systems should be capable of stopping all forms of speculation involving land. (*Report*, Vol.1, p.6).

3. *Report*, Vol.1, p.7.

4. *Report*, Vol.1, p.12.

5. *Report*, Vol.1, p.9.

6. In presenting the case material, I have followed the format used by the Lands Commission in its own presentation. As the *Report* is a public document, and as all parties in the cases were represented before the Commission at the sittings, I did not feel it necessary either to omit or change the names of the individuals involved. Page numbers mentioned at the end of each case refer to the relevant volume (by LGA) and the pages in the manuscript edition.

7. The term *gandu* refers both to the family production unit, and to the farmland which that production unit worked.

8. For details of forced labour policies, see M.M. Tukur, *The Imposition of British Colonial Domination of the Sokoto Caliphate, Borno and Neighboring States: 1897-1914*. Ph.D. Thesis, Department of History ABU, 1979, Chapter VII.

9. *Tukur*, Chapters I and II.

10. *Report of the Lands Investigation Commission*, Vol.1, p.12.

11. *Report*, p.13.

12. Based on the total complaints filed with the Commission, not on the number heard in public sittings.

13. Based on my own calculations from the complaints heard and documented in the *Report*.

14. For a detailed discussion of Nomijidi regulations, see *Report*, Vol.1, pp.25-28.

16. Capitalism, on the other hand, exploits and dominates *primarily* through the system of economic relations, and does so in a more universal way than does feudalism.

Female Urban Employment

A.B. Zack-Williams

This study is mainly concerned with the female construction workers of Jos Local Government Area of Plateau State in Nigeria. The paper is divided into seven sections: introduction; methodology; recruitment procedures; types of work and remuneration; workers' reaction to work insecurity; the views of the male workers; and conclusion.

Introduction

The visitor to Plateau State is struck by three peculiar features of the region: its mountainous terrain; the mild temperature; and the high predominance of female workers on the construction sites that are scattered all over Jos, the capital of the State.

Jos, a middle size town in northern Nigeria, was founded in 1915 as a direct result of the economic stimuli (mainly tin mining and commerce) from colonialism.[1] The town has experienced rapid growth, particularly since World War 2. The population in 1930 was put at 2,500[2], and in 1963 457,760 and the estimated figure for 1974 was 601,000[3]. Since the petro-Naira oil boom of the early 1970s Jos has developed into a major communication centre linking other important towns such as Kano, Port Harcourt and Lagos by road, rail and air. Today, Jos is a cosmopolitan urban centre with the population drawn from all over Nigeria "and almost all of the ethnic groups of the country are represented in proportions that are remarkably close to those for the nation as a whole".[4]

Even though there are women working on construction sites in south-western Nigeria,[5] Jos is unique among northern States in having large numbers of women working in this industry. As we shall see presently, there are various reasons why women have moved into this sector. Furthermore, as far as one is aware, no serious attempt has been made to study these women "operatives" within the building industry.[6] It is hoped that this paper will help to fill this gap.

104

Methodology

The research for this paper was carried out between January and May 1982. The methods used involved formal questionaire and informal "depth" interviews as well as non-participant observation. The interviews were conducted with the aid of three research assistants.[7] The lack of adequate information on female construction workers meant that a non-random sample of respondents had to be chosen. Indeed, interviews were conducted wherever one could find women on construction sites, and, one tried as much as possible to avoid duplication.

In all, 108 formal interviews were conducted: 54 of the respondents were women; 38 were men; and 16, contractors. 30 construction sites were visited spanning an area with a radius of over 40 kilometres. Eight of these were concerned with hotel construction, five with the construction of public buildings, three with churches, and 14 with private buildings. The work involved varied from the construction of three-bedroomed family bungalows to multi-storey high-rise buildings.

Among the information sought were: the age of female respondents; religion and marital status; whether they had children or not; and, if so, who looked after the children during working hours. One also wanted to know if working in the construction industry is a tradition for some families and ethnic groups. Thus we posed the question: "Does any member of your family work in the construction industry?" We were also interested in the ethnic and state origin of respondents[8], how they were recruited into the industry, why they left their previous jobs (if they had any) and how long they had been working in the industry. One also wanted to know whether they owned the tools which they worked with; the nature of their jobs; the security of their jobs; the length of the working day, and days a week; how and what they spent their wages on. Finally, one wanted to know if these women belong to a Trade Union and also their attitudes towards Trade Unions.

Recruitment Procedures

We now turn to look at some of the major findings of this research. Of the 54 women interviewed only four, representing just over 7% were Muslims, the rest being Christians. The fact that non-Muslims predominate is not at all surprising for two reasons. Firstly, Jos is a predominantly Christian town, though there is a significant Muslim minority. Secondly, a large proportion of Muslim women in northern Nigeria are put in seclusion (known as *kulle* in Hausa), which tends to prevent their participation in the formal labour force.[9]

All the women, with the exception of six (i.e. 11%), were married. Among the unmarried women were two high school drop-outs who had failed to gain admission to college; and a child of about 10 years old.

The age of respondents ranged from 10 to 42; with most respondents being under 30 years of age. Only one married woman replied that she did not have a child. If the number of single women (who had no children), are added, it means that almost 13% of our respondents had no children. Also of interest was the size of the family of these women. Their replies showed that 63% of the women had three or more children.

After finding out the number and age of the children, we wanted to know how they were cared for during working hours. An interesting conclusion emerged. Mothers with sucklings and toddlers usually took them to the work sites, whilst older children of school age (i.e. between 6 and 15) were left with older siblings, friends and relations.

All but one of the respondents were indigenes of Plateau State. The only non-Plateau respondent was a Chaiwo (ethnic origin)[10] from Kaduna State. The respondents came from various ethnic backgrounds with Miango, Rukuba, and Jarawa being the major ethnic origins of our respondents.[11]

Also considered was the question of recruitment of women into the industry. Both structured and unstructured questions were put to the women, male workers and contractors. From their answers given, it was concluded that there were three avenues through which female workers entered the industry. The first and most important avenue is through the *Yan Kamisho* system.[12] The *Yan Kamisho*, who is usually a woman, embodies a number of functions. She is both recruitment officer of the contractor, as well as the welfare officer of the women workers. Once a building contract is won,[13] the conractor would approach a *Yan Kamisho* to help in providing labourers. She would then go round from house to house and other informal channels (for example beer parlours) in search of women willing to work. At times, the *Yan Kamisho* would be approached by potential workers. Occasionally, she would have a gang ready, and would then move on straight to the site.

Once on the site, the *Yan Kamisho* is responsible for the welfare of the worker. She acts as a liaison between the *Alhaji* (contractor)[14] and the women. She ensures that the women are not exploited by being "over-worked", and protect them from potential bullies. The *Alhaji* does remunerate the *Yan Kamisho* at the same rate as the women. In addition she receives a commission of between 20k to 50k per worker per day.[15] This is quite a substantial amount when it is considered that in all the sites visited women represent over 60% of the labour force, and in some cases, the female labour force could be as large as 125.[16] Furthermore, this amount represents a serious deduction from their already scanty wages (see below). Though their wages are calculated on a daily basis, the women are paid either on a weekly basis or at the end of a "job".

The second method by which women are recruited into the industry is through the "sub-contractor" system. Under this system, a large contractor will sub-contract specific tasks, such as casting, floating or even fencing to a smaller contractor. The sub-contractor, if he does not already have his own gang of "women navvies", will move to the surrounding villages, such as Miango, Rukuba and Naraguta in search of potential labourers. Usually, a contractor tends to retain the services of his navvies, after a specific task has been completed; and they move around from site to site. One shall see presently that these women are very much socialized into the "wage-economy" and that they tend to show a high level of Trade Union consciousness.[17] The sub-contractor is responsible for the wages of the women, and the same conditions prevail as under the *Yan Kamisho* system, with the exception that no commission is deducted from the women's wages.

The third and final method of entering the industry is by individual women going round from one site to the other asking if their services are needed. These women, like most of those recruited by the *Yan Kamisho,* tend to be the least proletarianized and some of them even enter the industry with their implements of work — pans for carrying concrete and water.

Type of Work and Remuneration

Having identified the avenues through which the women entered the industry, one was also interested in knowing the nature of the job they undertook; how long women have been carrying out these tasks and their remuneration, in particular their wages as compared to their male counterparts.

From our interviews among all groups of building personnel and from our observations, there are two points which could be made about the types of jobs carried out by the female workers. Firstly, using the concept developed by Bromley and Gerry,[18] their job can be described as usual work". By this one means "any way of making a living which lacks a moderate degree of security of income and employment".[19] The insecurity of employment is shown by the fact that only the *Yan Kamisho* said that they were entitled to their wages in case of summary dismissal. Furthermore, it has been shown by a number of researchers that though the building industry is a large employer of labour in the Third World, yet this type of work is characterized by uncertainty.[20] Women in the construction industry in Jos have no contracts guaranteeing employment for a specific period. Contractors can terminate employment whenever work is not available. The work force will vary according to the number and size of projects under construction, and with the stage of completion of each site. The labour force will be reduced when construction on a site is complete; and workers will not be re-employed until new projects can be secured. As a result workers may be employed on a particular site for only a short period and will experience unemployment before securing a new job.

Secondly, the work carried out by these women remains largely unskilled. They are mainly carriers of water, blocks and concrete. A few women have "graduated" to the point where they now shovel and mix concrete. There were no women masons, bricklayers, or carpenters. The women are brought in to carry out specific tasks such as supplying masons with blocks and concrete, or carrying sand and water to masons. The unskilled nature of their job helps to increase their insecurity. Not only are their jobs threatened by "other reserve armies of the unemployed", but because of the volatile nature of the building industry in the Third World,[21] these women would be the first to lose their jobs in the event of a down-turn in the economy.

With regards to remuneration, given Bromley and Gerry's continuum: stable wage-work; through short-term wage-work; disguised wage-work; dependent work; and finally true self-employment, we can say that the work of the women in the construction industry in Jos is a form of short-term wage-work. As Bromley and Gerry noted, short-term wage-work is "paid and contractd by the day, week, month or season, or paid and contracted for fixed terms or tasks, with no assurance of continuity of employment..."[22] This type of work is recognized as wage work in law, though the benefits associated with long-term work (such as tenure) are not realized. Furthermore, the women in this industry do not enjoy the Federal Government's minimum wage provision of N200 a month.

Wages for women ranged from between 3 Naira and 5 Naira a day for an eight-hour-day, six-days-a-week job. It is a truism that both male and female workers in the industry are exploited by the contractors and the builders alike, for thom construction has become an important avenue of capital accumulation.[23] However, women as a (gender) group are much more exploited than their male counterparts. For example, not only were the wages of the male workers higher than women's, but even for the same job (e.g. concrete mixing), men received higher wages than women. This over-exploitation of female labour[24] cannot be resolved under the rubric of "relative skills". There are various cultural and structural variables which tend to undermine the position of these women. These shall be returned to in the next section.

Strictly speaking, these are women in the process of proletarianization and are not solely dependent on their wages for survival. For most of them (76%) this was their first job outside household chores or farming. However, 26 out of the 54 (48%) owned the pans and shovels with which they worked.[25] But for long "established" workers in the industry (i.e. those who worked for the contractors on a semi-permanent basis), and for those on large projects such as the construction of hotels or public buildings, the tools were owned by the employers. Furthermore, in order to find out if there was a tradition of women working in the industry, we asked the women how long they had been working in the industry. The response showed that over 82% had been in the industry for less than four years. The respondent with the longest stay in the industry claimed that she had been in the industry for eight years. the *Yan Kamisho*s tend to have stayed the longest. Thus it would appear that female employment in the industry is a relatively recent phenomenon.

It would appear that these women were responding to a boom in construction in Jos which led to a tremendous demand for unskilled labour. Since the extraordinary increase in revenue from petroleum products, successive Nigerian governments have embarked upon large-scale construction works. These include road-building, irrigation and hydro-electric projects, and the building of a brand new capital, Abuja Federal Capital Territory. One effect of these projects has been to attract skilled and unskilled workers from "peripheral areas" like Jos, to booming areas like Abuja.[26] It would appear that these women have moved in to fill this vacuum left by departing male workers.

Instability of Employment and Workers' Reaction

One has seen that the work on the building sites for the female workers is an exceptionally insecure position. One now turns to look at how women tried to adjust to this rather precarious situation. It must be borne in mind that for a large number of these women, their job was never a "matter of life and death", since they were not the bread-winners. When asked: "whilst working do you get money from your husband?", of the 48 married women only three said that they did not receive support from their husbands. They were further asked how they spent their wages; the majority — 42, claimed they spent their money on the children or for personal effects.

It has been seen that 35 of the women had no job other than farming and the "domestic economy" before entering the construction industry. The remaining 13 were asked why they left their previous jobs, (mainly trading and home-help), 11 claimed they were attracted to the building industry by the "high" wages to be earned.

It is clear that the women were attracted to the industry by the relatively high wages. This means that in spite of the poor safety conditions on several building sites, as long as there is a perceived high wage to be earned, the women will still come forward for employment. Furthermore, though the women spend long (eight) hours on the sites each working day, yet their work is not as regulated as their counterparts in factories. Persistent late-comers are not shown the door; children could be brought to the site; breaks are long and quite frequent; women carry only one block at a time and only a moderate amount of sand, concrete and granite. In short, social relations on the sites are not as alienating s those in the modern capitalist factories.

Now, though the women have tried to adjust and manage to make the best out of a bad situation, this does not mean that they are content. When asked, "what do you think of your job?", 34 said they were unsatisfied; whilst seven claimed that they were quite satisfied. The rest had no idea.

Still trying to assess the level of job satisfaction among women, we asked them, "would you leave your job if you could find another?" 51 said they would, whilst only three said they would stay on. Two of the three who said they would stay on turned out to be two of the oldest respondents interviewed. The third was only 15 years old and may have been influenced by the fact that her mother was working on the site at the time of the interview.

One tried to establish whether there was any form of Trade Union to which the women belonged. Whilst the men had their own Unions, one only heard once of a Trade Union for women called *Matakonkare*.[27] All the women interviewed said that they did not belong to any Union. When asked if they felt that a Trade Union would help improve conditions at work, most (26) felt that it would help; (20) felt that it would not make any difference, and the rest did not have any views at all. Most of those who "called" for a Union were those recruited directly by the contractors. These are the women who have worked the longest in the industry and they formed the core of the disgruntled in the industry. It is from these women that one should expect agitation for Unionism; and they will provide the vanguard for any such agitation.

The View of the Men

It is clear that women were not the only operatives in this industry. One would now like to look at how the men felt about having such a large number of women in the industry. The men can be divided into two: contractors and male workers. It is the latter group with which one is now concerned.

The men were asked if they felt that the women were performing their jobs as well as them. 20 (55%) said that they did not feel that the women were performing as well as the men. 14 (38%) felt that the women were performing just as well as men. The men were also asked why women were employed in the industry. The majority — 88% (29) — felt that they were employed "to do the lesser job". One went on to ask the men that if offered would they accept the jobs of the women. Over 55% (20) said they would not accept. In order to clearly assess the view of the men, we asked them how they felt about women working alongside them. The vast majority — 72% — felt that they were favourably disposed; whilst only 8 (22%) felt unfavourably disposed. They were also asked, "if you did the same job as a woman, would you be angry if you were offered the same wages?" Again the vast majority 72% (26) said they would not be angry.

One wanted to see if both men and women could work within the same Trade Unions to bring about a transformation in the industry. In order to test the male workers' reaction, the following question was posed: "Would you join the same Trade Union as women?" The vast majority of respondents (27 or 75%) answered in the affirmative. Finally, those who said yes were asked if they would join the same Trade Union as women and if they would vote for women as Trade Union Officials? 16 (61%) claimed that they would vote for women as Union Officials.

It is clear from the above that the attitude of the men in the building industry with regards to their female colleagues runs contrary to the general attitude of the wider public in and around Jos. They see their female colleagues as belonging to the *Talakawa* (toiling masses). It is only the Alhajis and the wider society that see the women as removed from the men. This is one important reason why women in the construction industry in Jos are paid less for the same job done by their male colleagues.

Conclusion

In this paper one has tried to examine how a section of the poor in Nigerian society (in the words of Bromley and Gerry) "make out" in a society with little opportunity of wage employment, and one where women are treated in the workplace as socially inferior to men. One has shown that one way of survival for these women was to pick up casual employment in the building industry. One has seen that though construction work is not one in which traditional northern Nigerian women have been employed, yet these casual workers have been used to carry much of the burden of risk, both economic and physical, within an insecure work milieu. They are drawn into the industry when there is a demand for extra labour and are laid off when the "order book" is low. This means that the women construction workers are only paid direct wages; and they forfeit the indirect wages needed for the period they are laid off.[28] In this way, one can say that the incorporation of female workers into the industry has tended to lower the cost of putting up buildings in Jos. Since the lower cost is not passed on to the tenants in lower rents one can conclude that these casual workers play an important role in the process of petty bourgeois accumulation in Nigeria. This type of accumulation clearly leads to the concentration of wealth in the hands of the few and the pauperization of the many.

With regards to the question of overcoming the over-exploitation of female labour within the industry, it is important to note that the state too contributes to their instability of income opportunities through its "exclusive" rather than "inclusive" legislation. In this respect, one has noted that the minimum wage provision does not apply to these workers, presumably because they are in the private "informal" sector. However, it is clear that no real change could occur in the position of these women without a total transformation of Nigerian society.

Notes

1. For a detailed topography of Jos town, see L. Plotnicov, *Strangers to the City, Urban Man in Jos, Nigeria:* University of Pittsburgh Press, 1971; also by the same author, "The Modern African Elite of Jos, Nigeria", in L. Plotnicov and A. Tuden, *Social Stratification in Africa:* The Free Press, New York, 1970, pp.269-302.

2. Plotnicov, 1970, ibid.

3. For 1963 figure and 1974 estimate see *Statistical Year Book, Benue-Plateau State,* 1974, published by the Ministry of Economic Planning, Statistics and Demographic Division, Jos; Table 10, p.11.

4. Plotnicov, 1970, p.271.

5. I would like to thank Ms. Abiola Ogunsola for pointing this fact out to me.

6. One exception to this generalization is the work of A.C. Emovon, "The effect of Women's Employment on Family Relations: A Case Study of Women Contractors in Benin City, Nigeria", mimeo, n.d. I am grateful to the author for letting me have access to this mimeo. One important difference between her study and mine is that her work could be defined as looking at the industry from top-down; whilst my work is concerned not with the contractors but with the "labouring women" in the industry.

7. I am particularly grateful to Vongjen Wazh for his assistance.

8. This was an opportunity to verify Plotnicov's assertion that "migrant labourers are insigificant in Jos". See his 1970, p.272.

.9. This does not mean that such women are economically inactive. For example, both Shea and Schildkrout have argued that women in Purdah (i.e. *Kulle*) are able to earn and control their own incomes so long as they do not infringe *Kulle* obligations. See P.J. Shea, *The Development of an Export Oriented Dyed Cloth Industry in Kano Emirate,* unpublished Ph.D. Thesis, University of Wisconsin, 1975, especially pp.69-71. E. Schildkrout, "Age and Gender in Hausa Society: Socioeconomic Roles of Children in Urban Kano", in J.S. LaFontaine (ed.),, *Sex and Age as Principles of Social Differentation,* pp.109-137, New York Academic Press, 1978; also her "Women's Work and Children's Work: Variations among Muslims in Kano", in S. Wallman (ed.), *Social Anthropology of Work,* pp.69-85, New York, Academic Press, 1979.

10. It is interesting to note that this group is also found in Plateau State. While this is not significant evidence to verify Plotnicov's assertion that migrant labour is insignificant in Jos, our data would tend to confirm such a conclusion.

11. These are all major ethnic groups in Jos metropolitan area. What is surprising is that only one respondent claimed to come from Birom, the largest ethnic group in Jos.

12. *Yan Kamisho* in Hausa loosely means the one who receives a commission.

13. It is important to note that the work of these women is not confined to the erection of dwellings, but they also work on putting up other physical structures, such as the fencing of the Bauchi Road Campus of the University of Jos.

14. The term "Alhaji" traditionally is designed for devout Muslims who have made the holy pilgrimage to Mecca. But, in contemporary Nigeria, this term has a sociological interpretation. It is used to refer to rich businessmen, both Muslim and non-Muslim, in particular to contractors and landlords, and other members of the merchant capitalist classes.

15. The currency in Nigeria is the Naira, which is equivalent to £.80.

16. Conversation with Alhaji A.B. Galla, a contractor who at the time of interview (January 1982) "employed" a *Yan Kamisho*.

17. This term is not used in the Leninist sense to differentiate it from proletarian consciousness. It is only meant to show that this group of workers tends to see Trade Unions as having a major role to play in ameliorating their working conditions.

18. R. Bromley and C. Gerry (eds.), *Casual Work and Poverty in Third World Cities,* John Wiley and Sons, Chichester, 1979.

19. Bromley and Gerry, p.5.

20. See for example, A. Stretton, "Instability of Employment among Building Industry Labourers in Manila", in Bromley and Gerry (eds.), pp.267-282; and P. Sylos-Labini, "Precarious Employment in Sicily", *International Labour Review,* Vol.89, 1964, pp.268-285, especially p.270 where he argues that "...persons engaged in (this) activity have no guarantee of stability either of their job or their income and hence have no definite prospects of ovement... wage labourers are precariously employed when they have no stable labour contracts or no contracts at all; they may have to change their masters; or if they remain with the same master, they are always in danger of losing their jobs."

21. See Stretton, p.281.

22. Bromley and Gerry, p.5.

23. Because of the serious housing shortage in Nigeria, there is a mad rush to erect houses and hotels, which are rented out at exhorbitant amounts. Some of these houses are so poorly and badly constructed that if not for the acute housing shortage, many would be condemned as unfit for human habitation.

24. For a more elaborate analysis of the question, see this author's "Female Labour and Exploitation Within African Social Formations: Some Theoretical Issues", paper presented at the Seminar on *Women in Nigeria,* A.B.U. Zaria, 27-28 May, 1982.

25. Too much should not be read into this, since carpenters and masons too, often carry their personal tools to their place of work.

26. It is common knowledge in Nigeria that Abuja is a contractor's paradise, and the average skilled or semi-skilled worker can easily expect to earn over five times the income of his counterpart in Jos. Abuja is less than 250 kilometres from Jos.

27. This was mentioned me me by Alhaji A.B. Galla, though I have not been able to verify this information. By *Matakonkare,* I suspect he was referring to the *Yan Kamisho.*

28. The cost of reproduction of their labour power is borne by the non-capitalist sector, since most of the women, 31%, claimed that their husbands were farmers.

Rapporteur's Report

A. Mohammed

The major theme that the papers and the discussion of the session presented was that of the "Double Oppression of Women", i.e. the exploitation and oppression of women as the members of different productive classes, i.e. the peasantry and the proletariat, and especially as members of the female sex.

It was noted that the surplus labour of women is exploited just like that of men among the proletariat. Hence, working-class men and women are pitched into the same camp against the bourgeoisie as far as the class struggle is concerned in a capitalist context,

In the rural semi-feudal setting, a similar situation obtains whereby both the male and female peasants are oppressed and exploited by the feudal aristocracy and their capitalist allies. But the session more specifically addressed itself to the issue of access to land. In this respect, as a community or as a class of the peasantry, women were found to be equally subjected to the oppression and exploitation of the arbitrary practices of the land-owning class with regards to the right to land ownership.

As for the other aspect of the theme, it was established that women are exploited and oppressed specifically in their position as members of the female sex. For instance with regards to their employment with particular reference to the construction industry, women are mainly engaged in unskilled labour as opposed to men who are engaged in skilled labour. Women are paid lesser wages than men and there are no conditions of service or fringe benefits attached to their labour. Thus women are treated as a labour reserve. Their exploitation in these circumstances is over and above the exploitation of surplus labour in a peripheral capitalist system.

With regards to the situation of women among the peasantry as far as access to land is concerned, the story is not any different. As a consequence of the status of women within the family and in marriage they are denied access to land. So, this is a classical case of the oppression and usurpation of the rights of women within the family. In this situation it is not the enemy class — the feudal elements or the capitalists that inflict the tyranny but rather it is the men of the peasantry.

As to what should be done about the "double oppression' of women in the society, Perchonock's paper concluded with a suggestion which seems to be a consensus of the session that:

> While women need to organize to obtain full rights within the family, it is obvious that this cannot be achieved without at the same time fighting against the total system of exploitative relationships which characterizes the society as a whole. *If the double oppression of women is to be overcome, the battle must be fought on two fronts.*

PART IV
Contemporary Experiences (1)

Women in Nigeria

'Molara Ogundipe-Leslie

On the Globality of Sisterhood

This essay will begin with a poem[1] by a distinguished male poet friend of mine who is a Professor of English Literature and a Malawian. His poem sprang from the many arguments and discussions we had on women, feminism and politics in Africa and the wider world while he was visiting Nigeria. Although he is Malawian, his poem is pertinent and instructive of some of the basic ideas and attitudes of men in Nigeria and Africa.

LETTER TO A FEMINIST FRIEND

I will not pretend
to see the light
in the rhythm of your paragraphs:
illuminated pages
need not contain
any copy-rights
on history

My world has been raped,
looted and squeezed
by Europe and America
and I have been scattered
over three continents
to please Europe and America

AND NOW

the women of Europe and America
after drinking and carousing
on my sweat
rise up to castigate and
castrate their menfolk
from the cushions of a world
I have built!

Why should they be allowed
to come between us?
You and I were slaves together
uprooted and humiliated together
Rapes and lynchings —
the lash of the overseer
and the lust of the slave-owner
do your friends "in the movement"
understand these things?

The wile of the coloniser,
the juggernaut of apartheid
the massacres of Sharpeville and Langa,
"interrogation" unto death
unreal inquests have
your friends seen these?
like the children of Soweto?

No, no, my sister, my love,
first things first!
Too many gangsters
still stalk this continent
too many pirates
too many looters
far too many
still stalk this land —
every inch of it should be sure
yet inch by inch
day by day we see it ceded
to forces beyond our control.

Where then do we sit
where build our tent
while sorting out
the faults between you and me?
Miracles still happen,
I agree,
and privilege and the underdog
can unite to undo privilege
but sister,
not every yawning of the privileged
amounts to a sacrifice!

When Africa
at home and across the seas
is truly free
there will be time for me
and time for you
to share the cooking
and change the nappies —
till then,
first things first!

Notice the use of the first person. It is his world that has been raped. The Promethean persona that endured slavery and the slave trade, colonialism, imperialism and neo-colonialism, does not have time for women's rights yet. The world has been built by "him" and he must attend to the pressing issues of colonialism, imperialism and neo-colonialism.

These attitudes hark back to the important feminist issue of the representation and understanding of women and their roles in history ably dealt with by feminists such as Mitchell, Rowbotham and Firestone among others.

And there is the black-white posing of issues which socialist feminists reject, insisting on a class view of history and human societies. The oppression of women, economic or personal, is not solely a white-black race confrontation although the oppression of black women is deeply tied to the variable of race in the history of imperialism. Similarly, we, Nigerian women who are Ibadan branch members of AAWORD (Association of African Women for Research and Development) argued this class view in a position paper presented in the group's research workshop in Lusaka, in December 1976. In the paper, we insist that the study of women must be done from class perspectives, taking cognizance of class differences in society, in particular in Africa. Such an approach, we feel, would yield a true picture of the woman's place in society.[2] The white women in the poem as wives of colonizers and collaborators with colonialism, imperialism and neo-colonial Africa and the United States are not sisters. In fact, we need to keep our minds firmly fixed on what is meant by sisterhood and the globality of sisterhood. Some feminists and activists would reject the terms of "sisters" and "sisterhood" outright. Are women oppressed first as women or in their roles in their societies deriving from their respective relation to the means of production in their various societies? Again, another feminist issue which has received much attention from feminist theoreticians. What about feminist aristocratic women within feudalism or bourgeois women in the ruling classes of capitalism and imperialism? Are they seriously oppressed or oppressed at all considering they have money and leisure to soften or remove many of the pains of male domination. In fact, there is greater financial collaboration with and inclusion of women in family rights among families with high levels of capital.

The poem ends on a final note irritatingly typical of male supremacists everywhere: to wit, that other issues exist which are more important and urgent than the liberation of women. Somehow, miraculously, you can liberate a country or society and later, turn your attention to the women of that society — first things first! Note also that the liberation of women is conceived as the desire of women to reduce men to housekeepers. Since most men despise manual work for feudal and middle-class reasons, women's liberation is feared as an effort by women to "feminize" men, that is, degrade them.[3] In the middle-class capitalist societies, mental labour is more respected than physical labour; in feudal society, the great man works not at all but makes others work for him. Hence, women's work is never respected. The poem feels women's liberation is about cooking and nappies. No, women's liberation is about the fundamental human rights of women in all areas of life, public and private.

Women in Nigeria: Problems and Realities

Most Nigerian women of the middle class whom I know and whom I have talked with argue that the basic situation of women in Nigeria is not intolerable or appalling because of the economic opportunities women have within the social system. These economic opportunities are not recent or post-colonial but pre-colonial. In fact, colonialism eroded many of the economic avenues women had.[4] Women had been able to engage in farming, fishing, herding, commerce and industrial labour such as pottery, cloth-making, and craftwork among other activities alongside their men, and they had the right to keep the financial proceeds of their work and earnings from the sale of products. The economic position, rights and gains of aristocratic African women in pre-capitalist societies are less known. Even in purdah, in Islamic northern Nigeria where Islam took away in the early nineteenth century many of the historically established and strong social rights of the Hausa women driving her indoors, even there, women work in purdah and sell their products through emissaries.

These economic opportunities and the right to work which the middle-class woman may be fighting for in other societies and in some pockets of post-colonial and post-Christianized Nigeria have, in fact, always existed. Today, these rights and attitudes have blossomed forth again and women have risen to pluck them, following independence in 1960 and the near cataclysmic change going on now. This deep social change is related to the civil war and the new oil-economy as it is related to the crisis of being governed by a black national and exploiting ruling class which is subjecting the total population to stress, anxiety, and insecurities of various kinds. Women, in response to the social situation, wish to secure for themselves and their children some financial viability and other gains of modernization such as formal Western education in a society where all forms of marriage are under crisis, and men may not wish to take complete responsibility for their offspring.

All women in contemporary Nigeria are under the stress of living in a Third-World, neo-colonial nation ruled by an indifferent, oppressive and wasteful black bourgeoisie. The reactions of the women differ from class to class. Women of the urban working class, the urban poor, and the peasantry have definitely different attitudes. They insist more on their right to work, as they very often have to live within polygynous systems, Islamic and traditional. They tend to ignore the biological and emotional oppressions they have to endure, in the view that men are incorrigibly polygynous and that women are socially impotent to correct them. They insist only on the right to have their children fathered, sexually and financially, while they expect little from men in terms of companionship, personal care and fidelity.

At a symposium organized by the Nigerian Association of University Women in 1974, with market-women of the city of Ibadan on the panel, the trading women revealed interest in problems patently different from our middle-class ones. They were, in fact, contemptuous of some of these problems, in particular, the resentment of polygyny by middle-class and Westernized women. They mainly felt men could not be expected to be loyal to one woman while some outrightly claim they needed helpmates in the form of co-wives to assist with housework. They needed younger wives to share or preferably take over the chores of kitchen and bed, so they, the older wives, can be freed to concentrate on travel for business reasons.[5] It may be argued that these trading women are victims of false consciousness and social brain-washing, but for them, the old pre-capitalist system exists, works, and is respected by them. We may ask if they have their humanity, their dignity, their human rights and self-fulfilment, guaranteed within this system. Their only objection was to the rupture or distortion of the older system of marriage where the older wife now is relegated to the background by an uncaring husband or where the younger wife would not keep her lower and deferent place within that system.

It is within marriage, however, that the Nigerian woman suffers the most oppression. More recently, illegitimacy was written into the 1979 constitution, making all children born inside and outside a marriage legal. This is surely an underwriting of polygyny in the society. This year, 1982, there was talk of cancelling the bigamy laws which forbade that the various kinds of marriage possible in the country — Islamic, traditional and Western ordinance — could be coincident while they forbade that within the Western marriage, one could marry more than one wife legally and officially. Members of women's groups stormed the parliamentary buildings that day to the hilarity of men who, in this country, often and generally react to women's issues with laughter and scorn. It is, however, also known that new forms of polygyny, displaced and new urban varieties, abound in the society today.

The oppression of women within marriage takes various forms. First, the woman loses status by being married bcause in the traditional system which is still at the base of the society, the woman as daughter or sister has greater status and more rights in her own lineage. Getting married, she becomes a client or possession, voiceless and often rightless in her husband's family except, in some groups, through what accrues to her through children. She also loses much of her personal freedom which she can only gain at prices expensive to herself such as the admittance of other wives or publicly acknowledged girl-friends. She also has to submit to dominance by her husband, or face execration and blame from the total society. She can, however, win by "stooping to conquer" as the generally-held cliché goes in the society. This means accepting subjection in order to "conquer" abstractly.

Men also tend to be less trusting of wives than they are of their own mothers and sisters, a situation which often alienates the wife throughout her marriage and makes her a stranger in enemy territory all her life.[7] In fact, men here lean emotionally more on their mothers, sisters, and aunts — the womenfolk of their own lineage or kin group than on their own wives. This situation gives some emotional power to women. Thus often women "take consolation from this fact and help to oppress other women" who come into their own lineages as wives. It is generally known that women in their own lineages form the emotional support of the men to the extent that the men cannot function without them. Yet such men will express in acts and words the most blatant notions of male dominance. Such emotional power often satisfies women to the point of preventing them from wanting to take other more public action or to resist the subordination they suffer within their own marriages. In addition to the power of female relatives within marriage, there exist the pressure and power of peer group values on the husband; values which often confirm male dominance and encourage even recalcitrant and would-be gentle and just husbands in the direction of male supremacy.

The subordination of women within marriage takes the various traditional forms though palliated by women's right to work. But the reality of this is that women are overworked. Generally, men do not do housework of any sort or care for children so the woman struggles on two fronts — the home and the working place. As a result, women of the middle class find that the most important problem they confront now is the problem of house-help in the home. The traditional support systems of grandmothers, siblings, younger relatives, and co-wives having been withdrawn by new social developments such as compulsory education, urbanization and capitalist atomization of the family, the middle-class woman is more frequently now marooned in her home and struggling with her job and house-keeping. The working-class woman is, of course, more burdened as often she has to struggle similarly but with less financial wherewithal to solve her problems. She is often more structurally and financially dependent on her husband particularly if she does only petty retail trading. She is therefore more subject to male domination while she has sometimes to care for her own children if she exists within a polygynous structure of marriage where she has to contend for personal and financial attention with other co-wives. Polygyny, not infrequently, leads to the financial neglect of children by a husband too poor to cope with the burden of a large family. So each woman has to care for her own children.

Not least of the biological oppressions women endure within marriage is the compulsion to have children. Childless marriages are blamed on women as men are never admitted to be sterile or infertile. The anguish of childless women is recorded in many a Nigerian literary narrative, traditional and modern. One finds that the childlessness of women is a recurrent theme in modern Nigerian women's writing.[8] A childless woman is considered a monstrosity as is an unmarried woman, spinster, or divorcee. She becomes the butt of jokes, scandal, and the quarry of any passing man, married or unmarried. She is often seen by males in the society as an unclaimed and degenerating commodity to be freely exploited in all ways — emotionally, sexually, and financially among others.

The greatest strength of women lies in their right and ability to work in addition to their resourcefulness and great capacity for emotional survival. The extended African family probably guarantees this or contributes enormously to it. The greatest gain made in recent years, particularly since independence in 1960, has been the widening of formal educational opportunities for women, resulting in chances in public life and a gradual change in men's attitudes that women can do as well as men, if not better, when given a chance. As a result, men more willingly educate their daughters in the Western tradition today.

It can be said that the main areas where women need to struggle now are those of national development and political representation. Abortion is not likely to be legalized soon. When the issue arose in 1981, the greatest opponents were, in fact, middle-class women who adopted very moralistic, even Sunday-school, unscientific attitudes to the need for legalized abortion in the society. Men proved more progressive about the issue. The issue of genital mutilation has not seen the light of day yet in the country. This is probably because not enough is known about its occurrence and the frequency of its incidence. Certainly, basic research needs to be done on genital mutilation in Nigeria for information and action. Female circumcision is only vaguely known to exist among certain ethnic groups in the country. Within marriage, where this paper argues women are most subordinated, laws exist to protect women's rights.[9] The hitch is that these laws are not always implemented or obeyed owing to the pressures of the past and the unwillingness of women to seek redress officially and publicly because of the mental subjection they have integrated into themselves historically. Males also tend to please themselves rather than go through formal legal processes. A male-dominated society guarantees them protection and instant sympathy even in the law courts.

Nigerian middle-class women have, however, to insist that there cannot be equality without the sharing of responsibilities. There cannot be dignity and the sharing of power without the sharing of the burdens of responsibility and power. Women therefore can only claim equality within marriage if they are willing to share the financial and other burdens of marriage. As emotional and financial dependents, they cannot claim equality with the husbands who support them. Strangely enough, though, my discussions with male colleagues over the years reveal that some men would rather shoulder their marital burdens alone in order to be able to give orders to their wives. Power is sweet. In reality, the women have to pitch in on food and school fees since frequently the men do not earn enough. But women still expect certain traditional male gestures of money, cloth and jewellery gifts. All in all, middle-class men do not seem grateful for the contributions to the home made by their wives. They in fact resent the contributions, I suppose, because they erode their total "hegemony", their ability to treat their wives as subordinates, slaves or possessions.

Politically, in modern life, the roles of women are negligible, though traditionally, avenues existed for the political participation of women.[10] Very often, dual-sexual political systems existed in pre-colonial societies[11] whereafter these systems were either distorted, suppressed or restricted in scope by the colonial administration which excluded women from its new patterns. Traditionally, structures of political participation, equivalent or parallel to those for men, existed for women whereby women's voices were heard, their opinions consulted and their participation guaranteed from the familial households to the councils in the larger society. Today, we behave and talk as if it is new for women to have any political voice, role or power.

Today in the presidential system, the woman's visibility and leadership opportunities are negligible, though the political and personal liberties of women are theoretically and fully guaranteed in the 1979 constitution.

In a recent public lecture, the notable Nigerian woman novelist, Flora Nwapa, delineated statistically the scanty number of women in visible positions despite the existence of women voters as the majority and the exploitation by political parties of women's enthusiasm to work during the election process.[12] Women are pre-empted from leading political roles by the attitude of men who cannot see women in leadership roles over them. Women were not considered fit to sit among the "fifty" and later forty-nine "wise men" who drafted the 1979 constitution, despite the large number of professional women in the country. Political parties are alleged to be unwilling to field women candidates. Women are also pre-empted by the lack of capital to conduct campaigns on their own steam if they are not fielded by the male-dominated parties. Women are additionally disadvantaged by their own unwillingness as mothers within a polygynous society to commit themselves totally to the vagaries of public life without the assurance that their children will be supported.

Some women would argue that women withdraw from politics because they are shy of public criticism and would wish to avoid the rough and tumble of politics.[13] Others put the reason down to the lack of dynamism among women and their inability to pull together and exploit their own potential.[14] These sociological observations, whatever their truth, must have their cause sought in social structures and institutions, in particular the structures of oppression including the effective subjection of women's minds within the society. Women become their own worst enemies and the worst enemies of other women in an effort to please males, as is typical of the psychology of servitude, the constant desire and anxiety to please the master until constant failure produces a dialectical and revolutionary change in the servant. Women also typically engage in self-flagellation, blaming their own oppression on themselves. Mea culpa! So effective has male domination and partriarchal ideology been within the country.

Can women be organized against the structures of oppression within Nigeria? Are there organized women's movements in the country? Various women's societies exist within society such as the Movement for Muslim Women, the Women's Improvement Society, the Nigerian Association of University Women among others, some of which come under the national umbrella of the National Council of Women's Societies, a government-recognized body, and some of which do not.[15] In addition, there are the women's wings of political parties, frequently only used to work for the party without compensation or political recognition for the women members. Women are best organized around definite economic, religious, professional, ethnic or class interests. The most lasting and effective bodies are organized around economic interests with immediate and concrete material and social benefits in view, such as those represented by market women's associations, and credit co-operatives etc., as well as religious interests represented by church societies which provide avenues for administrative powers and emotional support for funerals and such mishaps in urban situations where members may need the women's society to act in place of their own more distant families. Not negligible also are the ethnic groups and peer-group associations which attempt to maintain cultural continuity in the city among their members.[16] Class-based middle-class unions such as that of University Women or Old Girls' Associations are the most unstable perhaps because they have no concrete objectives, strategies or gains in view.

Most interviewees admit to the difficulty of organizing women. Some of the difficulty, I believe, springs from the overworked nature of women's lives, particularly of married mothers and the lack of time which results in an unenduring commitment and a consequent falling-off in participation. Such behaviour should not be explained by any self-blaming theory of the immanently and intrinsically inconsistent nature of women, as women themselves tend to do. Nigerian women are tired, emotionally neglected, socially stressed but brave women. The reasons for their organizational behaviour should be sought in their objective causes — in social structures which breed various forms of personal, emotional, psychological and *institutionalized* oppression, some of which are so integrated as to be almost unrecognizable, even by their victims.

Prospects

The future of feminism in this country depends on the raising of the consciousness of women to a greater awareness of their human rights in general and in relation to men, followed by a keener desire to know and act on the various possible modes of ensuring these rights. A certain fatalism, even masochism, about male dominance still prevails in women of all classes. All of them, however, believe in education as a way out of their differing oppressions. They all feel Western education will inevitably force men to a recognition and acknowledgement of their equality and abilities. Education, they feel, will provide the social and economic basis and security from which they can resist subjection and indignities. So resistance is being carried on individually now and not through collective and organized action. Bolanle Awe feels that women have to be taught today to understand power which men definitely do not want to share.[17] If women actually organized themselves and claimed their places, men would react violently and suppressively since the male attitude to women is born of a contradictory but explicable fear of and contempt for women. Chief Mrs. Ebun Oyagbola, the National Minister for Economic Planning, in a recent public statement said if women proved "arrogant", they would be neglected by the men and made to fail. Women of the urban working class and peasantry who also look so much to education will be radicalized, perforce, and may move into more radical action with men of their class, the more hopes are disappointed by the national ruling class and the more the national economy degenerates under the stresses of neo-colonial government.

It would seem that this writer is arguing that men are the enemy. No, men are not the enemy but the total societal structure which is a jumble of neo-colonial — (that is, primitive capitalist and intermediary consumerist economic formations dependent desperately on international capital) and feudalistic, even slave-holding structures and social attitudes. In fact, other forms of economic formations exist here which are not strictly within the usual Marxist categories of economic formations. As women's liberation is but an aspect of the need to liberate the total society from dehumanization and the loss of fundamental human rights, it is the social system which must change. But men become enemies when they seek to retard, even block, these necessary historical changes for selfish interests in power, claiming "culture and heritage" as if human societies are not constructed by human beings, or pleading and laughing about the natural and enduring inferiority of women, or arguing that change is impossible because history is static, which it is not.

I shall end with a stanza from one of my poems which says:

> How long shall we speak to them
> Of the goldness of mother, of difference without
>   home
> How long shall we say another world lives
> Not spinned on the axis of maleness
> But founded and wholed, charting through
> Its many runnels its justice distributive.

Notes

1. Felix Mthali: "Letter to a Feminist Friend". The poem will appear in a volume entitled: *Beyond the Echoes* (unpublished manuscript).

2. Awosika, & Ogundipe-Leslie, M., *Proposals on Research Priorities: A Nigerian Perspective.* Paper presented to the AAWORD/AFARD Lusaka Workshop on "Priorities in Socio-Economic Research on Women", December, 1976.

3. Other reasons can be adduced for the fear by men of women's liberation, a basic one of which is their fear of the loss of their property rights over their women and wives.

4. Sudarkasa, N., *Where Women Work: A Study of Yoruba Women in the Market Place and the Home* (Ann Arbor: Anthropological Paper No.53, Museum of Anthropology, University of Michigan, Ann Arbor, 1973).

5. Personal communication during an Interview with Professor Bolanle Awe, Professor of History of the University of Ibadan, leading activist in many Nigerian women's societies, former Commissioner for Education in Oyo State. She was herself present at this symposium. Ibo business women express the same views in

Flora Nwapa's latest novel, *One is Enough* (Enugu: Tana Press, 1981.)

6. Interview with Professor Bolanle Awe, cited above.

7. Nwapa, Flora, *One is Enough* (Enugu: Tana Press, 1981) p.30. Note also women's marital problems as dramatized in the work.

8. Nwapa, Flora, *Efuru* (London: Heinemann, 1966), *Idu* (London: Heinemann, 1970), *One is Enough* (Enugu: Tana Press, 1981). Emecheta, Buchi, *The Joys of Motherhood* (London: Heinemann, 1978).

9. See Akande, J., *Law and the Status of Women in Nigeria.* (Unesco Commissioned Monograph, 1979).

10. Paulme, D. *Women of Tropical Africa* (Berkeley: University of California Press, 1971) in particular A.M.D. Lebeuf, "The Role of Women in the Political Organisation of African Societies"; Johnson, Samuel, *The History of the Yorubas from the Earliest Times to the beginning of the British Protectorate* (1966 ed., Lagos, C.M.S. Bookshops, 1921); Awe, Bolanle, "The Position of the Iyalode in the Traditional Political System" in Schlegel, A. (ed.), *Sexual Stratification* (Columbia University Press, 1977); Mba, Nina, *Women in Southern Nigerian Political History* (1900 — 1965) (Ph.D. Dissertation of the University of Ibadan, Ibadan, 1978). Her impressive bibliography will be extremely useful.

11. Okonjo, K. "The Dual-Sex Political System in Operation: Igbo Women and Community Politics in Midwestern Nigeria" in Hafkin, N.J. & Bay, E.G., *Women in Africa* (California: Stanford University Press, 1976).

12. Nwapa, Flora, *"The Role of Women in the Presidential System"* Alumni Lecture, University Alumni Lecture Series, Ibadan, 19 March 1982.

13. Interview with Chief (Mrs.) G.T. Ogundipe, mother of the present writer. Retired researcher of trigonometry, elementary mathematics and literature in teachers colleges, wife of a retired Bishop, himself now a traditional chief of agricultural life in his native town of Ago-Iwoye. Currently and for the second time, the Lay President of the Ibadan Diocese of the Methodist Church of Nigeria, Chief (Mrs.) G.T. Ogundipe has called for the ordination of women and has written a booklet to that effect entitled: *The Ordination of Women* (Ibadan: Methodist Literature Department, 1977). As an active and leading member of many women's societies including business co-operatives, church societies and political party wings, she has been Deputy National President of the National Council of Women's Societies and founder of her own recognized group, The Women's Improvement Society, based in Ibadan. She is a major figure and sometime president of the Nigeria branch of the International Women's Alliance, for which organization she has travelled extensively in Europe, America and Africa. She toured Nigeria in the 1960s as a leader within the women's wing of a political party. A traditional chief of all women in economic life, in particular the markets, she sits and deliberates on the king's councils in her town and her husband's town. To keep herself busy and in touch with contemporary educational ideas, she runs a children's day-care centre in her home. She attended in July 1982 a Conference of the International Women's Alliance in Helsinki, Finland. Chief (Mrs.) G.T. Ogundipe is seventy-six.

14. Interview with Professor Bolanle Awe, cited above.

15. Interview with Mrs. Adeola Ayoola, current National Social Secretary of the Nigerian Association of University Women (NAUW), 26 March 1982. She reports how supportive government bodies are of her group and planned women's activities in general. Her view is that women members of some organizations need to be more committed and consistent.

16. Interview with Professor Bolanle Awe, cited above.
17. Awe, interview cited.
18. Chief (Mrs.) Ebun Oyagbola, *Punch,* 19 March 1982.
19. Omolara Ogundipe-Leslie, "On Reading an Archaeological Article on Nefertiti's reign and Ancient Egyptian Society". Poem to appear in Ogundipe-Leslie, Molara, *Sew the Old Days and other Poems,* (London & Ibadan, Evans Brothers Publishers, June 1982).

References

1. Adekanye-Adeyokunnu, T., *Women in Nigerian Agriculture,* (Unpublished Monograph 1982. Department of Agricultural Economics, University of Ibadan, Ibadan, Nigeria).
2. Akande, J., *Law and Status of the Nigerian Woman,* (Unesco Commissioned Monograph, 1979).
3. Ardener, S., ed., *Perceiving Women* (John Wiley & Sons: N.Y. 1975).
4. Hafkin, N.J. & Bay, E.G., *Women in Africa,* (California, Stanford University Press, 1976). Has important essays on the political position of women in some Nigerian groups.
5. Hill, P., *Rural Hausa* (London: Cambridge University Press, 1972).
6. Smith, M., *Baba of Kano* (London: Faber and Faber, 1954). On the socio-economic role of the northern Nigerian women.
7. Sudarkasa, N., *Where Women Work: A Study of Yoruba Women in the Marketplace and the Home,* (Ann Arbor: Anthropological Paper No.53, Museum of Anthropology, University of Michigan, Ann Arbor, 1973.)

Contemporary Positions and Experiences of Women

Bene E. Madunagu

The notion and expression, "The Oppression of Women", has been widely abused and emptied of all meaning and determination by petty-bourgeois and pseudo-radicals as well as feminists, shades of honest progressives and humanists. Despite this and perhaps partly as a result of this, the oppression of women remains a stubborn reality in our society. There are several manifestations of this oldest of all oppression.

Today in the Nigerian social context, women suffer oppression not only as human beings living under the historical social structure, called neo-capitalism or peripheral capitalism, but also as that section of the Nigerian people called women.

Although we shall attempt to separate the two forms of oppression, in reality dichotomy is impossible since they largely and continuously reinforce each other. This objective mutual reinforcement is what many feminists and anti-feminists often fail to appreciate.

Let us first examine the overall social terrain on which women are oppressed as women. The social reality of Nigeria today is that she is embedded in the periphery of the world capitalist economic system which has been created and is continually being recreated by, and in the interest of, the central capitalist countries of America, Japan and Western Europe. Nigeria, by this position, continues to be permanently forced to develop in a direction which serves the needs of the "metropolis of capitalism". Neither the social forces of production nor the social relations (including the man-woman relationship) can develop freely under this condition.

The material oppression of the working people of Nigeria has its roots in the world capitalist economic structure in which Nigeria is embedded. Both men and women are subjected to this oppression but under other specific conditions. On the level of day-to-day life, what is the objective contemporary situation of Nigeria, 22 years after what is now popularly known as "Flag Independence"? What have been the experiences of Nigerian women?

Let us take up the objective contemporary situation first. The situation today is that Nigeria still provides raw materials on an unequal basis for the imperialist industries. The "modern" sector of the Nigerian economy is essentially that of buying and distributing luxury consumer goods among the various strata of the Nigerian ruling class and elites, namely: businessmen and businesswomen; party leaders; members of the legislative, executive and judicial institutions; executives of parastatals and other economic institutions, etc. The interests of this class rule, over the basic and elementary needs of the rest of society (roughly 95%) and women constitute the majority of the "underdogs".[1]

Nigeria today harbours hundreds of foreign companies and banks through which a large part of our national surplus is transferred daily abroad while the working and toiling people are subjected to harsh economic deprivations. The vast majority of our toiling and working people still live below subsistence level and reproduce their lives in physical and mental conditions not better than their conditions before 1960. While the toiling and working people are subjected to a minimum wage much below subsistence level (in the face of mounting inflation) capitalist employers, "public officers", leading members of the state apparatus continue to allocate to themselves millions of Naira in fraudulent contracts, allowances and "contingency funds".

Nigerians have always been promised increased and better housing, more food, "qualitative" or "free" education, "free" or "qualitative" medical care, etc. In short, verbal promises of "life more abundant" is what the Nigerian ruling class has for the masses. In reality, however, every policy turns out to be at best illusory and empty and at worst, manifestly anti-people.

A stratum of the Nigerian ruling class (a small fraction of parasites who, however, control the means of producing and expropriating the wealth of our country) literally live in obscene affluence. On the opposite side of the "paradise on earth", there exists mass poverty for the working people — a reality which is continually being reproduced and intensified by policies and measures such as the so-called "austerity". These are, of course, meant to ensure the continuity of the affluence of the opposite extreme.

There are some forms of oppression imposed essentially on the working and toiling people of Nigeria by the neo-colonial (or peripheral) capitalist structure of the economy. On the most general (i.e. abstract) level, working and toiling people of both sexes suffer these forms of oppression. This, we think, is the correct starting point for the consideration of the specific oppression of women in our society.

The specific oppression of women in Nigeria can be considered under the following categories:

(a) oppression by the state, i.e. socio-political oppression;
(b) oppression within the family;
(c) oppression in the "civil society".

We shall not follow this division strictly — as this is almost impossible — although we appreciate its analytical value.

The various agencies and institutions of the state operate from, and on, the premise (explicit or implicit) that a wife occupies a subservient position in relation to her husband. Countless examples can be cited. We pick out only a few. In an institution such as a university, where medical services are provided for the workers, a wife can be treated on the ticket of the husband if the husband is the employee. But if the wife is the employee no such privilege is extended to the husband. The assumption here is that the wife is an appendage of the husband. It is the working wife who feeds and clothes her family and sometimes pays fees for the children but her tax is higher because the employer assumes that the husband caters for the family.

Several categories of positions in private and public institutions are exclusively for men. Some institutions will not employ women because of the time lost to the employers when working women go on maternity leave. These positions are occupied by men who go on endless non-productive tours. The sum total of the time thus fruitlessly consumed by a "senior" male official in a year is often greater than the period of maternity leave. These same employers who detest women going on maternity leave would divorce their wives if they did not bear children. Thus the ability to bear children, that is, to reproduce the human species, has been transformed into a liability. There are several other forms of discrimination against women as regards privileges granted to employees. The evolution of the institution of marriage and especially the monogamous transformation of the nuclear family established the family as a basic economic unit of society within which a woman and her children — through exploitation of biological and emotional factors — become dependent upon an individual man.[2] The fundamental element of this transformation was that women became the "beasts of burden" in the mundane task of ensuring the day-to-day care of the family. Arising in conjunction with exploitative class relations, this transformation resulted in the well-known and all-pervasive forms of oppression of women that have persisted to the present day.

The subjugation of the female sex can therefore be traced to the transformation of an important socially necessary labour — housework — into private service through the separation of the family from the clan.[3] It was in this context that women's domestic and other work came to be performed under conditions of virtual slavery, that is, without recognition or remuneration. It is crucial to the organization of women for their struggle for liberation to understand that the monogamous family[4] as an economic unit is basic to women's subjugation. Several revolutionary conclusions can be drawn from this. In ancient communal society, decisions were made by those who would carry them out. Thus the participation of women in socially necessary labour did not place them in a position of subjugation (as it does today) since women also took part in decision-making. It is therefore a paradox in European history that the only public area in which individual women claim equality with men is that associated with stereotypes of masculinity — leadership, power and decision-making.

In Nigeria, the socialization and domestication of the female sex on the material, ideological, and psychological levels start in the family and are continued, extended and intensified by the state and the society at large. A girl is from the cradle trained to assume a role similar to that of her mother. Result? Perpetuation and reproduction of the same subservient relations. The society regards a woman as incomplete without a husband; but a man without a wife is tolerated — and may even win public applause. It is regarded as normal for a man to have an emotional relationship with his housemaid but abnormal for a woman to do the same. A radical woman is regarded as eccentric or she engenders condemnation or murder for being an embarrassment to a bourgeois husband. Where a radical woman is not stoutly opposed, she meets with a mixture of applause and surprise. In the latter case, derogatory explanations are offered for her activities. It is a historical fact that not only bourgeois men but socialists and revolutionaries as well justify and *live* these sexist stereotypes. This is a sad indicator of the level of consciousness within the revolutionary movement of our time.

Constitutionally, women are equal with men but practically today women are still regarded as appendages of men. 1975 was declared International Women's Year. That same year in Nigeria, an important "national event" — the formation of the Constitution Drafting Committee (CDC) — took place. It is on record tht no woman was included in the CDC even though the CDC was to draft a constitution for the entire Nigerian population, 50% of which is female.

The Nigerian President and Vice-President are both men. (The Nigerian ruling class could not even pretend to concede the position of "Vice-" to a woman as they do in many institutions.) Nigeria is divided into 19 states, and the political head of each state — the governor — is a man. Of the 449 seats in the House of Representatives, very few are occupied by a woman. There are 95 senators — all male! The Chief Justice of the Federation is a man, etc., etc. Thus, even on the level of the bourgeois concept of women's emancipation, Nigerian society is still men's exclusive domain — at least on the level of government. It is however, also part of the Nigerian social reality that there are even more staggering differences in positions and opportunities among women themselves. There are women in our society who occupy senior posts in economic, social and political institutions, government and para-government departments, and enjoy comparable privileges as their male counterparts.

On the other hand, a large percentage of our women serve as slaves for the privileged few, just like the working and toiling people of the male sex. A large percentage of our women still scratch the land to support a bare existence. Therefore, given these realities, we must be careful when we talk of women's oppression in general. The question is:

When we talk of oppression, which group of women are we referring to? Is it the 5% that aid the ruling class in exploiting the labour of the other 95% or is it the down-trodden 95%?

We are not by any means anti-feminists. Those women are oppressed as a sex, everyone agrees. The point we are making is that the experience of this oppression is not even. However, no amount of verbal denunciation of the present condition of women will negate the reality of the existing social inequality of men and women, nor can we hope for bourgeois laws which will ensure the equal involvement of women in social affairs.

According to Lenin:

> The chief task of the working women's movement is to fight for economic and social equality, and not only formal equality for women. The chief thing is to get women to take part in socially productive labour, to liberate them from domestic slavery, to free them from their stupefying and humiliating subjugation to the eternal drudgery of the kitchen and the nursery.[5]

Conclusion

Historically the oppression of man by man has been based on the institution of private property and division of labour. Before the emergence of the institution of private property, there had been divisions of labour along physiological lines, not class lines, e.g. along man-woman, strong-weak, adult-child lines.

With the development of productive forces and the emergence of social classes and private property, the social division of labour assumed a new form of class-physiological forms.

Today in the world capitalist system to which Nigeria belongs, the social division of labour is primarily along class-lines, with the physiological division being relegated more and more to the sphere of the nuclear family. This has not made the social burden on women any lighter. If anything, it has become heavier. The oppression of women did not originate under capitalism but took a most alienating form under capitalism where all things including human beings and their values have become commodities. It has now become historically necessary to pose a concrete alternative to the oppression of women in particular and other forms of social oppression in general.

There must emerge a movement whose central demand would be that the Nigerian working and toiling people[6] should assume the role of *directly* and *collectively* controlling the economic, political and social affairs of Nigeria. Such a movement must evolve specific programmes and tactics for the mobilization of women for their liberation. Such programmes must take cognizance of the additional dimensions of women's oppression while at the same time also recognizing that even these additional dimensions cannot be completely superseded without the liberation of society as a whole.

Notes

1. Since women constitute more than half of the population, and the ruling class is dominated by men, it follows that women constitute the majority of the "underdogs" — the popular masses.
2. Frederick Engels, *The Origin of the Family, Private Property and the State.* (International Publishers, N.Y. 1975), pp.137-138.
3. Ibid.
4. By monogamy, we mean strictly "monogamy for women".
5. V.I. Lenin, *On the Emancipation of Women,* (Progress Publishers, Moscow, 1972), p.81.
6. More than half of whom, as we have said, are constituted by women.

References

de Beauvoir Simone, 1969, *The Second Sex* (New English Library, London).
Firestone, S., 1970 *The Dialectic of Sex: The Case for Feminist Revolution* (First Morrow Paperback, N.Y.).
Friedan, B., 1963, *The Feminine Mystique* (Penguin).
Hamilton, R., 1978, *The Liberation of Women: A Study of Patriarchy and Capitalism* (George Allen and Unwin, London).
Kramnick, M., *Wollstonecraft: Vindication of the Rights of Woman* (Penguin).
Mitchell, J., 1975, *Psychoanalysis and Feminism* (Penguin).
Mitchell, J. & Oakley, A., 1976, *The Rights and Wrongs of Women* (Penguin).
Montagu, A., 1975, *The Natural Superiority of Women* (Collier Macmillan Publishers, London).
Rowbotham, S., 1975 *Woman's Consciousness, Man's World.* (Penguin).

How Relevant is the Western Women's Liberation Movement for Nigeria?

Elizabeth Obadina

How often do you hear the words, "I'm no believer in women's liberation but…" or "I wouldn't call myself a women's liberationaist, but…" and the speaker invariably goes on to say that women should have equal rights with men, that girls should have access to as good an education as boys and that a mother's lot should be much improved.

That "but" belies a women's liberationist, but it is voiced by a vast number of women throughout the world who cringe at the tag "Women's Lib". How is it that the women's liberation movement (WLM) has got itself such a bad name? In part, of course, it's due to the bad reporting from the male-dominated press, which focuses on the bizarre and the extraordinary aspects of the WLM to the exclusion of more mundane achievements, and who reinterpret the term, "women's liberation" to mean "female sexuality on display"! Such methods belittle the more altruistic concepts of the WLM.

However I must opine that the bad image of the WLM is in part due to the direction the Western WLM has taken. A direction which focuses increasingly on female sexuality and female separateness. Most of the women who organize themselves in the mainstream WLM in the West seek to live quite apart from men, seeking emotional, sexual and domestic satisfaction from other women. They are radical feminists amongst whom a woman who chooses to share her life with a man, especially if that relationship is a happy monogamous one, finds herself an oddity; someone who must be saved from selling her soul down the river of male chauvinism and oppression.

Needless to say, such an attitude has alienated the majority of Western working class women from the WLM They cannot afford the luxury of abandoning conventional social mores. The WLM as such as been left by and large to a relatively small group of middle-class, educated feminists who have the means to experiment with alternative lifestyles and lack the social pressures to conform.

Despite the drift of this vanguard of women's liberationists to a remoter plane of existence it can nevertheless be said that modern Western women espouse female suffrage, support women's right to work and to equal pay and do battle with their husbands over who should wash the dishes, cook the meals, bath the baby, attend PTA meetings and so on. In effect women are seeking to liberate themselves from the shackles of domesticity and to take an equal share in determining their future. Surely that's what women's liberation is all about?

Here in Nigeria women constitutionally and, it must be said, in theory, have all the rights Western women have had to battle for decades to obtain. Officially there are no barriers to women attaining high office, and indeed women like Mrs Janet Akinrinrade can quite legitimately and without being laughed at declare their aspirations to the presidency itself.

How does the emancipation of a host of prominent women reflect upon the lives of ordinary Nigerian women? Does their existence indicate that there is no need for a women's liberation movement in this country? In fact the enshrinement of the principle tenets of the WLM in the Constitution defuses much of the steam for a Nigerian WLM — there is no great national crusade, as for female suffrage, to organize around and to fight for, yet there is clearly a crying need for improvements in the lives of the majority of Nigerian women.

Nigerian women have to decide upon their priorities for campaigning. If they copy the tendency displayed by the rest of society they will surely turn to the West for inspiration. This is why in this paper I shall seek to indicate some of the pitfalls of such an approach.

Women in the Economy

In the West a massive battle was fought around the turn of the century for a man's right to earn enough to support himself and his family. The concept of the "family wage" was born and the wives of workers no longer had to take degrading and debilitating poorly paid employment to help make ends meet. Their role became that of servicers and producers of labour. A role which was accorded high moral status but little financial recognition by the state.

As the years passed by, many of the forms of employment men had sought so strenuously to protect their women and children from — coal mining, taking in laundry, sweat-shop tailoring and so on — became history. A vast range of modern and attractive employment opportunities arose that women wanted to avail themselves of, spurred on, unfortunately, by the deepening economic recession which has overtaken most Western economies, forcing women to go out to work to supplement the family income.

Thus were born in the 1960s the campaigns for the right to work, for equal pay for equal work, for job evaluation studies in the areas of predominantly female employment, for creches for working mothers, and more stridently for abortion for those who didn't want to become unwilling mothers, and for "wages for housework" for those who stayed at home.

By contrast, in Nigeria women work and have never been really marginalized in the economy as Western women have been. Whether she is engaged in cottage industry from the confines of purdah, or is a farmer, or is one of the super-rich Alhajas trading in all manner of goods, the Nigerian woman enjoys her own income and a degree of financial independence from her husband. Motherhood is no reason, as I have personally discovered, to cease gainful financial employment. Indeed under the degraded forms of polygamy being increasingly practised throughout the country today, men are taking on more wives than they can afford to keep and women have no choice but to work or see their children starve.

The notion of a woman's right to work has little relevance here, but a campaign for an improvement in the nature and conditions of female employment would have far-reaching resonance.

Housework

In the West mothers are isolated and solely responsible for the maintenance and routine care of the home. It is their personal responsibility. The campaign to make this a political issue of which the Wages for Housework campaign is a part strikes a chord amongst most Western women. For women here it is a secondary consideration, their main activity lies elsewhere and thanks to the extended family system, daughters and young female relatives carry most of the burden of housework and childcare secure in the knowledge that the day will come when they too will have their own households to direct.

Women don't contemplate shouldering the entire burden of housework alone. Even if they lack young family helpers there is a vast pool of cheap labour upon which to draw for domestic help. In the West only the upper class women can afford the luxury of freeing themselves from domestic drudgery for other pursuits. Here most adult women are relatively free.

There is little basis for a Wages for Housework campaign. But with the growth of urbanization and the siphoning off of children to schools, women are increasingly being left to manage the housework removed from traditional sources of help and without the products of a high technology culture which so aid the housebound Western woman.

Nigerian women enjoy a degree of economic independence and freedom from housework that is quite foreign to Western women. This is laudable, but as feminists we shouldn't close our eyes to the conditions those who do perform the housework labour under. Foreign housegirls and child servants fall outside of the limits of employment legislation and trade union organizations. They are an invisible and highly exploited force yet upon their shoulders lies the responsibility for servicing the labour force of the nation.

One unfortunate by-product of the relative emancipation of the Nigerian woman seems to be, paradoxically, the nurturing of overinflated male egos. In the home I have watched Nigerian men being spoilt and pampered like overgrown babies by women whose strength of character and independence can find few equals in the West. Why do they do it? Why do they allow such a monstrous flowering of male chauvinism amongst their husbands and their sons? I can only presume that it is because they do not have to do most of the running around after their men themselves. They can direct others to service the man's need for a beer, a clean shirt and so on. Certainly in my own household the fire of many a "who does what" argument has been put out since we employed a servant. My husband gets away with far more than he ought to in domestic matters! Sadly that seems to be held as a virtue, especially amongst more traditionally-inclined women who see the male person as sacrosanct. What man is going to counter such a position? Yet unless such attitudes are undermined by a women's movement, women here will be seen to have dug their own graves as they juggle with the impossible task of running house, children and a job single-handedly.

How Women are seen by Society

The prevailing view of women in the West is as girlfriends, wives and mothers, or whores. Here I would hazard to say women are labelled more by what they do than by their relationship to men. Marriage is the overriding norm, concomitant with motherhood, and it is taken for granted that women "just are" married and mothers, unexpectedly freeing them to be portrayed in a far greater range of images, as businesswoman, trader, doctor, politician and so on.

Of course with the explosion of high-technology news and advertising media this is changing to reflect more the Western conceptions of womanhood. Young girls are presented models of carefree "Joy" girls to identify with before graduating to become an "Omo" mum. Products are increasingly being marketed by exploiting female sexuality at the expense of other female attributes. The most glaring offender has to be my own newspaper with its offensive "Page Three Girl".

More and more, women are coming to be seen purely as functions of their sexuality. Wives in polygamous households no longer hold their position due to economic expediency but rather as a measure of their husbands' sexuality. They are little more than sexual ciphers.

Women have responded to the altered perception of their kind and there are some women who, desirous of material consumables beyond their means, use their own bodies to secure promotions, school certificates, degrees, contracts, cars, holidays, and all manner of things. Sex for sale seems to be a burgeoning feature of daily life, particularly in the cities. Such quasi-prostitution is an anathema to female self-respect, a negation of traditional self-reliance, and an impediment to the development of the image of women as being more than just sex objects.

Women Organizing

How women should organize is the one issue that has split the Western WLM asunder. So far I have avoided any mention of the differences that exist between women, concentrating instead on what very many women hold in common. Certainly there are innumerable issues which affect all women to greater or lesser extents and which can form the basis for women to act together as a group. Should women then organize themselves into a Women's Party as radical feminists might propose? Should they recognize their common problems and resort to put-pressure-on-your-husband politics as happened when the marriage bill amendment was defeated? Or should women see themselves as part and parcel of a class embracing both sexes whose fortunes will affect them more directly than their situation as women? I leave you with a contentious question. Was the defeat of the marriage bill amendment really a victory for the majority of working class women? Most ordinary women pass their lives in polygamous households which might enjoy constitutional validity, but the women are denied legal matrimonial rights which only women in a one-man, one-wife relationship enjoy. As feminists can we say that the defeat of the bill to recognize all forms of marriage was in the interests of most women?

The Labour Market Implications of the Access of Women to Higher Education in Nigeria

Rachel Uwa Agheyisi

Introduction

A cursory look at the Nigerian labour market reveals a number of imperfections. Perhaps the most obvious of these anomalies are the problems of unemployment (especially in the urban areas) and shortages of crucial skills. However, there is a third and rarely mentioned imperfection, that of a dichotomy of the labour market into "male" and "female" occupations; an anomaly that breeds segregation and non-competition between the sexes. For instance, there tends to be a concentration of women in the clerical and service industries while men are in more technical industries. In countries where similar patterns exist, it was noted that segregation of employment by sex helps to make women's jobs less well paid, less stable, less skilled, and having fewer promotional prospects than the jobs occupied by men,[1] The barriers facing women either as individuals or as a group in the labour market can be grouped into three.[2]

Direct Discrimination. This may occur in cases when a woman fails to get a particular job or gain entry into a particular training school because of her sex.

Indirect Discrimination. This applies in situations when in the process of the "normal" operation of the labour market, some individuals (women) are adversely affected. For instance, there exists subtle discrimination when systems of training and promotion, though ostensibly neutral, favour one sex over the other. Such discrimination is often hidden behind rules — for example, rules about height requirements — which males can comply with more easily than females.

Educational Opportunities and Socialization. The choice of the path of educational training made early in life by young girls under the strong influence of families, peer groups, etc., (reflecting social attitudes) often closes many opportunities to women and propels them towards the direction of traditionally socially-approved, "female" careers or segments of the labour market. This, in my opinion, has the most profound consequences for women's role in the labour force because it dictates not only their presence, but also the type of role they can actively play. To our mind, this is the most pervasive type of barrier facing Nigerian women.

This paper looks at the labour market and development implications of the access of women to higher education in Nigeria. Higher education is narrowly defined here as university education. This is essentially consideration of the supply side of the Nigerian labour market, i.e. the type of training (skills) women acquire for sale in the market especially in modern sector employment. It is our view that generally in Nigeria, women's access to higher education, and consequently to specialized skills, is very limited and often restricted to some disciplines. The remaining part of the paper is organized into three sections. Section I, gives an overview of the Nigerian labour market and female involvement in it. Section II I presents data on the pattern of female participation in university education while Section III draws the conclusion.

The Nigerian Labour Market

The population of any country constitutes that country's human resource potential, and its size, structure and other characteristics are influenced by such factors as fertility and mortality rates and also the pattern of migration. The labour force is confined to persons between the ages of 15 and 55 (60) years in Nigeria although the active labour force is conventionally defined to exclude students, physically and mentally handicapped persons, and full-time housewives.

Current data on the size and characteristics of Nigeria's population are hard to come by and often unreliable. The 1963 population census which is the officially accepted figure puts the country's population at 55.7 million people in that year. Projecting this figure on the basis of a 2.5% annual growth rate (assuming unchanging fertility and mortality patterns), the population was estimated to have increased to about 82.9 million people by mid-1979.[3]

A breakdown of the 1963 figures showed that women constituted about 49% of the total population accounting for 27.6 million (see Table 1). However, of the 18 million persons in the labour force then, women accounted for only 4.4 million or 24% of the economically active population as against the males' almost 50% share.

The 1966-67 Labour Force Sample survey further confirmed this pattern. As shown in Table 2 below, the labour force participation rate for all age groups is higher for males than for females. This fact is also corroborated by figures in Table 1. Labour force participation rate is defined as the percentage of working age population who are actually in the labour force.

Table 1
Nigeria's Population by Sex & Age Group, 1963

Age Group	MALES			FEMALES			TOTAL		
	Total Population	Economically Active Population Number	%	Total Population	Economically Active Population Number	%	Total Population	Economically Active Population Number	%
-15	12,235,411	–	–	11,600,175	–	–	23,925,586	–	–
15-19	2,501,434	1,404,182	56.1	2,749,750	528,068	19.2	5,251,184	1,932,250	36.8
20-24	3,153,836	2,704,399	85.7	3,769,352	961,747	25.5	6,923,188	3,666,146	53.0
25-29	2,606,386	2,506,115	96.2	2,964,199	866,224	29.2	5,570,585	3,372,339	60.5
30-44	4,759,917	4,627,429	97.2	4,454,271	1,383,368	31.1	9,214,188	6,101,797	65.2
45-49	682,464	667,895	97.9	485,584	170,095	35.0	1,168,048	837,990	71.7
50-54	682,577	668,007	97.9	534,322	187,173	35.0	1,216,899	855,180	70.3
55-59	277,241	267,762	96.6	186,235	63,667	34.2	463,476	331,429	71.5
60-64	447,156	431,869	96.6	338,636	115,769	34.2	785,792	547,638	69.7
65-	675,430	609,098	90.2	475,679	142,943	30.1	1,151,109	752,041	65.3
Total	28,111,852	13,886,756	49.4	27,558,203	4,419,054	16.0	55,670,055	18,305,810	32.9

SOURCE: ILO, *Year Book of Labour Statistics, 1975*; ILO, Geneva, p.12.

145

Table 2
Nigerian Labour Force Participation Rates by Sex, 1966-67
(% of population in labour force)

Age Group	Male	Female	Total (as % of population)
15-17	73.6	50.8	62.2
18-23	89.6	56.6	69.1
24-29	97.9	66.1	77.5
30-35	99.1	68.5	81.4
36-40	90.0	72.8	85.8
41-45	99.0	72.0	86.5
46-50	98.0	72.8	87.0
51-55	96.0	69.7	85.2
Total	94.2	64.8	77.8

SOURCE: National Manpower Board, *Labour Force Sample Survey, 1966/67,* Lagos, 1968

While overall, 94.2% of the males between 15 and 55 years of age were reported to be economically active, the corresponding figure for females was 64.8%. In addition, for each age group, the female participation rate was lower than the total. Fapohunda in her study[4] reports substantial variations in women's labour force participation rates throughout the country with the rates generally higher in the southern part of the country than in the northern.

An obvious conclusion that stems from the above analysis is that based on official definitions, there is a general under-utilization of almost half of Nigeria's human resources i.e. those embodied in her women. If we include the officially excluded activities such as street hawking and canteen operations, etc., the general pattern may change somewhat but from the point of view of vital skills needed in the process of economic development, the contribution of "female labour" remains essentially marginal.

It would have been helpful to examine the distribution of male and female employees by industry but such data are not readily available. But in terms of the type of employer, Table 3 shows that for each of the major employers, (governments and private sector), female staff were less than 18% of total staff, with the private sector, the largest single employer, employing the smallest proportion. Overall, females constituted only 13.2% of total employees in these sectors. It would therefore appear that over 80% of the economically active women are in the informal and intermediate sectors; in one form of self-employment or another e.g., as petty traders, sewing mistresses, hair plaiters etc. Modern sector participation remains poor.

Table 3
Distribution of Total Employees by Type of Employer as at April 1977

| Type of Employer | Employees | | | Female as Percentage of Total |
	Male	Female	Total	
Federal Government (Civil Service)	154,099	22,468	176,567	12.7
Federal Government (Corporations)	93,715	16,059	109,774	14.6
State Governments (Civil Service)	159,717	33,631	193,348	17.4
State Government (Corporations)	54,112	9,520	63,632	15.0
Local Governments	53,225	9,571	62,796	15.2
Private Sector	366,718	42,504	409,222	10.4
Total	881,586	133,753	1,015,339	13.2

SOURCE: National Manpower Board, 1977, *National Manpower Survey Report,* p.3.

Table 4 further confirms the general low participation of women in skilled jobs. The proportion of women in the technical, scientific, and professional manpower categories was less than 7% for all occupations, and for engineering and aircraft operations less than 1%. It is not unusual to find these women performing mainly administrative duties rather than actually practising their skills. Even in jobs usually termed "women's jobs", such as confidential secretaries and stenographers, men rather than women predominated.

Table 4
Employment in Selected Occupations, by Sex, April 1977

Occupational Categories	Men	Women	Total	Women as % of Total
Administrative & Managerial Manpower				
General Managers and Managing Directors	2,835	116	2,951	3.9
Economists	443	42	485	8.7
Confidential Secretaries and Stenographers	5,180	2,977	8,157	36.5
Technical, Scientific and Professional Manpower				
Architects	255	14	269	5.2
Town Planners	160	7	167	4.2
Quantity Surveyors	326	15	341	4.4
Land Surveyors	449	19	468	4.1
Estate Surveyors and Valuers	215	16	231	6.9
Engineers	11,383	59	11,442	0.5
Aircraft Pilots and Navigators	420	3	423	0.7
Agricultural Manpower				
Agricultural Engineers	116	4	120	3.3
Veterinarians	442	11	453	2.4
Medical Manpower				
General Practitioners	1,089	193	1,282	15.1
Obstetricians and Gynaecologists	131	10	141	7.1
Paediatricians	85	12	97	12.4
Pharmacists	425	117	542	21.6
Dieticians and Nutritionists	29	156	185	84.3
Nurses	2,615	10,581	13,196	80.2
Artisans and Craftsmen				
Fitter Mechanics	9,225	7	9,232	0.1

SOURCE: Extracted from NMB, 1977, *National Manpower Survey Report,* pp.7-13.

The situation in the universities was no different. As at April 1977, of the total of 3,608 Nigerian lecturers employed in 12 universities that respondended to the NMB questionnaire, 3,400 (i.e. 93%) were males, meaning that only 208 or 7% were females.[5] A breakdown according to selected disciplines presented in Table 5, shows a concentration of these female lecturers in the arts, education (arts), and medical faculties with almost total non-representation in the Faculties of Engineering, Environmental Studies, Veterinary Medicine, Management Studies, and Law.

Table 5
Distribution of Teaching Staff by Discipline & Sex, April 1977

Discipline (Faculty)	Nigerians	
	Male	Female
Arts	527	46
Education (arts)	238	33
Law	84	1
Science	638	31
Medicine & Related Subjects	546	54
Social Sciences	417	13
Engineering	259	–
Environmental Studies	53	1
Management Studies	105	4
Veterinary Medicine	86	1

SOURCE: NMB, 1977 *National Manpower Survey Report*, p.50.

Many factors are responsible for the observed low participation of women in Nigeria's labour market. A blanket factor may be the fact of the underdeveloped status of the economy making it impossible for job opportunities to expand faster or as fast as population growth. The competition for the few available places is very keen. One may, there-fore, be led to hope that as economic development progresses, jobs will increase, and so will the number of Nigerian women occupying positions in the modern sector. However, such hope may not be realized in the light of other factors militating against more active and extensive participation of women in the labour force. These factors are the social status of women as defined by Nigerian society and the type of access Nigerian women have to education and skills acquisition.

Traditionally, Nigerian society has carved out the women's place to be in the home, regarding her as an "object" to be seen and admired (and used) but not heard! Consequently, her job is child-bearing and rearing and performance of *all* the household chores. Since these functions are usually "full-time", there is little or no time for most women caught up in this role to acquire skills that would enable them to participate effectively in the labour force. The women who have "outside" jobs find themselves in a persistent struggle to find a working arrangement for the efficient performance of their household chores and their office jobs.

The other major obstacle to fuller female participation is the fact that most Nigerian parents' attitudes to (higher) education is biased against their female children. They are often readier to make financial sacrifices for their sons' than for their daughters' educational pursuits.[6]

Even in cases where the negative social attitudes do not outrightly deter girls from pursuing higher education, the social attitudes of their families, peer group pressures, and adults who serve as role models define their educational choices, and point young women in the direction of traditionally "female" careers.[7] It is against this background that we view the type of access Nigerian women have to education especially at the higher level.

Access of Women to Higher Education

As far back as 1962, the Nigerian Association of University Women (NAUW), Ibadan Branch, conducted a survey of women's participation in all tiers of the education system. It was found that the female population was generally small, and at the university level the number increased at a "very slow and unsatisfactory rate".[8] The survey also revealed that female students were largely in the Faculty of Arts.[9]

More recently, Ojo (1980), in his study, observed a low rate of female participation in Nigeria's educational system. His findings show that between 1969 and 1972, female population at the primary school level was less than 40%, about 33.7% at secondary school level, and persistently less than 15% at the university level.[10] The significance of such data lies not only in revealing the fact that there are fewer females than males in all stages of schooling, but also in pointing out the fact that the number of female students tends to drop as they move up the educational ladder.

Detailed statistics on female participation in Nigerian universities are not readily available. Here, we use data from ABU, which we hope illustrates the general trends of female student population in Nigerian universities.

General Trend

Table 6 shows that there has been a steady, though small, increase in the number of female undergraduate students over the 1972-80 period rising from 322 in 1972/73 to 897 in 1979/80; a 178.6% increase.

However, there were wide fluctuations in the annual growth rates ranging from 3.1% to 49.4%. As a percentage of total students, female undergraduates constituted between 11.7% and 15.7% over the period.

However, there were wide fluctuations in the annual growth rates ranging from 3.1% to 49.4%. As a percentage of total students, female undergraduates constituted between 11.7% and 15.7% over the period. These are low proportions and they imply that, for instance, in 1979/80 when the female population was highest, for every female undergraduate there were about six male undergraduates!

Table 6
Distribution of Students by Sex 1972/73-1979/80
*(Undergraduates only)**

Year	Male	Female	Total	% Increase in Female Share	Female as % of total
1972/73	2,358	322	2,680	–	12.0
1973/74	3,613	481	4,094	49.4	11.7
1974/75	–	-	–	–	–
1975/76	4,063	656	4,719	–	14.0
1976/77	4,551	679	5,230	3.5	13.0
1977/78	4,866	745	5,611	9.7	13.3
1978/79	4,627	768	5,395	3.1	14.2
1979/80	4,803	897	5,700	16.8	15.7

*Figures are for first-degree students only and exclude diploma and School of Basic Studies students.

SOURCE: ABU Academic Office Files.

At the graduate level, the males dominated again with the female share being persistently below 9% of total graduate students' population. Table 7 below shows that the number of female undergraduate students especially in the 1977/78 academic year was almost negligible.

Table 7
Distribution of Students by Sex 1976/77-1978/79
*(Graduates only)**

Year	Male	Female	Total	Female as % of Total
1976/77	305	24	329	7.3
1977/78	369	22	391	5.6
1978/79	635	59	694	8.5

SOURCE: ABU *Development Office Files;* ABU *Digest of Statistics,* Vol.1, 1979, p.9.

Table 8
Distribution of Undergraduate Students by Sex & Faculty, 1972/73-1979/80

Faculty	1972/73 M	F	1973/74 M	F	1974/75 M	F	1975/76 M	F	1976/77 M	F	1977/78 M	F	1978/79 M	F	1979/80 M	F
Administration	202	8	242	15	n/a	n/a	271	27	326	39	354	50	390	46	456	68
Agriculture	80	n/a	121	2	n/a	n/a	182	5	152	1	170	9	169	11	159	13
Arts & Soc. Sc.	573	154	904	196	n/a	n/a	1,062	172	1,292	157	1,274	150	1,164	201	1,331	278
Education	244	66	542	134	n/a	n/a	771	256	766	252	797	259	687	253	581	248
Engineering	367	4	533	5	n/a	n/a	376	3	428	5	488	7	479	5	431	6
Env. Design	133	–	165	3	–	–	229	10	297	37	418	48	424	51	472	41
Law	133	14	184	21	–	–	279	37	302	44	303	50	251	53	296	70
Medicine	239	36	298	46	–	–	319	46	342	51	366	49	360	44	344	41
Pharm. Sc.*	–	–	–	–	–	–	–	–	94	47	126	95	133	53	161	51
Science	251	38	385	55	–	–	400	117	355	61	370	59	376	37	370	69
Vet. Med.	136	2	177	2	–	–	175	7	197	5	200	5	194	14	201	12
Sub-Total	2,358	322	3,613	481	–	–	4,063	656	4,551	679	4,866	745	4,677	768	4,803	897
Total	2,680		4,094		–		4,719		5,230		5,611		5,395		5,700	

*Faculty of Pharmaceutical Sciences was part of the Faculty of Science until 1976/77.

SOURCE: 1. ABU *Information Office Files*
2. ABU *Development Office Files*
3. ABU *Digest of Statistics*, Vol.1, 1979, p.6.

Distribution by Faculty

Consciously or otherwise, a dichotomy into "men's subjects" and "women's subjects" has been the case at ABU. As depicted in Table 8, the Faculties of Arts and Social Sciences and Education, (especially the arts-based subjects), have over the years proven to be the women's favourites; whereas the Faculties of Agriculture, Engineering and Veterinary Medicine have been almost exclusively men's. In the 1979/80 year, for instance, 74% of the female undergraduates were found in the arts-based disciplines of administration, arts education*, and law. Of this, 59% were in the Faculties of Arts and Social Sciences and Education. This meant that in that year, only 26% of female under-graduates were to be found in the remaining seven science-based faculties.

The same pattern of distribution was observed at the graduate level (Table 9). However, a significant proportion of the female population were in the Science Faculty with Education and Arts and Social Sciences Faculties recording large shares also.

Table 9
Distribution of Graduate Students by Sex & Faculty
1976/77-1978/79

Faculty	1976/77		1977/78		1978/79	
	Male	*Female*	*Male*	*Female*	*Male*	*Female*
Administration	38	–	50	2	68	3
Agriculture	27	–	16	–	55	5
Arts & Soc.Sc.	115	5	114	9	137	10
Education	36	8	49	3	68	13
Engineering	12	10	28	–		
Env.Design	35	6	92	5	168	9
Law	13	–	7	–	7	1
Medicine	–	–	–	–	–	–
Pharm. Sc.	–	–	–	–	11	–
Science	29	5	31	3	63	–
Vet.Med.	–	–	–	–	30	15
Sub-Total	305	24	369	22	635	59
Total	329		391		694	

SOURCE: ABU, *Development Office Files.*

*Though education is not totally arts-based, a survey showed that only a negligible proportion of females in education opt for science-education courses.

This pattern of low female student population and high concentration in a few disciplines observed at ABU compares well with findings for Ghana. Amon-Nikoi reports that there has been a small but fairly steady growth in total female population in Ghanaian universities. In the University of Ghana, Legon, she observed that women predominated in the Faculty of Arts and Social Studies.[11] Chabaud (1970) also reports that in more than half the countries of the world, there was a proportionally smaller intake of females in technical education, and that under the existing conditions and the influence of tradition, women students generally tend to take up arts subjects and very often enter sections preparing for occupations which are of only marginal importance from the point of view of economic development and the progress of science and technology.[12]

It would therefore appear that the traditional societal prejudice against formal education for women, especially at higher levels, is gradually giving way; but it seems only to be leaving room for yet another strong prejudice i.e. the kind of education women should get. Just as for ages formal education was regarded as the preserve of males, it now appears that modern technological and scientific studies, and consequently know-how, remain in most cases the privilege of men. This prejudice tends to limit the scope of opportunities to professional training and advancement opened to girls and women. It is common knowledge that Nigerian men are often afraid to marry women who are "too well educated" — implying women in scientific and technological professions. This fear indirectly influences the educational choice of girls and impedes their access to higher education in general and scientific and technical studies in particular. They (the girls) do not want to swot themselves out of the marriage market! Invariably, therefore, most female students tend to follow the traditionally expected pattern of acquiring sufficient general education to be able to discuss things with their husbands, bring up their children, and obtain jobs that fit their traditional role, and forgo the pursuit of any rigorous profession. This accounts for the clustering of female students in the arts and other "soft" courses (as they are labelled) at both the secondary and higher educational levels.

The experience of an American female student aptly summarizes the situation of many aspiring female students today.

> Ever since my childhood, I have been attracted by science. I was preparing to study bacteriology and to take up cancer research. But I changed my mind and took up domestic economy instead. This interests me less than bacteriology, but I realized that it was better to change so as to have a social life. I realized that I should not be so serious minded. I am going to go back home and work in a shop until I marry.[13]

What a tragedy! The reason this student completely changed her line of education, and consequently career, was not because she lacked interest or motivation, but the underlying strong current of social prejudice and expectations as to the place of a woman! Her career prospects are altered essentially because she is a woman! Many Nigerian women faced similar situations and have taken similar decisions to conform with the social expectations.

One is not saying that only the scientific and technological professions offer avenues for self-fulfilment and fruitful opportunities. What is being stressed here is that women students should be allowed to pursue any course of the arts, sciences, or technical areas without bearing the tag of a deviant. The narrow social view as to which disciplines and careers suit the woman must be eliminated. In fact, in the face of serious and urgent problems arising from a shortage of graduates in science and technology, the under- and mal-utilized human potential represented by the woman, is an intolerable wastage.

Nigeria should learn from the experiences of countries that have created avenues for their women to make careers for themselves in branches of science and technology apart from the traditional "women's subjects". For instance, in the Soviet Union, women have proven themselves equal to the task. They constitute 36% of engineers, 45% of scientific workers, 70% of teachers, and 80% of the medical profession.[14]

Summary and Conclusion

Apart from the more obvious anomalies of urban unemployment and manpower shortages, the dichotomy of the Nigerian labour market along sex lines should attract more attention. Such a dichotomy breeds segregation and non-competition between the sexes. Added to this problem is the observed general low female participation in the Nigerian labour force, an indicator of under-utilization of about half the nation's human resource potential. A major explanatory factor of this low female participation is the type of access to education women in the country have, which, in turn, is defined to a large extent by social expectations.

From available data, it can be concluded that the issue of higher education for women is no longer a fight for a right to that education but a fight for what kind of education. This is vital because the kind of education significantly determines what skills women acquire and, consequently, in what area and at what level they feature in the labour market and the development process.

If women in Nigeria are to develop to their fullest capacities and contribute meaningfully to the overall development, then no doors should be overtly or covertly shut to them in their quest for knowledge. In fact, incentives should be worked out and implemented to attract and encourage women into the educational system and into the sciences, starting at the lower tiers of the system. Proper, enlightened, and progressive career guidance is indispensable in this respect. There is nothing wrong with efforts being made specially to encourage girls to take a keener interest in mathematics, science, and technical subjects. Women already in one "woman's" job or the other, but who are desirous of further studies, should be given vocational counselling and encouraged to look at the wider range of occupations that are available, including the so-called "men's jobs", as long as these women have the necessary aptitudes. Experience elsewhere has shown that abilities and aptitudes are human, not sex-typed. Nigerian society stands to lose if women are continuously shunted into "soft" courses and careers while the country continues to suffer acute shortages of skilled scientific and technical manpower.

Notes

1. OECD, *OECD OBSERVER,* No.104, May 1980, p.7.
2. Ibid.
3. Federal Republic of Nigeria, *Digest of Statistics,* Lagos, Federal Office of Statistics, Vol.27, December, 1979, p.1.
4. Eleanor Fapohunda, "Urban Women's Labour Force Participation Rate Patterns in Nigeria", mimeo, Lagos, University of Lagos, 1976, p.4.
5. National Manpower Board (1977), *National Manpower Survey Report,* September 1978, p.50.
6. Folayan Ojo, *Education and Manpower in Nigeria,* Human Resources Research Unit, University of Lagos, 1980, p.11.
7. OECD, op. cit.
8. The Nigerian Association of University Women, Ibadan Branch, *Survey of Women's Education in Western Nigeria,* Ibadan, 1963, p.13.
9. Ibid. p.14.
10. F. Ojo, op. cit.
11. Gloria Amon-Nikoi, "Women and Work in Africa", in U.G. Damachi & V.P. Diejomaoh (eds.), *Human Resources and African Development,* New York: Praeger Publishers, 1978, p.201.
12. Jacqueline Chabaud, *The Education and Advancement of Women,* Paris, UNESCO, 1970, p.10.
13. Betty Friedan, *The Feminine Mystique,* New York, 1963.
14. J. Chabaud, op. cit., p.100.

Rapporteur's Report:

Jibo Ibrahim

The discussions in this session were very lively. Many issues concerning the contemporary experiences of women were raised and debated. The question of the types of jobs women are stereotyped into was elaborated upon. It was shown, for instance, that in the colonial era men were doing jobs like nursing and typing, which they claimed were too demanding for women. With independence, men moved into "senior service" jobs, and suddenly these other jobs needed the correct feminine touch.

It was pointed out that this system of female oppression was all-pervasive. It affected professional and working-class women who are denied many privileges and fringe benefits. It also affected peasant women who have limited access to land, fertilizers, loans, etc. However, it was demonstrated that women from the upper classes tend to have their oppression ameliorated through employing househelp, labour-saving devices, etc. However, they too suffer a certain degree of oppression.

The question of sexist literature and media was also raised. Although a few of the participants felt that some of these, like the *Punch* "Page Three girl" (a semi-nude pin-up appearing daily on page 3 of the *Punch* newspaper) simply projects the higher aesthetic figures of women, most participants felt that it is simply a manifestation of the general abuse and commoditization of women. It was also felt that many women have come to accept the material value system in the society and, therefore, accept oppressive situations like purdah and polygamy either for the fringe benefits like cars and dresses, or because they feel they have no alternative.

Another issue that was raised is that women, like men, are involved in business, the professions, smuggling, etc., so they have equalized (in the bad things); it was further argued that this is one of the chauvinist approaches to destabilize the women's liberation movement, i.e., if the women have equalized, then what is the struggle about? It was stated that the majority of women are not in business or the professions, and there is no escape but to admit that they are oppressed.

Another issue that was raised was the relationship between Islam and women. It was argued that Islam is manifestly discriminatory towards women on issues such as inheritance. In fact, some participants noted that Islamic law conceives of women as legal minors, and the evidence of two women (in court) is equivalent to that of one man. This is compounded by the fact that women are not even listened to except on marital and family issues. Others also noted that while a husband can divorce his wife by simply saying he has done so, women can get a divorce only after a rigorous judicial process. The lone suggestion that Islam gives more to men because they have more responsibilities to the family only reinforced the argument that Islam sees women as second-class citizens. The further suggestion that women are subjective and emotional at critical moments drew nothing but disgust from most of the audience. It was stressed that since religion is based on faith, Islamic women are bound to accept the conditions stipulated by their religion.

Some of the more concrete medical problems that women face were also raised. These included the marriage of under-aged girls and the consequent physical damage that occurs due to early childbirth. Genital mutilation was also discussed and condemned.

The session stressed the necessity for women to participate more in politics and the professions. It was argued, for example, that when Mrs. F.Y. Emmanuel was the Permanent Secretary in the Federal Ministry of Establishments, she abolished some of the policies that were discriminatory towards women. As if to demonstrate the persistence of the system, the policies were reversed by her successor when she was transferred.

The session stressed that this should not lead us into a purely sexist analysis of the woman question. The oppression of women must be understood as part of the oppression and exploitation of a class-divided society.

PART V
Contemporary Experiences (2)

Marriage and Family

Grace B. Aluko and Mary O. Alfa

Introduction

Before going into any serious talk on this sub-title, we would like to define some of the key concepts we would come across in the course of this presentation.

Family. The family system has no specific definition in the Nigerian context. This is because various people define the family system in various ways. While some may refer to the nuclear family which consists of a man, his wife, and children, others may refer to the extended family which consists of the nuclear family and the relations of both the man and the woman. In spite of this confusion, one thing is certain and that is, the family system intersects the sex role system at two critical points:–

1. The family of orientation, and
2. The family of procreation.

One's family of orientation includes parents and siblings, as defined by family of birth, while one's family of procreation comes into being at marriage and includes spouses and children.

The two systems, family of orientation and family of procreation, are not independent.

Marriage. Another concept that needs clarification is marriage. When asked why marriage exists, most lay persons will answer in terms of individual needs for love, companionship, sex, children and homelife. Yet these answers are all time- and culture-bound to an extraordinary degree and they ignore the fact that marriage is part of the social structure, not just a matter of individual option. It is the union of a man and a woman which is legalized officially in every society we know of, and has some sort of prescribed type of marriage, whether it be monogamy, polygyny or polyandry.

Housewife.

> A housewife is a woman responsible for running her home, whether she performs the task herself or hires people to do them. This distinguishes her from an employed housekeeper who maintains a dwelling belonging to someone else without having final responsibility for it. Many other people may undertake the tasks of housewives, but they are socially recognized as substitutes, assistants or deviants... Thus, all housewives are women. But not all women are housewives.[1]

Inheritance. Inheritance system is defined as the way by which property is transmitted between the living and the dead and especially between generations. Transmission refers not only to the means by which reproduction of the social system is carried out but also to the way in which inter-personal relationships are structured. The linking of patterns of inheritance with patterns of domestic organization is a matter not simply of numbers and formations but of attitudes and emotions. The manner of splitting property is a manner of splitting people. It creates a particular constellation or conciliation of ties and cleavages between husband and wife, parents and children, sibling and sibling as well as between wider kin.

Having classified some of the concepts used in the paper, we shall now proceed. Home socializing contributes to the development of human sentiments, self-awareness, the ability to be responsible and understand others, the capacity built upon speech and thoughts to analyse situations abstractly, and to plan actions and complex behaviour patterns. Schooling adds to this store of knowledge and prepares individuals to live in a complicated society. Although most formal educational programmes are supposed to be transmitted to children of both sexes in the same way, home, self, peer and teacher tend to differentiate between boys and girls and result in great differences between the behaviour patterns of the sexes.

Feminine behaviour is directly socialized into and observed by the child, assisted by a variety of home and school procedures. Unfortunately, the main occupational role of most women — that of housewife — is not evaluated by girls as an exciting and desirable life goal.

According to James Coleman, girls do better in school than their restless brothers but they become directed away from study during adolescence and turn towards "popularity contests" among themselves. Girls' attention has become focussed on general manners or domestics, while boys become increasingly achievement-orientated. Although unprecedented numbers of young girls are currently in colleage and universities, they restrict themselves to a limited number of fields culturally approved for their sex. Men still outnumber women — radio 5:3 receiving BA degrees, 7:3 in MAs and 25:3 in Ph.Ds.

The role of wife is neither automatically learned nor easily performed, owing to cultural differences between spouses, a lack of training of both partners, the emotional and behavioural individualism into which both have been socialized and an absence of guidelines. In addition to undertaking the roles of wife and housewife and placing her in central positions, a young woman is expected to add several other roles, such as that of daughter-in-law. She must modify her role of daughter, push into the background that of friend, change her relations at work and generally relate to all from the new perspective of "Mrs" or "married woman". Symbolic is the change in domicile and in name indicating a break with the past.

In a nuclear family, the wife has the total responsibility of child-care. This stage requires a great deal of work to be planned, organized and executed by the same person. The young mother feels that time is a problem as she complains "work is never done" or "there are no set hours" or "I just don't have time to myself". The less highly-positiond women do all the work of caring for the house and children virtually by themselves and without many labour-saving devices or baby-nurses. Some young mothers (especially those not working) are lonely and isolated.

Motherhood is a source of many problems and frustrations to modern women because they are aware of the increasing psychological and developmental needs of children, they suffer from a lack of relevant guidelines. At the same time motherhood is a source of satisfaction whenever worries turn out to be unfounded and children measure up to expectation. Thus, patience is considered by many to be the most important virtue of the ideal housewife.

Division of Labour

All known societies of the world have developed a division of labour between sexes. Most, if not all, have assigned the function of home maintenance to women. There are three notable different areas between male and female labour:

1. the life, or better, family-cycle is more dependent on women's work as opposed to men's.
2. the considerable income differential between male and female workers reflecting the differences in occupational status and prestige.
3. the number of part-time, as opposed to full-time, job opportunities for women.

The most glaring sex role difference which in a sense is the precursor of all the rest is the first: the broken nature of female work participation.

A study by Garfinkle indicated that, "the birth of a child reduces the average number of years a married woman can be expected to spend in the workforce by about 10 years. The birth of each additional child appears to reduce further the work life expectancy from two to three years for each".[2] The issue here is "who shall care for the children?"

The difficulties of childcare should not be underestimated. But two points need to be made. First, why is childcare defined as a female responsibility and why does it interfere with female career development, not males? Secondly, the problem of childcare is self-limiting to any given case, and today engages a smaller part of the woman's actual life span and potential work life.

The division of labour according to sex roles does not end with childcare or household chores. One would see that in any social obligation such as funerals, marriages, and naming ceremonies, the bulk of the preparation and cooking is done by the women. The men emerge only when the cooking is done and everything is set and the most "valuable" thing they (men) do in such ceremonies is to consume the food and drink.

Inheritance

Virtually everywhere, the rule existed that property descended from males to males in the family. In Europe, where women became heiresses to land they did so in order to attract marriage partners. One implication of this is that women varied in their attractiveness as marriage partners according to their endowment, encouraging a tendency to make matches between individuals of similar wealth and status. In a sense, women were more valuable as wives than they were as daughters, since, in the latter capacity, they had to share in the estate.

However, in Nigeria the situation is different. Property passes between members of the same sex rather than between men and women. For instance, if a woman's husband dies, although she is entitled to a share of the husband's property by law, she is usually not given anything and her case is even worse if she is without children. What the law stipulates is quite different from what she obtains. The result is a great separation between the sexes; a separation that is evident in the ordinary social intercourse as well as in the management of the family estate.

Bedroom

In the 1920s in Europe, the definition of proper womanhood changed from "educated motherhood" to woman as "wife-companion". It was a romantic and sexual definition, moving woman from the nursery to the bedroom even if it kept them at home.[3] They were to find fulfilment not in the role of mother or wife but in their own accomplishment. One woman recounted "I wash the dishes, run the older children off to school, dash out in the yard to cultivate flowers . . . help the youngest child to build a block house, spend 15 minutes skimming the newspapers, so I can be well-informed . . . By noon, I'm ready for a padded cell."[4]

Sex was the only thing that gave the woman identity and life in the family and marriage relationship. A woman's right to her own person included the right to define and to choose her own life style. In the family, the issue of liberalized abortion may be best for the rights of women, but it was not necessarily in the best interest of the husband or of society in general. This is even if it is in the interest of the woman to abort; she cannot do so if the husband does not consent, unless of course she does it the other way without his knowledge. The emphasis therefore, is on children's rights regardless of the cost to others. Even in the bedroom, the woman has no control over her body. Hence, one finds "Family life as a zero-sum game".

The contemporary definition of family life is that it is a battleground, each member trying to gain his or her own personal victory. Since the family is a battleground, each should have and does have its own Clausewitz. One assumption that is common to all family life is a zero-sum-game — some interests must be sacrificed for others and usually it is the woman's interests.

Conclusion

In conclusion, a time allocation study of four couples (two elite families and two non-elite families) was conducted to reinforce the fact that women are exploited and subjugated to their husbands. From the study, we deduced that suburban housewives (non-elite housewives) had become prisoners in their own homes, not enjoying privacy but suffering solitary confinement. Table 13 confirms this.

The women only leave their houses when going out to shop, chauffeur their children or attend social engagements with their husbands, preoccupied by the endless routine of household chores. They have lost self-respect. As one woman put it: "The problem is always being the children's mommy, the minister's wife, and never being myself". That is, a woman finds fulfilment vicariously, through the achievement of others. This curse of lack of self-direction and self-satisfaction in the mother would be visited on the children.

What a Christian or Muslim woman expects from her husband are orders and what she is expected to give is total obedience. The relation is a power-based one. The duty of the man to command his wife is embodied in his right to correct her by physical beating or refusal of sexual intercourse with her. The tables reflect how women are used as slaves in their own homes.

Comparison of Time Allocation by Gender in Elite and Non-elite Families

Table 10
Elite family (i)

Activity (elite family)	Average time allocated (in minutes)	
	Woman	Man
A. *Household*		
1. Cleaning, Cooking	220	0
B. *Crafts and other Professions*		
1. Office*	585	535
2. Tailoring	40	0
C. *Personal needs*		
1. Meals	65	65
2. Personal hygiene and other needs	200	20
3. Rest, relaxing	60	90
D. *Free Time*		
1. Media (TV)	30	30
2. Social Obligations (Games & Club)	0	240
E. *Other activities**		
1. Night sleep	390	420
Total Work (A, B.)	845	535
Total personal needs and free time (C, D, E.)	745	865

*Observation was not based on direct participation observation.

This woman has four children. Three are schooling and one is not yet of school age but he is no longer nursing. When asked how she manages in the house where she uses over 14 hours (i.e. 845 minutes) for working she said, "at times I feel as if I wasn't a working mother, I don't have enough time for my children, myself . . . I am thinking of resigning soon."

I went further to ask her if her husband helps with the household chores and she said, "My husband is a typical Nigerian man who believes in pushing all the domestic work to his woman — if he helps today then till the year of our Lord before his hands touches anything again." Although this might sound funny, this is actually what happens in many homes, and one may come across men stating: "Why else did I marry — if not for the woman to work in the house?" Looking at the table critically again, one would see that the man has enough time for social functions like going to the club or going for games but the woman hardly even takes siesta let alone going to any social functions.

Without saying it, we would all by now realize that the woman is the "lackey" of the house. We might all ask a burning question: Why should the woman even work at all in the office since her husband is working? Well, let us turn to a non-elite family on Table 11 and we shall be more enlightened.

Table 11
Non-elite family (i)

Activity (non-elite family)	Average time allocated (in minutes)	
	Woman	Man
A. *Household*		
1. Cleaning, Cooking	180	0
B. *Crafts and other Professions*		
1. Selling	480	0
C. *Marketing (shade)*	10	0
D. *Personal needs*		
1. Meals	100	100
2. Personal hygiene and other needs	40	40
3. Rest, relaxing	0	120
E. *Free Time*		
1. Conversation	0	20
2. Visiting	60	510
3. Religion	20	0
F. *Other activities**		
1. Night sleep	680	480
Total Work (A, B, C.)	670	0
Total personal needs and free time (D, E, F.)	900	1,270

*Observation was not based on direct participation observation.

Table 11 Analysis

The woman is a trader. Although trading is considered as work, it is not in the sense that one would view a white collar job. The woman here is the "man" instead of the "woman". She works for 670 minutes and rests for 900 minutes while the man does no other work than to wait for his pension money every month because he is an ex-serviceman.

So all in all he rests for 1,270 minutes, which is over 21 hours a day.

When the woman was asked why the man rests so much she said bitterly: "My husband is a good for nothing man. Now that he is not working, he doesn't help me in the stall where I sell food or in the house; all he does is sleep, drink, and when it's time for food, he comes for it."

The couple have four children; one is married and three are schooling. I asked her if the man uses his pension money to pay for the children's school fees, and she said: "pension money? I pay the school fees, buy foodstuffs, and cook the food in this house." I was puzzled as to what the man uses his money for and she said: "The man, my husband, divides his money into two halves; he uses half for drinking and now he is talking of marrying a second wife, so he gives the other half to that other woman."

Not to say much we would see that in spite of the fact that the man does no work in the house, he is, at the same time, a liability to the woman because before the 12th day after the receipt of his pension money, he comes back to the woman for money, and if she refuses, a fight may ensue.

Thus, whether the woman is working in an office or inside her home, she is still subjugated to and exploited by a working or non-working husband.

Table 12
Elite family (ii)

Activity (elite family)	Average time allocated (in minutes)	
	Woman	Man
A. *Household*		
1. Cleaning, Cooking	150	0
B. *Crafts and other Professions*		
1. Nursing & Civil Service*	440	530
C. *Marketing*	40	0
D. *Personal needs*		
1. Meals	75	75
2. Personal hygiene and other needs	130	65
3. Rest, relaxing	90	120
E. *Free Time*		
1. Media (TV)	100	0
2. Social Obligations (Games & Club)	0	240
3. *Educational activities (taking children to/from school)*	0	30
F. *Other activities**		
1. Night sleep	380	360
Total Work (A, B, C.)	630	530
Total personal needs and free time (D, E, F.)	775	890

*Observation was not based on direct participation observation.

Table 12 Analysis

The third couple, this time an elite family, reinforces the fact that no matter the level of the education of the couples, especially the woman, she is still subjugated to her husband. The relationship here is more egalitarian for the husband helps with washing the kids and cleaning the house on Saturday. The woman is a nursing sister and the man is a civil servant. They have two children, both at a nursery school.

The total work (A, B, C.) on Table 12, shows that the woman works more than the man, when one excludes the office hours work from the total work, the woman works for 190 minutes in the house and the man, zero.

When asked why she does so much work without the assistance of her husband, she said with regret: "My mother-in-law caused it, when we came back from Europe in 1978, my husband was very considerate and loving, but after about two visits from my mother-in-law, she warned her son never to enter the kitchen and he obliged, and his friends' talk at the club made him change drastically." She claims that he still helps in bathing the children and getting them ready for school when she is sick or very busy.

The woman wakes earlier than the man and sleeps less in the afternoon during siesta. Regarding total personal needs and free time, (D, E, F), the man spends 890 minutes while the woman spends just 775. I asked why she doesn't go to the club or go for games. She said: "Since Baba Ayo doesn't stay at home with the kids even for 10 minutes to watch telly with them, I feel I should be around them always. I can't leave them alone in the house and go for games or club — I just don't have the time."

From this table, we see that at times men are willing to help their wives at home, but the social system will not allow them, and the influence of friends, mothers-in-law and cousins prevent this kind of relationship.

Table 13
Non-elite family (ii)

Activity (non-elite family)	Average time allocated (in minutes)	
	Woman	Man
A. *Household*		
1. Cleaning, Cooking	285	0
B. *Crafts and other Professions*		
1. Farming*	0	0
2. Others (arranging kiosk)	30	0
C. *Marketing*	120	0
D. *Personal needs*		
1. Meals	85	40
2. Personal hygiene and other needs	60	20
3. Rest, relaxing	0	120
E. *Free Time*		
1. Media (radio)	0	10
2. Conversation	0	40
3. Visiting	40	0
F. *Other activities**		
1. Night sleep	580	650
Total Work (A, B, C.)	735	420
Total personal needs and free time (D, E, F.)	765	880

*Observation was not based on direct participation observation.

Table 13 Analysis

The last time allocation was carried out on a couple who are non-elite. The man is a farmer and the woman is a petty trader.

The woman's kiosk is in front of the house, which makes things worse for her, for automatically she is around the house for 24 hours except when she goes to the market. The man, on the other hand, wakes up at about 5 a.m. and leaves for the farm, returning home at midday.

Throughout the day, the woman is busy doing one thing or another. She gets up at 6 a.m. and cleans the house, cooks the breakfast etc. This woman has four children. The man comes back from the farm, eats his lunch, and rests for 120 minutes while the woman is still busy either washing up or selling in her kiosk. When asked why she doesn't find time to rest in the afternoons, she said: "rest ke, my sister, when I have to make sure the things in the kiosk are properly sold and also make sure that the kitchen is in order". Then I said, "Why don't you tell your husband to help you supervise the children at times?" She said: "Last week, I asked him to bring me some pepper on his way home from the farm, he just slapped me — how much more telling him to sit in the kiosk while I sleep?"

She confirmed further that "He does not help me in doing anything and all the gains I could have made on the items I sell, he utilizes e.g. by just going to the kiosk and taking a packet of cigarettes." The woman said bitterly to me: "My pickin, I am tired of living with this man but my parents will not let me leave him."

In terms of personal needs and free time, the women only spend 40 minutes visiting friends while the other 721 minutes are spent on personal hygiene, meals and other needs. The man spends 780 minutes either conversing, visiting his friends or drinking.

This data shows that exploitation of women is not a class phenomenon but a gender phenomenon. The women are never treated as equals in the house, they are seen and treated as sex objects, slaves or foolish human beings. Their duty is to produce and baby-sit, and the duty of the man is to enjoy life.

Finally, the subjugation and exploitation is gender based and it would take a radical social shift in sex-role concepts to define childcare as appropriate for any person other than females.

Notes

1. H.Z. Lopes, *Occupation: Housewife*, p.3.
2. S. Weitz, *Sex Roles: Biological, Psychological and Social Foundation*, p.133.
3. S.M. Rothman, *Women's Proper Place — A History of Changing Ideals and Practices (1870 to the present)*, p.5.
4. Ibid, p.227.

References

1. Shirley Weitz, *Sex Roles: Biological, Psychological and Social Foundations*, Oxford University Press, New York, 1977, pp.115-140.
2. Jack Goody, et al. (eds.), *Family and Inheritance: Rural Society in Western Europe 1200-1800*, Melbourne, Australia; Cambridge.
3. H. Lopata, *Occupation: Housewife*, New York, Oxford University Press. 1971, pp.3-44.
4. S.M. Rothman, *Woman's Proper Place — A History of Changing Ideals and Practices (1870 to the present)*, New York, Basic Books Inc. 1978, pp.221-253.
5. Fatima Mernissi, *Beyond the Veil: Male and Female Dynamics in Modern Muslim Society*, 1975.

Shugaba-ing Rawlings: An Appraisal of the Marriage Institution (A woman's point of view)

Ifeyinwa Iweriebor

Nigerians are, without a shadow of doubt, some of the greatest law-lovers in the world. They love the law so much that they frequently resort to violent law-making behaviour to demonstrate their love for the law.

As law-lovers, Nigerians are consequently very conservative. They resist with all their might (vocal might mainly) any attack on the Constitution, which is, after all, the supreme law, which they as its worshippers have pledged to invoke at the slightest opportunity.

Perhaps in a bid to soothe its fellow citizens' pathological hatred of things unconstitutional, the Nigerian military softened its image by wearing flowing civilian robes, and compensated for its rape of the Constitution by involving innumerable civilians in its system of patronage and reward.

The law-lovers however, remained adamant. Power, they insisted, belongs to the civilians.

Also as law-lovers, Nigerians are inevitable law-givers, for, since every fourth black African is a Nigerian, who has better right to lay down the law for citizens in other countries as to who should be their rulers?

Consequently, having "wrested" constitutional civilian freedom from the military, on a platter of gold, Nigerians are naturally anxious to ensure that fellow human beings taste and feed well on a similar repast. Thus it was no surprise that the first ascension of Flight Lieutenant Jerry Rawlings in nearby Ghana, was met with derisory hoots and cat-calls from within this country.

When the phenomenon repeated itself last December, Nigerians' fury knew no bounds. Where the "unconstitutional" military had maintained aloof and disapproving silence in 1979, constitutually-elected representatives of the Nigerian peoples refused to be muzzled.

Resplendent in his constitutional garb of free speech, one such Honourable went on Nigerian national network news to denounce the Ghanaian Head of State as a "hybrid bastard who should be deported to Scotland". His adam's apple choking against his stiff white collar, and sweat coursing down his face, the Honourable, duly encased in a woollen suit spluttered with rage. "No white man should be allowed to rule black Africans!", he declared.

In a rejoinder published in some national dailies, an official of a political party rebuked the Honourable for his uncouth language, pointing out that much as his party abhorred the military interruption in Ghana, it must be realized that the matrilineal system was in operation there. Hence, he continued, Rawlings, by virtue of having a Ghanaian mother, was fully entitled to full Ghanaian citizenship, rights, privileges and responsibilities.

This, he implied, did not apply to Nigeria which practised the patrilineal system. So, apparently, did the authorities who ordered the deportation of a prominent member of one of the so-called opposition parties, Alhaji Shugaba Rahman, majority leader in the GNPP-controlled Borno State House of Assembly.

In one of the most glaring examples of the workings of the Nigerian male mind as regards the intricacies of the patrilineal system, the prosecutors argued as follows:

Alhaji Shugaba's father was a Chadian who, though resident in Nigeria, had never acquired Nigerian citizenship, and therefore was deemed to have lived and died a Chadian.

Alhaji Shugaba, despite the fact that he had been born in Nigeria, and despite the fact that his still living mother is a Nigerian, was deemed by the fact of the prevailing patrilineal system to be a Chadian.

It is interesting to note that in deciding in favour of Shugaba, the emphasis was more on the fact that Shugaba had long been recognized as a Nigerian, e.g. issuing him a passport, his prominence in Nigerian politics, etc., than on the fact that his mother happened to be a Nigerian.

According to the Nigerian 1979 Constitution, one is entitled to Nigerian citizenship if either parent is a Nigerian.

However, like several similar provisions that go against the grain of constitutional traditional norms, this is hardly ever invoked, or translated into reality.

Birth certificate forms place more emphasis on the name, origin, and occupation of father, than that of mother. Passport forms, scholarship forms, school forms, application forms of all sorts are more concerned with the father of the person in question than the mother.

The translation of the patrilineal system into modern reality takes on the most absurd implications. For one thing, official cognizance is not taken of the fact that women do contribute financially and otherwise to the upkeep of the home and family, as demonstrated by the tax laws that compel women to pay more tax than their male counterparts. Discrimination in the award of fringe benefits which prevents a woman from taking her children and husband to health clinics provided at her place of work is another.

In fact it becomes most ludicrous when a pregnant female worker cannot benefit from her company's clinic because her pregnancy belongs to her husband. And even when she goes to the government maternity hospitals, she is not entitled to subsidized rates unless her husband is a civil servant. No cognizance whatsoever is taken of the fact that she might be a civil servant herself. The relevant forms do not even ask anything about her. Thus you have the contradictions of women civil servants married to self-employed men or even unmarried, having to pay exorbitant maternity bills, while their male counterparts, who are but remotely concerned with the actual burden of making a baby, can turn in countless wives to the hospitals literally free of charge.

In his opening address to the Seminar on the Role of the Zimbabwean Women in the National Struggle, run by the Zimbabwe African National Union (ZANU) in 1979, Robert Magabe, now Prime Minister of Zimbabwe, commented on the ironies of the patrilineal system:

> The child born of a woman, despite the nine months spent in her womb, was never hers by customary right of ownership, and remained her child only as long as the marriage between her and her husband was good.

The inequalities of the traditional African form of the patrilineal system have not only been reinforced by the European version but have been cleverly packaged in what some have termed mixed grills of both cultures.

Now, even the woman who has opted to bear the burden of looking after her husband alone in a monogamous marriage has no guarantee that she alone will share the benefits of her life-time investment. The Constitution clearly allows the man to recognize any children he may have whether so-called "inside or outside wedlock", children who by virtue of being entitled to inheritance can still act as insurance policies for their mothers who never entered the shackles of marriage. The women who do marry are, by tradition, not entitled to anything in the event of their husband's demise unless they have children, in particular males. Thus whether a woman is married or unmarried, children are the insurance policy of their old age. That is, of course, if the children are recognized. The law, however, gives the man the right to recognize or not to recognize the child at his whim. It also gives him the option to have the benefit and pleasure of a relationship with a woman without the accompanying responsibilities.

A man who has scorned a woman for years, leaving her to bring up a child alone, can suddenly, when the child is a young adult with a bright future, turn round to acknowledge its existence to the embarrassment of the so-called wife in the house. Ironically, in their successful bid to cause the still-birth of the proposed marriage bill, women, in their reluctance to give the men legal freedom, have merely opted to continue with the status quo in which the man can still "eat his cake and have it". Rather than fight to keep the man in the home, women should be fighting to keep the home independent of the man. Rather than compete to be the tax allowance for the husband, women should concentrate on ensuring that they get adequate tax relief for the responsibilities and burdens they bear.

Rather than submit children as insurance claims to inheritance benefits, women should concentrate on getting revoked traditional laws and modern norms that prevail against daughters unconditionally inheriting land and property from their father, or married women earning property in their own right with no strings attached. Regulations that force a married woman to apply for her husband's permission to get a bank loan or a passport, are all cases in point. Rather than seeking men to own and acknowledge their children, women should fight for the legal backing of a natural biological law. Children are women's gifts to men. They should not be used as pawns in the power struggle, or as weapons to keep the woman down. At the moment, if I may quote from an article by Stella Balogun in the *Sunday Concord* of 4 April 1982, p.15: "In marriage men are like the amoeba. They embrace, absorb, and entirely devour the entity of their partner, her name, state of origin, private property and a whole lot more."

In conclusion, therefore, I urge our sisters to work for a marriage that is a genuine partnership, based on mutual respect for each person's intrinsic human value. This is not tantamount to having two captains on a ship, as detractors may argue. Rather, to be effective, a leader should ensure enlightened followership, as a head with a paralysed body is next to useless.

Rather, therefore, than persist in a contradictory situation, where, since men are regarded as our life-line, we struggle to keep our stranglehold on them, thereby warping ourselves and producing stereotypes known as "nags, witches, leeches and such like"; I urge fellow womenfolk to rise above the debris and seek, with the cooperation of our men, to build a society committed to the higher ideals of human nature.

Hausa Traditional Birth Practices and the Health of Mother and Child

Mairo Alti-Muazu

Confinement Period

When a Hausa woman is in labour, she is given some traditional medicines which are supposed to aid her in delivering her baby safely and without too much delay. Actually, some of these medicines are supposed to be taken by the pregnant woman from the seventh month of pregnancy. One of them is called *maganin zaki* in Hausa. It is supposed to make the pregnant woman lose "excess sugar" which is called *zaki* (sweet). There is a general belief among the Hausa women that if a pregnant woman does not lose this sugar, she will have a painful and difficult labour. Thus an expectant mother is discouraged from taking too many sweet things. The *maganin zaki* is called *sobarodo* in Hausa, that is, the flowers of the sorrel plant. When they are dried, they will be soaked in water and the expectant mother will drink the water. She drinks this medicine not just once, but several times. The women told me that after the pregnant woman has been taking the mixture, she will actually begin to discharge something from the vagina which resembles sugar syrup. When she loses this excess sugar, it is believed that she will have an easy delivery.

The Hausa people have a tradition called *goyon Ciki*, whereby a young girl, expecting her first child, goes back to her parents' house during the seventh month of pregnancy, so that her own kin can look after her properly.

This only happens during a woman's first pregnancy as subsequent children are delivered in the husband's house. A girl's mother or grandmother helps during labour, delivery and also teaches her how to look after herself and her baby properly. That's why parents insist that their daughter return home to have her first child. This is a good custom, health-wise, because the majority of these girls are usually no more than children themselves at the time of their first pregnancy. It is good that an experienced person should be at hand to help and direct them, otherwise both the young mother and her child will suffer in many ways through the ignorance of the new mother.

Therefore, all the medicines that are supposed to be taken before and during labour will be prepared for her by her kinswomen. The older woman who has had some experience will prepare her own personally. Some Hausa women (e.g. in Katsina) drink raw beans soaked in water to aid them during labour. The beans will first of all be roughly ground, then soaked in water for about an hour and the woman in labour will drink it. This is supposed to help speed the labour period.

A particular practice that expatriates and even Nigerians who are non-Hausa find hard to believe is that Hausa women (and Fulani also) are supposed to bear the unspeakable pain of childbirth silently, without any complaint. If a woman dares show any sign of the pain she is having, let alone screams, then she has committed a very shameful thing, and she will never hear the last of it, especially if she has co-wives. That is why some of these women will be in labour for days, suffering a lot of agony, but they dare not complain. This is rather too much to expect of anybody. This sort of practice has its disadvantages in that the woman in labour may be having some difficulties, but since she does not speak out or complain, people assume everything is alright and she stays like that until she finally collapses before any action is taken. This practice can cause a lot of harm to the mother as well as to the baby. Many Hausa women told me that their co-wives never even know that they are in labour. They only hear the crying of the baby when it is born, and they live in the same compound.

Another practice similar to this found among the Hausa and Fulani women is *kunya* in Hausa. Here, a young woman expecting her first (and, frequently, her second) baby is expected to keep quiet about it and the forthcoming birth is not discussed at all, so such women keep quiet even if they are in difficulty, which usually results in a lot of complications, and sometimes in fatality.

The Hausa women do not like having their babies in the hospital. They prefer to have them at home. They only use the hospital as a last resort, usually when childbirth complications have already occurred. The men do not like the idea of their wives being exposed to a male doctor, which is often the case in our hospitals. They feel it is not right and it is against the Islamic religion for any man to see the wife of another man naked. Hausa women have their babies kneeling down, in contrast to the practice in the hospitals, where a woman is made to lie down on her back. Again, these women have been brought up to be modest and shy and never to expose their bodies in public. So, when they go to the hospital, they feel really strange, especially when they are asked to take off their clothes in order for them to be examined.

Another practice related to the first two is that Hausa women, or the majority of them, are in seclusion. Therefore, it is obligatory for a wife to have the permission of her husband in order to attend hospital. Often, this permission is not granted. Moreover, if the husband is away from home, when she falls ill or is in labour, she will not be allowed to go to the hospital until his return. These practices are bad as far as the health of the pregnant woman is concerned, because these women just remain at home and are in labour for days. Some finally give birth to still-born babies while others die along with their babies as a result of exhaustion and infection.

If any complications are suspected, then a *yankan gishiri* — cut — may be administered. "This is usually done by an elderly woman recognized to be proficient in this skill. *Gishiri* is the Hausa word for salt, but in the context of illness, refers to diseases of the vagina." (Murphy, M. and Baba, T., 1981) Murray Last (1976) describes it as "the omnibus complaint for women of childbearing age irrespective of whether they are or have ever been pregnant."

"It is treated by an incision into the anterior wall of the vaginal orifice." (Murphy, M. and Baba, T., 1981)

The Hausa believe that a "*gishiri* cut" is particularly helpful in relieving obstructed labour. The sad thing about this practice is that often the cut is made too deep, and it damages some nearby organs, for example, the bladder; and is often a direct cause of vaginal fistulae, where the unfortunate woman just leaks urine continuously and cannot control it.

Moreover, the razor or sharp instrument used in making the incision is not sterilized and thus can cause some infections.

Post-Natal Period

"Normal pregnancy lasts for about 40 weeks, and if, after this time, the mother is delivered of a healthy baby, there is celebration both in the family and local community." (Harrison, K.A., 1978)

Among the Hausa too, the safe delivery of a healthy child is an occasion that calls for celebration. However, the new mother's ordeals are by no means over. There are many traditional rites that she has to perform in order to regain her health and strength.

The Hausa believe that exposure to cold may cause serious ill-health in a woman who has just had a baby. All possible precautions are therefore taken to see that a new mother and her baby are kept warm. Therefore, new mothers are made to have very hot baths twice daily, and to sleep in overheated rooms for several months after childbirth. A fire is kept burning in her room, or a container with hot charcoal. In Zaria and its surrounding villages, a special mud bed is made for the new mother with a fireplace underneath the bed. A mat is spread on it and the woman is expected to lie on it and turn from one side to another, so that her body gets the heat of the fire underneath. Among the Hausa women in Katsina, the mud bed is not as popular as in Zaria. They only put hot charcoals near the woman's bed. From time to time, the new mother is told to kneel over the hot charcoals so that her genital area gets the heat. This is supposed to help the place heal fast. If she does not do this, it is believed that her inside will become rotten and her husband will have no further use of her sexually.

Apart from dwelling in an overheated room, the new mother takes hot baths twice daily. These baths are taken with practically boiling water. Before the bath, she will sit next to the container of very hot water, cover herself and the container with a thick cloth, so that she gets all the steam coming from the hot water. After that, without further delay, she begins her bath using leaves from the neem tree or the cassia-simea tree. She dips the leaves in the water, shakes them a little then beats her body with the leaves so that the water gets all over her body.

After the water has cooled down a little, the woman will sit inside the water so that her genital area can get more heat. In the Zaria area, a woman who has had other children before, will take these hot baths for as long as three months, whereas a woman who hasn't had any children before, will take the hot baths for as long as five months, twice daily, i.e. morning and evening.

In Katsina town and its environs, the period of the hot baths is not as long as in Zaria. There, the new mother bathes with hot water for forty days. If the child is her first, she may add 10 extra days making fifty days, but it is not compulsory. During the post-natal period, called *jego* in Hausa, a woman should not drink cold water at all. She should not even touch cold water if she can avoid it. Both she and her baby drink warm water.

These hot baths are very important to the Hausa women. I have seen a case where a grandmother cried bitter tears, because her educated, "modern" grand-daughter had refused to take the hot baths. The Hausa women firmly believe in them. A woman who does not take the hot baths is believed to be inviting trouble for herself. The women say that such a woman will start to swell all over and may die as a result or else her genital area will just rot away and she will start to emit an unpleasant smell. As a result, they go to all lengths to make sure *Sun gasu sosai*, that is, "they are well roasted" which is literally what happens.

The dangers of these practices are clear enough. Harrison (1978) said, "This custom obviously recognises the need for personal hygiene at this time, but unfortunately injuries from scalds and burns sometimes result from these practices. Some of these injuries can produce serious effects, for example, we have seen burn scars on the breasts preventing breast-feeding." Ahmadu Bello University Hospital has seen a large number of such cases — where the mother or baby or some other member of the family (especially children), accidently falls into the fire or gets scalded by hot water. Sometimes both mother and child suffocate due to lack of oxygen in the room, since the door and windows are kept closed and a fire is kept burning at night. No fresh air gets in at all.

There was a case in Shika village (near Zaria), about four years ago, where a woman lying on a mud-bed, with a fire burning underneath, got so badly burnt that the skin of her back was stuck to the mat. She died as a result. It has been confirmed by doctors that hot baths can and do cause heart failure among Hausa and Fulani women. Of the taking of the hot baths, Salawu said, "This is practised widely among the Hausa and Fulani women, and it results in the Clinical Syndrome of Peripartum Cardiac failure which is known to be commoner in Zaria than in any other centre in the world." *(ABUMED*, Vol.1 No.5, April 1977, p.37)

Lastly, the women who take these hot baths become very black even if they had been light-skinned before. They just become very dark as a result of too much heat. Some of them develop skin rashes; their babies too, often have rashes, especially if they are born during the dry season.

Post-Natal Diet

This diet includes an in-take of highly-spiced foods and also a high potash (Na_2Co_3) diet. After having a baby, a Hausa woman is required to eat highly-spiced foods.

Just before delivery time, the pregnant woman's mother, mother-in-law or some other close female relation will prepare these spices for her. They include a lot of small red peppers (hot chillies), cloves, ginger, garlic, etc. They will be ground into powder and the new mother must always add a generous portion of this powder to whatever she is going to eat or drink. She even adds some to tea. When she is eating or drinking, she sweats profusely. The food must be hot from the fire, as well as hot because of the addition of spices.

The new mother takes a lot of nutritious food which includes: meat, honey, cereal, cow-leg or chicken pepper soup. But all of these foods must be seasoned well with spices. It is said that when she takes her food with plenty of spices, she will have more milk in her breasts with which to feed her child.

This practice is good in one way but it has its disadvantages too. Nutritionally speaking, the new mother eats well. She eats plenty of meat which is a good source of protein and it will help her to regain her health faster. However, the addition of too much pepper and other spices may do her and her suckling infant harm. Too much pepper can cause dysentery and it can also aggravate stomach ulcers.

Another thing that is added to the new mother's diet at this time is potash (Na_2Co_3). She is supposed to drink *Kunun Kanwa*, that is, potash pap, at least twice daily, or whenever she is hungry. As the name suggests, this pap or cereal is made of millet and plenty of potash *(Kanwa)* as well as the inevitable spices. Again, this practice is more popular among the Hausa women in Zaria and Kano. In Katsina, they make their own *kunu* without the potash. It is called *Farin Kunu*, that is, "white pap", because there is no potash in it. They only add the spices.

Potash (Na_2Co_3) and salt (NaCl) have been confirmed scientifically to aggravate hypertension or high blood pressure, especially when taken in large quantities. That is why many people in the U.S. have now either reduced their salt intake or given up salt completely. (*Time* No.11,

15 March 1982, pp.54-61.) Therefore, the new mother's health can be affected by the intake of too much potash and salt.

Traditional Practices Performed on a New-Born Baby
Immediately a baby is born, the umbilical cord is cut by the midwife (*unguwar zoma* in Hausa). These traditional midwives are usually old women experienced in such things. The services of a midwife are required during the confinement period as well as during the post-natal period. Where a woman has no close kin at hand, the midwife will take their place and offer every possible help to the woman in labour. Midwives are very valuable people in the Hausa society.

Even though the midwife may be an experienced one, the instrument used in cutting the cord is often dirty and unsterilized. Her own hands may be dirty too. In this way, the new baby may get infected with some bacteria within a few minutes of its entrance to the world. The new baby, too, has to undergo the hot baths just like its mother. Although the water is allowed to cool slightly, unlike in the mother's case, it is still too hot for such a delicate and small body.

The Hausa women say that unless the baby is washed thoroughly, initially, it will not be strong and later on in life she/he will have an unpleasant body odour. As a result, as long as an hour is spent twice daily on bathing the baby thoroughly with hot water.

Although the room is usually warm, babies do catch cold because of the lengthy time taken in bathing them. Some get pneumonia from constant exposure. Moreover, babies are kept naked — just wrapped in an old piece of cloth. Some Hausa mothers do not put any clothes on their babies until they wean them. This is because the babies soil the clothes. One can imagine the consequences of such a practice on the health of a baby that was used until birth, to the agreeable conditions of its mother's womb.

After the umbilical cord has been cut off, what is left of it is treated twice a day by the midwife, after the baby has had its bath. This is so that it will fall off quickly and the place will heal fast. This is done by placing the metal part of a hoe *(hauya)*, into a fire until it is red hot, then the midwife will dip her right hand in cold water, then tap the hot metal with the palm and quickly place her palm on the baby's cord. She repeats this over and over until the metal is cold. This practice is to be frowned upon because the baby can be infected because the metal hoe is often dirty, and it's not even washed, let alone sterilized. The midwife's hands may be dirty too. Many Hausa babies get tetanus as a result of this practice and I have seen cases where the umbilical cord of the baby becomes septic.

Another practice which should be discouraged because of its effect on the baby's health is giving the baby some of the water with which he/she is being washed to drink. This water, which is soapy and dirty, is often further contaminated by the baby urinating in it. However, it is still given to the baby to drink so that it will be strong and big. When the baby's umbilical cord has fallen off, the mother will keep it. It will, henceforth, be soaked in water and given to the baby to drink whenever the baby has stomach-ache. It is no wonder these babies suffer from frequent stomach upsets, since they are made to drink dirty, soapy water.

Naming Practices
The Hausa people do not give a new baby a name until she/he is seven days old. On that day, a ram will be slaughtered, prayers will be said, and the baby will be given a name. The meat of the ram is meant for the mother of the baby to eat. After the baby is named, its head is shaved by the local barber. Traditional or "tribal" marks are also made on the face and stomach. *Beli* (epiglottis) is removed. The people believe that if *beli* is not removed it may cause a lot of trouble later on in life. The person will become thin and a swelling in the throat will prevent the person from speaking clearly, until he has it removed.

The local barber uses a knife to perform this operation through the mouth of the baby, without pain. If the baby is a girl, in addition to the above operation, her ears will be pierced, and a little bit of her clitoris is cut off (female circumcision). However, this latter practice is fast becoming outdated. Not many people circumcise their daughters nowadays.

All these minor operations are performed by Hausa barbers using unsterilized knives, razor blades and needles. The baby is therefore likely to get tetanus or some other infection, and apart from the pain caused when performing such operations, some babies bleed a lot which is a bad thing health-wise.

The Baby's Diet
The first thing a baby is given on its arrival to this world is a drink, *rubutu*, with a verse from the Holy Quran. The verse will be written on a slate by a Malam. Water is then used to wash the writing off the slate and the water will be given to the newborn baby until it is finished. The hazard of this practice is that the writing is done in local ink, the water used in washing the writing off is not boiled and the hands of the Malam as well as the container may be dirty. Such a mixture may well cause the baby stomach upsets.

For three days after its delivery, the new baby is not allowed to feed on its mother's milk. Instead, the mother presses out all the milk in her breasts and throws it away. The baby will be given either cow's or goat's milk to drink whenever it is hungry. The latter milk, however, is the more preferable of the two because the Prophet Muhammad was said to have drunk goat's milk as a baby, before feeding on his mother's milk. The Hausa, being predominantly Muslim, aspire to emulate this practice. They also believe that for the first three days, the new mother's milk is contaminated and therefore is unfit for the baby.

Whatever its religious significance, this practice is a very dangerous one, because often the cow's or goat's milk is *not* boiled before it is given to the baby. Many bacteria feed on milk as we do, so unpasteurized milk is not safe even for adults, let alone small babies. Tuberculosis (T.B.) can be caught through drinking unpasteurized milk.

Another thing is that the baby is deprived of a very good source of nourishment that nature has provided for it. There is nothing to compare with the mother's natural milk, which has all the essential nutrients in the right quantities — even the temperature is just right for a baby. It has also been scientifically confirmed that the first milk from the new mother's breasts is an excellent start for the baby. Nothing can compare with it. It is, therefore, such a shame that such an excellent and nutritious food is wasted in preference to goat's milk that may well cost the baby its life.

Another drink the Hausa women give to a new baby is *dauri*. This is a drink that is made by soaking the bark of a tree, called *hano* in Hausa, in warm water. After the water has cooled down, the colour will become red, and the liquid is given to the baby from time to time, so that "it will grow strong and healthy and will not have too much trouble when teething". I often wonder how safe this mixture really is for a new-born baby, not to talk of the cleanliness of the pot in which the bark is soaked.

Visiting the New Baby
As soon as it is known that a woman has been safely delivered of a child, women begin to arrive in large numbers to see the new arrival and congratulate the mother. They come to see them at all hours and these women also insist on carrying the baby. So, the baby is passed from one person to another throughout the day and even at night. The bad thing about this particular practice is that some of these women may come with their own children who may be suffering from some infectious disease like measles, whooping cough or a cold. It is therefore easy for the baby to catch an infectious disease, especially as it has not built up any resistance to such diseases at such an early age.

The mother too is highly susceptible to infections at this time. Both mother and baby need to rest after such a traumatic experience as childbirth, but their visitors do not give them a chance to do so. Many babies are often so tired after so much handling that they cannot sleep at night. They only cry and cry, and of course the mother is kept awake also. Many hospital staff in this part of the country have a hard time trying to keep visitors away from the maternity wards, or at least to limit their numbers because they know the disadvantages of this custom.

Recommendations
The basic fault in the Hausa traditional birth practices results from a lack of education on the part of these women and a lack of education on

the part of these women and a lack of understanding of the rules of basic hygiene. The Hausa women need to be enlightened about the importance of attending ante-natal clinics when they are pregnant. They should also be encouraged to have their babies in the hospital.

Some of the midwives found in the Hausa society are very knowledge-able as far as the delivery and care of babies are concerned. However, they need to be trained about the importance of sterilization of their instruments. Their own personal hygiene should also be stressed. They should also be taught the anatomy of the human body. This will help the situation concerning the *gishiri* cut.

The women should know that while there is a need for personal cleanliness after childbirth, there is no need for things to be carried to the extreme — i.e. bathing with boiling water twice a day for three to five months. Lectures on nutrition should be given at the ante-natal and child welfare clinics. Finally, Hausa women should be made aware of the danger of being in labour for over a day. "Normal labour should not last longer than 24 hours, but in some of these women it has been known to go on for as long as nine days". (Harrison, K.A., 1978)

They should therefore try to go to the hospital for help and not wait until things get bad. Husbands and other relatives can be appealed to for help. There is no need to wait for a husband who has travelled to come back before his pregnant wife is taken to the hospital — it may be too late. An apt quotation to bear in mind here is: "Never let the sun set twice on a labouring woman".

There should, therefore, be a mass campaign on the radio, television, in adult education classes, in our hospitals, and in any other possible way, to educate women on the few points raised, and any others that will help them deliver their babies safely, and care for them efficiently without too many health hazards.

References

1. Harrison, K.A. (1978), "Childbearing in Zaria". (A Public lecture in ABU Zaria on 20 March 1978.)
2. Murphy, M. & Baba, T. (1981), "Rural Dwellers and Health Care in Northern Nigeria".
3. Salawu, S.A.I. (1977). "The Effects of Marriage Practices on Maternal Health Care in Northern Nigeria".
4. Verbal interviews with women in Jama'a and Koraye Villages (Hausa and Fulani settlements very close to ABU Main Campus).
5. "Salt: A New Villain?" *Time* No.11, 15 March 1982.

The Role of Women's Associations in Nigeria's Development: Social Welfare Perspective

Arlene Bene Enabulele

Introduction

Historically, women's associations have always made tremendous efforts in contributions to their country's development. In the West, social welfare has always been the major concern of voluntary organizations. These organizations took the major responsibility of catering for the needs of the sick, poor and disabled in society. Only with the advent of social welfare policies (the Victorian Poor Law and Social Reform 1905-14), did government begin to play a major role in the delivery of social services.

The role of women's associations may be defined in terms of their participation, whether direct or indirect, within their existing communities. The purpose of this paper is to examine the role of women's associations in Nigeria's national development. A background of women's associations in Nigeria will be presented. Following this section, the structure of women's associations and the contributions made by women's associations in Nigeria, will also be covered. The paper will conclude with a summary and recommendations.

Background of Women's Associations in Nigeria

There is a paucity of data on women's associations in Africa. The few studies which have been done are a result of anthropological efforts. In many works, it has been explained that there have always been difficulties in making contact with "womenfolk", which may be due to the paucity of material concerning African women. However, the writer of this paper does not hold the above rationale, since gaining access to information is based on who is doing the probing and for what reasons. Traditionally, our people do not take kindly to "outsiders" asking too many questions. This traditional nature of the community vis-a-vis answering probing questions from unfamiliar, outside persons must be respected and understood.

However, the associations which have received the most attention in the literature are those of the secret societies of the Mende of Sierra Leone and the market women's group of the Yoruba (Leis, 1964).

In her study, she found that many of the Yoruba and Ibo women's associations control the market, whereas the Patani associations, according to her research, are engaged in cleaning the environment of refuse. She found that there are many associations which focus mainly on the lending of money or, as it is commonly referred to, "Osusu". Studies of urban formal associations in Africa have focused basically on those joined by immigrants from rural areas (Little, 1951). It has been found most often in rural settings that women's organizations are parallel to those of the men and each operate within their own boundaries (Lebeuf, 1963).

Historically, Nigerian women's associations have always played important roles within society. The Lagos Ladies' League, a voluntary women's club, played a major role in combating the high rate of fatality from malaria in Lagos around 1897. This group was selected to act as the health visitor under the then Governor Glover.

Lebeuf (1963) contends:

> while it is a general tendency for women to form groups for the purpose of carrying out their various activities in wealthy and populous areas like Southern Nigeria, such groups, owing to the importance of women in commerce and agriculture, have become powerful organizations which have been in existence for a long time.

The author further cited the following examples: Oyo associations around 1914 were often consulted by political authorities to make or contribute to important decisions within the community. Ibo villages had various women's councils, which were responsible for agricultural concerns and the interests of women in general. These councils mobilized the known historical event in Nigeria in 1929, namely the Aba Riots or, as they are sometimes referred to, the "War of the Women". Demonstrations concerning the rumoured introduction of tax on women's property spread through two provinces, Owerri and Calabar. As a result of these riots, the British sent two women anthropologists to study the cause of the riots and to uncover the organizational base that permitted such spontaneity and solidarity among the women. Studies by Leith-Ross (1965) and others resulted from the British investigations.

Women's associations in Nigeria before World War II, such as the Young Women's Christian Association (YWCA) and the Girl Guides, followed the interest and activities of similar organizations of the British. Generally, they were founded and headed by the wives of British administrators or by women belonging to the local elite in contact with the British administration. Local "Ladies Associations" differed little in function and structure from women's social and philanthropic associations in the West on which they were modelled. The primary objectives of these associations were to undertake social welfare work during the war years as well as holding literacy, cooking and sewing classes. Sanda (1981), in his analysis of the major characteristics of Nigerian social policy, places a great deal of emphasis on the remedial services; the significant role of voluntary organizations; the transplanting of the British tradition of social services, and the over-concentration on urban-related social problems.

There have been attempts on the part of women to bring the various women's associations under one council. Such a council would be used as a forum for women in Nigeria. Such an attempt was initiated by the National Council of Women's Societies, Nigeria, which was founded in 1958. The major aim of the Council was to create a federation of non-political Women's Organizations and assist women in towns and villages in their important role as homemakers, and nation-buiulders.

> The council seeks to create among its members an awareness of good citizenship. It aims at being an umbrella for coverage of its affiliates, a bridge for linking the women of Nigeria irrespective of creed, tribe or class, a platform for disseminating women's opinions and a liaison between the women and the government. In short, it is the voice of the women of Nigeria.
>
> (*Sunday Times*, 16 May 1982, p.9.)

The council laid the foundation for creating unity and sisterhood among the varied women's associations.

Structure of Women's Associations

The information for this section is based on data gathered by the author from a small random sample of 50 women's associations in Benin City. Women's associations are variously styled as bands, committees, groups, clubs, guilds, unions or societies. They may range in structure from very informal to formal associations, with size varying from as few as five members to over 500 members. However, it seems the larger the size of the association the more structured and formalized it becomes.

Most women's associations are basically volunteer associations. These are far more common in Nigeria where there are multiple roles such as:

(a) assistance in obtaining employment;
(b) learning to master or adjust to city life;
(c) mutual aid;
(d) recreational and social outlet;
(e) capital accumulation and maintenance of village ties;
(f) conserver of morals;
(g) a strengthener of family life, and
(h) in some instances they serve as socio-status conferrals.

189

Each association phrases its own goals or purposes somewhat differently. Perlman and Jones (1967), in their study of organizations, have isolated four general objectives of most organizations:

1. to provide social and psychological benefits to participants;
2. to provide self-help and mutual aid;
3. to increase the effectiveness of service delivery;
4. to achieve institutional change.

Objective 1:
The social and psychological benefits must be realized in order to keep the participant committed to the organization. These needs may be met through social contact and a sense of well-being and fulfilment gained from interaction with women of similar interests and backgrounds.
Objective 2:
Most women's associations function as informal support networks to their members. This form of informal support often takes shape in donations and contributions of various types such as clothes, money, food, moral support, etc., to members in need. This informal support is provided by all of the 50 women's associations reviewed.
Objectives 3 & 4:
These are accorded to the more structured and formalized organizations but not limited to them. The increase in the effectiveness of service delivery here relates to the extent to which the association has identified and fulfilled its community outreach goals. This takes into consideration the effectiveness with which the organization realizes its community targeted goals. These goals may be identified as providing goods and services to individuals or agencies assisting in the elimination of various social problems such as delinquency, housing, mental health, poverty, and donating equipment to schools, hospitals and various charity institutions. *Objective 4* may be viewed as the extent or degree to which the organization's social action has affected or impacted on the targeted social problem within the community. This objective serves as a continuous effort on the part of the association.

Women who join associations come from various backgrounds as well as socioeconomic and educational levels. Their reasons for joining are various and range from wanting to belong to a group, to the fact that their friends are members, to wanting to do something meaningful in the community or sheer psychological fulfilment. Rosaldo (1974) states: "Extra-domestic ties with other women are, then, important sources of power and value for women in societies that create a firm division between public and domestic or male and female roles."

The personal experience of such division has taken root and is spreading fast in Nigeria due to our new technological awareness and development. The amount of participation, both male and female, in a volunteer association varies directly with both the number of benefits (rewards or satisfaction) offered by an organization and the degree to which the benefits are contingent upon participation. Balchuck and Booth (1969) feel women, on the whole, appear to have more stable patterns of participation in voluntary associations then do men. Women on the whole tend to retain their membership in the same organization for longer periods of time.

Contributions Made by Women's Associations in Nigeria

As noted in this paper, Nigerian women's associations have always made and will continue to make significant contributions to the national development. The contributions are varied and diversified, and for the purposes of this paper we will consider those in the areas of health, education, and other social services. Of the 50 associations reviewed, the following community actions were identified:

Health
● the monitoring and support of inoculations and health campaigns throughout the country.
● donating money and equipment to clinics, health centres and hospitals.
● undertaking environmental clean up campaigns; fostering healthy mental attitudes amongst members.

Education
● fostering the need for young girls and women to play a major role in their nation's development through the attainment of education.
● providing scholarship and funds to deserving students.
● equipping schools with books and furniture, etc.
● establishing and maintaining day-care centres and nursery schools, in order to assist working mothers.

Social Services
● functioning as informal support networks to members and their relations.
● providing assistance to orphanages (donating clothes, toys, etc.)
● visiting those in hospitals and prisons.
● buying Christmas gifts and donating equipment to the physically and mentally handicapped.
● maintaining a healthy morale of family life amongst its members.
● fostering awareness and concern for the needs of the disadvantaged.
● maintaining and promoting cultural ties.
● providing recreational centres and events.
By the type of contributions made by women's associations in Nigeria, one is justified in saying that women's organizations have been the vanguard in the social welfare movement in Nigeria. For the community self-help approach has been and is being implemented in meeting the

needs of the people. These associations cannot carry the entire burden of the country's social welfare problems, but can continue to augment the programmes and policies of the Federal, State and Local Governments. These contributions of women's associations are necessary and are a viable tool in any nation's development.

Summary and Recommendations

This paper has attempted to provide a background on women's associations in Nigeria. Women's associations are not a new phenomenon in Nigerian history. As indicated in the paper, these associations have played and will continue to play an active role in Nigeria's development. From the contributions of the Lagos Ladies' League of 1897 which functioned as the health visitor in combating the high rate of fatality from malaria during that period to the period of 1929 when the Aba Riots or "War of the Women" brought women to the attention of policy-makers in the country, it has been noted that women's rights should not be taken for granted. The attempts of the National Council of Women's Societies, Nigeria in the unification of women's associations must not be overlooked. The council laid the foundation for creating unity and sisterhood among the varied women's associations.

The structure of women's associations ranges from bands, committees, groups, clubs, guilds to unions or societies. They may range from very informal to formal associations with size varying from as few as five to over 500 members. Most women's associations, regardless of their structure, function as informal support networks to members and their relations.

In the final analysis, the overall contribution of women's associations in Nigeria may fall into three major areas: health, education and social. Women's associations continue to augment the role of social welfare agencies in their respective communities. However, it must not be overlooked that the Federal, State and Local Governments have major roles to play in the area of social welfare in Nigeria's development.

In the past we have ignored the contributions made by women's associations in society. However, given the political and social climate in our country, we must begin to look to the associations to assist in finding solutions to some of the social needs and social problems. It is incumbent on the society to recognize and encourage women's associations in their continued contributions to society.

Efforts should be made by professionals and academicians in social work to provide technical assistance through workshops, training seminars, symposiums or conferences to bring these associations together for purposes of providing basic organizational skills and the knowledge of the dynamics of change in Nigerian society vis-a-vis women's associations. These skills should provide the associations with the knowledge of organizational structure, defining and targeting meaningful goals, fund-raising techniques: the basic skills which will improve their function as viable community associations.

In recognition of members' relentless contributions to the community, there should be a forum where these associations can come together to discuss issues and problems, as they relate to women and society. At this forum, which could be an annual event, members of the various associations should be cited, through nominations for awards or certificates, for their outstanding contributions to their community in that particular year. This forum, once a year, would serve as an incentive to these associations which under normal circumstances are not formally recognized by society. It would also develop a sense of comradeship and togetherness among the many associations. An annual updated directory of women's associations providing pertinent information on each association could be an outcome of the annual forums. This directory would be useful to professionals, social welfare agencies, and community leaders, who might wish to contact a particular association for its assistance in various community endeavours. We stand to gain a lot by such an inter-sectoral approach to finding solutions to our pressing social issues, such as care of children, care of female adolescents and care of the aged. But we may stumble if due recognition and patronage are not given to our womenfolk in national development.

References

1. Babchurch, N & A. Booth, 1969. "Voluntary Association Membership: A Longitudinal Analysis", *American Sociological Review* 34, No.1, pp.31-34.
2. Faniran-Odekunle, F., 1978, "Nigeria's Social Welfare Serivce: Past, Present and Future", *Nigerian Behavioural Sciences Journal,* Vol.1., No.384, p.180.
3. Foster, G.M., 1973, *Traditional Societies and Technological Change,* New York, Harper and Row Publishers.
4. Gary, L.E., 1978, "Support Systems in Black Communities: Implications for Mental Health Services for Children and Youth", *IUAR Occasional Paper* Vol.3., No.4., Institute for Urban Affairs and Research, Howard University.
5. Ifeka-Moller, C., 1975, "Female Militancy and Colonial Revolt: The Women's War of 1929, Eastern Nigeria", in Shirley Ardener (ed.), *Perceiving Women,* Halsted Press, New York.
6. Iglitzin, L.B. & R. Ross (eds.), 1976, *Women in the World: A Comparative Study,* Clio Press, Oxford.
7. Leis, N.B., 1974, "Women in Groups: Ijaw Women's Associations", in M.Z. Rosaldo and L. Lamphere, *Women, Culture and Society,* Stanford University Press, California, pp.223-242.
8. Leith-Ross, S., 1965, *African Women,* New York.
9. Ogbuibe, T., 1982, "Women's Council Hold Convention", *Sunday Times,* 16 May, p.9.
10. Perlman, R. & D. Jones, 1967, *Neighborhood Service Centers,* U.S. Department of Health, Education and Welfare, Wash.D.C., pp.49-51.

11. Sanda, A.O., 1981, "The Nature of Social Services and the Evolution of Social Policy in Nigeria", in Dele Oluwa (ed.), *The Administration of Social Services in Nigeria: The Challenge to Local Government,* University of Ife.
12. The Wellesley Editorial Committee (eds.), 1977, *Women and National Development: The Complexities of Change,* Chicago, The University of Chicago Press.

Rapporteurs' Report:

Renée Pittin & Norma Perchonock

The discussion opened with an altercation. The chairperson refused to recognize an individual who insisted on addressing her as "Madam Chairman". His response, that he "didn't think it made any difference" generated heated comment and was flatly rejected by the seminar participants.

Most of the papers revolved around the institution of marriage and the subordination of women within the family structure. In the discussion of the paper by Aluko and Alfa, contributions centred particularly on the ways in which women may contribute to the subordination of other women, through reinforcement of traditional family roles, as in the case of the woman who forbade her married son to assist his wife in the kitchen. A strand running through the discussion concerned the fact that individual women, regardless of status, must devote many hours each day to family and household work, and therefore never have the leisure time or opportunities for social activities that men enjoy.

A number of issues were raised in response to the paper presented by Ifeyinwa Iweriebor. Several participants attested to the validity of her statement that women do not have rights over their children and that, moreover, even their role in bearing their children may be denied if politically and socially expedient. Participants contested the presenter's suggestion that in any marriage one spouse must lead while the other must follow, and also the statement that children are women's gifts to men.

The paper by Mairo Alti-Mu'azu elicited much discussion about the medical problems faced by women, especially in the process of childbirth. A doctor in the audience gave a detailed explanation of some of the local medical practices that may cause permanent damage to women, especially *gishiri* cuts. These are performed when either a woman in labour, or her relatives, decide that there is an obstruction or other reason for prolonged labour. The vagina is cut with a razor, supposedly to make the birth easier. In the process, however, the urethra, bladder and other internal organs may be damaged, leading to a condition known as vesico-vaginal fistula, in which the woman leaks urine continuously. This condition can also be brought on by prolonged labour, especially common when the married women are very young and not physically developed enough to allow easy childbirth. The VVF condition, as it is called, can only be repaired by extensive surgery. Meanwhile, the women who suffer from it are usually divorced by their husbands, and become social outcasts as a result of the abnormal leakage of urine.

One commentator made a plea for the more extensive training of midwives so that women could deliver children safely in the home. The point was made that home delivery is more "natural", eliminating the hospital type of atmosphere. In reply, several individuals pointed out that the lack of medical and communication infrastructure in Nigeria makes it very difficult for women to get to the hospital in time, should any problems arise during childbirth that the midwives cannot cope with.

The final paper of the session, given by Arlene Enabulele, focused on women's associations in Nigeria. Commentators noted that the functions of the associations described tend to centre on philanthropy and social welfare, and thus tend to reinforce the notion that women are expected to play primarily nurturant and maternal roles in society.

PART VI
Contemporary Experiences (3)

The Role of Women in Nigerian Society: The Media

Thérèse Nweke

The Fourth World Manifesto of 1971, among other things states: "women, set apart by physical differences between them and men, were the first colonized group." Colonial situations are generally marked by a number of variables, such as the majority group being regarded as the minority, the colonized having no voice in the decision-making process, their forming a cheap labour pool, and the visible, normally physical, sign of differences between the colonizers and the colonized. This differentiation then forms the basis for discrimination, segregation and humiliation.

But whereas in classical colonialism the struggle is based on that of regaining the land, the peoples' traditions, and the old way of life, the major difference between the classical colonialist position and that of women is that the old way of life is the very thing which colonizes. Sexism, as the colonizing agent, is the major differential which forms the basis for discrimination, exploitation and oppression. And it is sexism which creates a colonial mentality by which women see their colonization as natural and normal to their daily lives.

In colonial society, position and status are irrelevancies, class lines are generally blurred, and both bourgeoisie and workers, despite varying perceptions, regard the colonialist as the common enemy. Hence our nationalist movements and liberation struggles are basically irreconcilable class groups which eventually unite, if only temporarily, to fight a common cause.

Women are in a similar position and cannot afford to be deceived by those Marxist theoreticians who regard the feminist movement as representing limited interests. The struggle is not really along class lines. For while there is room for appreciation of the labour movement, as well as awareness of its inherent sexism and prejudices, there is a more pressing need for female solidarity. It should also be realized that separatism, at this stage, and not assimilation, will guarantee that female interests and needs are better served.

"Position" is generally seen as a person's place within a social structure, and "status" is the prestige accorded to that position. In Nigeria, most women have no place in the social structure, not even at the bottom. They are outside the structure, and this is regardless of their education, their birth, their wealth, their class or even individual achievements. Thus, despite the tokenism of female ministers, commissioners, directors and a plethora of Nigerian professional women, when all is said and done Nigerian males regard females as "only a woman". An argument involving an illiterate *danfo* or *molue* driver and a female graduate on who really hit whose vehicle, eventually boils down to bystanders advising the illiterate male to "leave her alone, after all she's only a woman". Cross swords with any male colleague at work, or even a husband at home, and the basic consensus among well-meaning friends and relations alike, is "don't mind her, act like a man, she's only a woman". Thus the idea is to humour, to tolerate, not to take seriously, not to behave as if both parties have equal rights, since one is inherently inferior.

The basic contention here then is that Nigerian women (like women everywhere) are discriminated against by virtue of their sex. And it is that basic sexism which causes a certain unity, though qualified, of women in various cultures everywhere to fight differences whenever they exist in the legal, economic, social, political and cultural status of women and men. In Nigeria, the structure of the society, its values, traditions, and institutions all have an in-built discrimination against women. Women are regarded by everyone as weak, irrational, passive, and thus inferior. And even when educated, they are believed to share the same behavioural patterns and personality traits of their less educated sisters, simply because they are women. Most Nigerian men claim that no matter the level of education women achieve, they are still inferior to men (all men) because they are women. They contend that once stripped of her professionalism on the job, a woman reverts to being and behaving like a woman when the chips are down.

The fact that women as a group are perceived to have, and indeed are forced to have, a different kind of personality and a different pattern of behaviour as a group, has grave consequences for the position of women in Nigerian society. For this does not merely create differences between women and men as groups, but it also creates inequalities. Therefore, as long as this sexism persists, Nigerian women will continue to remain inferior. And even if a reformist attitude were to be adopted, and changes perceived to be important were made within the system, reforms will merely alleviate and the old attitudes will continue. Where such attitudes persist, it is almost impossible for development to take place.

If it is accepted that women as a colonized group should overthrow the shackles of male-colonizer domination, what then are the options? At present there is no concerted action, because as yet women are unaware of their rights. Some do not even realize that they need to bargain or require a bargaining weapon. And even though they are regarded as an undifferentiated mass, they do not even have the power of numbers, or even a power base, although they are seen to have one.

The only commodity over which they have productive monopoly is their bodies and the ability to perpetuate homo sapiens.

On surveying the record of women in the Nigerian media, one can see that Nigerian women over the past thirty years have invaded a former sacrosanct male profession. Yet their progress there is marginal and tokenistic. In the mid-fifties, among the first group of 100 trained Nigerian broadcasters in the Nigerian Broadcasting Service, there were less than ten women. Today there are approximately 100 chief executives of broadcasting stations who constitute top management. Of this number, not a single one is a woman. On scanning the list, one sees:

  2 DGs of Federal Radio and TV
10 MDs of Federal Radio and TV
21 GMs of Federal TV
21 GMs of Federal Radio (prospective)
19 GMs of State Radio Stations
19 GMs of State TV Stations (prospective).

The *Daily Times* newspaper organization, Nigeria's largest, is said to have about 300 journalists, one quarter of whom are women. Of this number, there are exactly three female editors and one acting editor. The News Agency of Nigeria (NAN), which began operations almost four years ago, has approximately 127 journalists of whom only eight are female. None occupy senior management positions. Of NAN's 10-member board of directors, only one is a woman. FRCN Lagos has a 35-per-cent female work force. However, in the senior management cadre, of the six assistant directors, only one is a woman, and she is a graduate with almost thirty years' experience in journalism.

In advertising, the story is not much different, although female advertising executives should be in a better position to understand the needs of consumers, since they cater for most consumers in the society. However, it has been estimated that there are not more than ten client service directors in any of the 30 advertising companies in Nigeria.

Scanning the Nigerian media scene, the situation is disturbing and depressing, but not much different from that in societies like America, where women have agitated much more for equality. As far back as 1790, one Mary Goddard, who served the Continental Congress as the printer of the first official printing of the Declaration of Independence, was removed from her job as Baltimore postmistress after 14 years of service. She was replaced when a new postmaster-general directed that her job be taken over by a man. She made passionate pleas for justice and failed. Almost 200 years after the Goddard incident, the American media women are still badly served. In a recent survey of individuals occupying "key positions of authority" in four of America's major news organizations — Major Newspaper groups 107, *New York Times* 11, News Magazines 32 and Networks 43, totalling 193 media directors, only nine were women, and all but one were in the print media.

Here, our index of "key positions of authority" is that of Domhoff[1] who defines authority within media institutions as constituted in the posts of president and membership of the boards of directors. Domhoff sees control residing in the hands of the boards who meet once or twice a month to decide upon the major policies of the organization. He also considers the boards decisive, because despite their need to delegate minor decisions and technical research, they make major decisions, such as those of investment and financing, and selecting the people who will carry out the daily operations. And while one must realize the significance of publishers, editors and reporters in the day-to-day decision-making process, these decisions are subject to review and change at board level, including the replacement of the managers themselves. In the study of social characteristics of institutional elites by Dye and Pickering,[2] the authors noted that top decision-makers in politics, the federal government, the military and corporations tend to be male, older, well-educated, affluent and upper and upper-middle class. With very little variation, this definition can be extended to the Nigerian situation and includes its media organizations. But whereas this "elite" perspective is less familiar in mass communications than in sociology and political science, it does exist.

In Australia, the number of women teaching electronic media courses in universities is 34, or 21.5 per cent of media instructors. At the University of Nigeria, Nsukka, only one woman is a member of the faculty of the Mass Communication Department. At the University of Lagos, Akoka, there are no female lecturers. And at the Nigerian Institute of Journalism, Lagos, of the ten lecturers (and this includes full- and part-time) only three are women. Yet another aspect to reflect on is that of tokenism and superstar status. Thus one can be deceived by examples of those who "made it" and confuse this with progress. Such was the case of America's Barbara Walters, the highest-paid news personality, who in 1976 left NBC's *Today* show to join ABC with a five-year contract of $5 million. There is also the case of Jeane Kirkpatrick, the US Ambassador to the UN, and the first American woman in the post. But she too has her complaints. According to Kirkpatrick, she has encountered more "rank sexism" at the UN, especially among the Press, than in any other public arena she has known. Referring to descriptions of her in the press, Kirkpatrick said: "Nobody called (former UN ambassador) Pat Moynihan 'Schoolmarmish', Nobody called Henry Kissinger 'Schoolmarmish'. They called them 'professional' and they call me 'Schoolmarmish'. I take that to be 'rank sexism'." It is pertinent to note that both Moynihan and Kissinger previously taught at Harvard. Kirkpatrick taught at Georgetown. All three are professors.

And then there are the typical male jokes on women, such as that in one edition of *Time* magazine where "many of Thatcher's colleagues believe that the experiences of being Prime Minister will temper her iron lady toughness. They should know that iron, tempered, becomes steel." Thus, while criticism in the Third World has been especially harsh against Britain in its war with Argentina over the Falklands, it is possible to argue that given the feeling of superiority and contempt Third World man has for women, if Thatcher had been a Heath prosecuting the war, the tone of criticism would have been less accusatory and strident.

So whilst women as a group are weak, irrational, emotional, frivolous and not to be trusted in key positions of authority, once they are allowed as individuals to enter former male sacrosanct territory, they are described as "wicked, ruthless, frustrated and hard-hearted". Therefore, from Golda Meir to Indira Gandhi and Margaret Thatcher, these female power brokers have been dismissed as "wicked" despite their acknowledged competence as national leaders.

Meir's political successes were written off as emanating from her failure as a wife. Gandhi, who jailed foes and detractors as any man in her place would have done, and muzzled judges and imposed states of emergencies at will, was universally and happily relegated to political oblivion when the inept Janata government came to power. Her return has often been atributed to her cunning and ruthlessness, not competence. In their study of "Women in the Nigerian Media"[3] Opubor and Osanrumwense found that in general, women in the broadcast media tended to have slightly less formal education than other media women. However, broadcasters tended to have more years of experience, and therefore to have risen through the ranks. Their experience, not educational qualification, determined their salary, although female graduates appeared to have made faster progress.

In the print media, greater emphasis was placed on university or higher educational qualifications. But despite this women were poorly represented in top management positions and were in effect discriminated against. One reason for this is marriage and its attendant responsibilities for women. One senior editor at the *Daily Times* recently told this writer that no woman could ever successfully hold the job of Chief Sub-editor in the newsroom there. According to him the hours were long, inconvenient and sometimes irregular. Moreover, as any journalist knows, the newsroom is usually the most hectic and chaotic section in any media organization. For him, the *Daily Times* newsroom was too taxing for a woman, no matter how professionally sound. How then can a woman successfully juxtapose the demands of a career against the backdrop of her role as wife, mother and housekeeper!

Sociologist Ann Oakley[4] contends that neither education nor paid employment are in any sense avenues to liberation. Both school and job function in ways which systematically limit the options available to women. To her, "women's employment is a red-herring, half an equation, a piece of double-think and is not a path to paradise". She believes that equality has to be pursued in the area of domestic relations.

For Oakley, the home is the model of the larger society, and that is where the battle must first be fought and won.

But it is here that Western and Third World concepts of feminism diverge. Here in Nigeria, motherhood is a high status sought by all women. But while most women do feel oppressed by the demands of child-bearing and rearing, and by male subjugation and exploitation, they are always proud of being mothers. Ask any Nigerian woman whether she wants her husband to do the job of "nurturing and caring" for her children? She would be scandalized! So, until the Nigerian media woman successfully balances familial demands with the more challenging roles in her organization, she will perpetually be excluded from the decision-making process. Yet another constraint is that of the straitjacket created by programmes and pages of media material directed towards women, which the male-dominated media organizations feel should only be produced by women. Hence female journalists have for a long time fed female audiences with articles on love, gossip, fashion, decorating and food.

In two studies undertaken by the Department of Mass Communication, University of Lagos, on media content aimed directly at Nigerian women, it was found that very little attention was paid to education, women's equality movements, and development issues. Instead the emphasis was on the three Ps — pats, pants and panties.

Some media women have even campaigned for the retention of women's programmes with their narrow outlook; as in 1975 when three senior broadcasters actually protested the absence of the *Feminine Fancies* programme. Meanwhile, this attitude effectively excluded female journalists from handling desks such as politics, technology, and religion, which would have made them easier promotion material.

Media women also need to educate other women on issues affecting women. These involve topics such as government agricultural policies which are especially significant, since the majority of agricultural workers in Nigeria are subsistence farmers and women. Therefore, when media practitioners write or conduct programmes dealing with traditional female topics, it further widens the gap between men and women. If women are illiterate, or are informed only in these areas, they will be unable to participate in the development process in the same way as men, whatever their capacities.

This brings one next to the image of women in the media. Here we find them at times invisible, and then visible they are characterized as sex objects, as passive, frivolous people. They are also projected in relation to men; this implies that whether or not the relationship is positive, women have no sense of identity apart from men. Thus in Nigeria, women are newsworthy as the wives, mothers or daughters of men in the news. Other "newsworthy" women are either entertainment or fashionable figures.

Iweriebor, in her study of women in Nigerian films,[5] states that their image is characterized by an absence of direct power or initiative. She argues: "In her most active roles, she portrays the unpleasant and undesirable. Otherwise she is generally supportive and passive." Citing examples from films such as "Aiye" or "Jaiyesimi", Iweriebor says that in these films, women have been given active roles as protagonists in the eternal supernatural duel between good and evil, but notes, that where women have some of the most active roles in Nigerian films, they do so as personifications of the devil. And even when they achieve their most active societal roles within the supernatural realm, the heads of the realm remain male, whether as satan or "God". This imbalance is seen to be linked to the male concept of women by those who control Nigeria's film industry, especially in the fields of scriptwriting and production. It is also a reflection of the society's overall view of women; a society which also sees women as a rib taken from the side of man.

This brings into focus the question of strategies to be adopted for meaningful change. On 17 December 1979, the United Nations General Assembly adopted a resolution approving the Draft Convention on Discrimination Against Women. The articles cover measures to be taken by states to eliminate discrimination in various fields, including political and public life, the right to nationality, education, employment, health, marriage and family. The rights of rural women were also given special attention, as well as the elimination of stereotypes. But resolutions and legislation are only a means to an end. And whereas they represent one way of contributing to the advancement of women, they do not guarantee fundamental freedom on an equal basis with men. Women's demands for the governmental concession to legal rights, equal employment and full access to education, etc., are merely attempts to wrest some of the authority men have arrogated to themselves.

One finds then that although Sweden was "the first country in the world" to frame a government policy of achieving equality between the sexes by changing the role of men as well as women — a policy declared in a 1968 statement to the UN and implemented with laws and governmental initiatives — policy is one thing, practice is another. The fundamental attitudes held by people, especially Swedish men, did not change much. The country's efforts towards equality were also undone by its mass media which are male dominated. Therefore, if change is to be effected without recourse to revolution, traditional male attitudes must be ventilated, examined, and changed. Women must also identify their needs and discover ways to achieve their objectives. Self-reliance is the first step to freedom. These may seem like lofty platitudes which may well founder on the rocks of practicality.

Women in Electronic Media

Hauwa Sani Dangogo

Good morning ladies and gentlemen. It's my pleasure to present this paper which I have given the title "Women in the Electronic Media". I chose this topic to throw more light on the type of duties women are made to carry out in the media and how far they have gone in pushing their way through to the management cadre.

We broadcasters are often criticized for talking too much. Listen to women broadcasters on radio or watch them on television; the question often asked is: "Yes, she has a fine voice but why doesn't she do anything more than just announcing programmes off and on or reading somebody else's work?" Well, I have worked for my radio corporation for nearly a decade now, and I can assure you that WE women do more than just sign programmes on and off or talking from some other people's scripts.

Radio broadcasting began in Nigeria 50 years ago (1932) and it was only 25 years later, that is 1957, that we had our first television station in Ibadan. For a long time after the introduction of Radio and Television Broadcasting to our homes, most of our women were either announcers or presentation assistants. They of course worked as typists, cooks and clerks and so on. Our menfolk performed the more important tasks of putting together programmes and gathering the news. They also formulated policy guidelines for the effective running of media organizations. In fact it was only towards the beginning of the last decade that women were allowed to read the ten-minute news bulletin on a regular basis.

It was believed that they had short breath and shrill voices which made them unable to talk a long script live without pausing for deep breaths.

But like I said at the beginning of this talk, I have been in broadcasting for nearly a decade and I can confidently declare that things are gradually changing for the better. I am currently with the News and Current Affairs Department of my Corporation having spent some time with the programmes division.

You will notice that I didn't say that things have changed for the better. If I had said so some of you would wonder why there isn't a woman heading any broadcast medium in the country today. In the FRCN

Kaduna Zone, where I work, there isn't a single female controller, the lowest position in the managerial cadre of any broadcast organization in the country. I have to admit, though, that in other radio and television corporations, and indeed all the other zones of the Federal Radio Corporation of Nigeria, we have been heading some important departments. However, compared to men there are certainly very few; they could be counted on the fingers of one hand.

The truth is that the Nigerian society today is yet to discard the notion that women are unequal to men. As far as society is concerned that includes women. I might add, there are certain duties specifically designed for each sex and it would be wrong to preach or argue for an interchange of roles. Because all broadcast media are governed by social ideals, members of managements cannot but reflect the thinking of the generality of our country's population in the conduct of affairs.

There used to be a time in our newsroom when I was often asked to visit a very large hospital in Kaduna to take stock of the number of babies at the beginning of every new year. Yes, I am a woman, and I ought to be interested in children since I have some myself, but why couldn't a man have gone round to record these births? Isn't a man involved in child rearing and isn't it proper for him to take an interest just like a woman? I am sure that there are women in other media organizations that could recount similar situations. Virtually all women are restricted to women's columns in newspapers or to the women and children's units of all radio and television stations. Where women own and operate magazines, these magazines generally deal with topics that would engage the attention of women and men who care to know about them. What this means of course is that although a woman may be better able to handle a complicated press briefing by some important personality, a man who probably earns equal pay but with less experience and competence may be preferred in the belief that women are generally lazy or always nervous when it comes to taking quick decisions.

This, you might say, is an obvious case of sex discrimination, and who am I to blame you for arriving at that conclusion. There are a lot of academically qualified women who spend their time and energy producing and presenting programmes dedicated to children and women. A lot of the time, they have very little to tax their brains or to stimulate them to be more creative.

Just as in other professions, too few women in the broadcast media are prepared to prove society wrong. A great number of women would foolishly and publicly declare that some tasks are exclusively the preserve of men and so wouldn't attempt them. That is why there are too few women in all news and current affairs departments of radio and television organizations. Women seem to be preoccupied with the notion that only men are able to spare the time to keep abreast with international occurrences. Yes, what I am saying is that women are generally inhibited from utilizing themselves to the full, and they too contribute to their lack of fulfilment.

I have very little doubt that it is the same set of criteria that is applied to promoting and disciplining all members of staff in the media, be they male or female. We might then return to the question I asked earlier: why isn't a woman heading any broadcasting medium in Nigeria? My answer will be that it isn't because we are being discriminated against but that because of our late entry into the profession, women would for a little while trail behind in managerial capabilities.

I must point out here that we are cheated a lot of times. This normally happens if our bosses, usually male, take our refusal to conduct ourselves modestly rather than seriously. One can point to a lot of such incidents in other occupations and establishments in all parts of the country. It is also sad to note that some women would prefer to climb the ladder through coquettry rather than using their brains, simply because they are lazy. These shameless women make it difficult for honest dedicated women to be exonerated from the erroneous impressions of our menfolk that we are weak and incapable of fending for ourselves. You can now see how we contribute to our own subjugation or exploitation.

Before the return to civil rule, one always used to see society categorized in our news slots into low-, middle- and high-income groups.

But since the re-emergence of party politics, we now hear of the masses as opposed to the bourgeoisie, the "haves and the have-nots". One is either rich or poor. While I must accept that this is the most appropriate way of classifying our society, I find it difficult to identify with the view and see the subjugation or exploitation of women in this country and the world as a whole as the handiwork of people bent on fuelling class divisions.

Poverty cuts across the sexes, so also does the appetite for acquiring riches. A woman either owns large sums of money or great property or is married to a man who does. She either has no means of sustenance or is married to a man who has no hope of seeing tomorrow. She is also of a high or low class with sophisticated or cheap tastes. I say this to justify my claim that if women are exploited at any of our broadcasting houses, it is certainly not because they are considered to belong to the less privileged class. To my mind, our subjugation in the media is demonstrated by our having to be assigned to perform tasks thought to be exclusively for women rather than being allowed to follow the dictates of our consciences. We, depending on the areas we are assigned, work the same hours as our menfolk and get our entitlements if and when due.

Like I told you earlier on in my talk, women in the electronic media are now beginning to diversify their interests. They write their own scripts and put together their own programmes, programmes which are not necessarily concerned with purely feminine issues.

The reasons for this development are obvious. With educational facilities and opportunities being continuously extended to Nigerian women, we are becoming more aware of more avenues previously preserved for men. Economic realities today, make it incumbent on Nigerian men to disinherit completely their socially acquired rights as the breadwinners of their families, hence husbands of media women complain very little when their wives have to work at odd hours either as announcers or reporters and editors.

I have a strong belief that in the not too distant future, managerial positions in all broadcast media in the country will cease to be occupied by men alone. My optimism stems from the fact that apart from the educational strides made by women in all fields, they have also shown themselves well able to cope adequately with changes. No culture has ever remained static. Social values are constantly changing to reflect social, political, and economic realities of the moment. And as we women continue to witness great strides in all aspects of our social life, broadcasting houses will have no alternative but to recognize our new and improved positions and reflect these developments in their treatment of women staff members. Our aim therefore should be to ensure that this happens in the shortest possible time. We can only achieve this objective by not shying away from areas that would prove very taxing. We should not for example shy away from taking up positions in the news and current affairs divisions of media organizations nor refrain from embarking on projects which would involve a lot of travelling and reading.

Women in all professions should always have at the back of their minds that to feel less exploited or subjugated, we must free ourselves from thoughts that would run counter to our sole aim which is to live and work side by side with our men to produce a healthy and wholesome society for the future generation. Thank you.

Nigerian Women in Politics: Problems and Prospects

Bilkisu Yusuf

To define politics is an elusive undertaking. Politics, being the very essence of survival, is subject to varying definitions. No realm of human activity is completely devoid of it, whether religious, social or economic. Certain intellectuals have defined politics as "the pursuit of the good life", while others define it as "the systematic reflection of power", and finally "politics is who gets what, when and how". If these definitions of politics are acceptable in any discussion of politics, the mind of Nigerian women is at a discount today. One is bound to question the fact that they undertake any systematic reflection on power because the societal set-up is far from conducive. This is a lag between the ideal social and political institution that democracy desires them to participate in and install, and the institutions which the predominantly male world has fashioned and developed in the course of history with an almost complete neglect of the role of their womenfolk. There is a lag between the life as enjoined on them by the society and the life they have tried to devise for themselves.

Thus looking back at the political development of this country, an independent observer will hastily conclude that women have contributed next to nothing in this very important aspect of human life. As in many other fields, the role of women in politics is minimal. Reasons for this vary, depending on which parts of the country one is looking at. However, irrespective of the area, one thing is true: when it comes to assessing the role of Nigerian women in politics, they have been relegated to the background. The only time they seem to become important is during the campaigns preceding elections when their vote is a crucial factor in deciding "who gets what".

What are the factors responsible for this? Is it lack of enthusiasm on the part of the women? Are women contented with the minimal role carved out for them? We have all heard of the phrase "it's a man's world". This phrase sums up the sexist and discriminatory attitude of most men towards women who have taken up the challenge in their effort to prove that it is also a woman's world. Discrimination against women is a world-wide problem and the struggle to end this is akin to that embarked upon by other deprived minorities. The odd thing, though, is that women are not a minority as such; rather they have been made a minority group in a male-dominated world. Apart from this widespread discrimination against women, certain socio-cultural factors in the society have contributed to the lack of enthusiasm on the part of the women. To make a successful entry into politics and to continue to tread the path of success requires certain skills and resources that are not easily accessible to the average Nigerian woman, who apart from competing with male chauvinists also has to fight off the myth that women must be seen and not heard. To succeed in politics women must be seen and heard. To succeed in politics women must be seen and heard. The few women who insist on being seen and heard are seen as deviant cases because they become a departure from the norm of a society fashioned predominantly by overbearing men who believe they have all the answers to society's hitherto unsolved problems.

The initiation and subsequent emergence of Nigerian women into politics can be divided into three stages. The first era I will call the era of inactivity, the second stage is the awakening, and the third is the breakthrough. Each of these stages, as the name implies, is characterized by certain peculiarities that differentiate it from the others.

The Era of Inactivity
This stage covers the colonial period, the struggle for independence by the nationalists, and the granting of independence. it covers the longest period and it is the least eventful in terms of involvement and participation by women. The Nigerian political scene was at this time completely dominated by the men and their foremost preoccupation was achieving independence for the country. Before the granting of independence, the British and the nationalists agreed that there should be political parties to serve as an ideological base and a rallying point for the people. This era therefore witnessed the formation of the first political parties without any visible role played by women. Nigeria cannot boast of a female nationalist. The political parties that came into being — the NPC, NEPU, AG and the NCNC — all grew out of cultural organizations (an aspect where women are usually in the forefront) yet none of these parties had in its fold a woman of national repute. Contributions made by women like Mrs Margaret Ekpo and Mrs Funmilayo Kuti cannot be forgotten but they never occupied major political posts, neither could they have influenced politics especially to favour women. What they did was to open up the hitherto unvisited political wilderness to their fellow women by their illustrious examples.

The Awakening
This stage covers the 1959 election period, the granting of independence through the First Republic. I call this period the awakening because it marked the stirring of women from their seeming slumber in the political arena. One factor that paved the way for their awareness of the

role they could play in their country's political development was the enfranchisement of the women in the south. The fact that women in the north were denied the right to vote should have increased their political acumen and provided them with a rallying point. It is pathetic that nothing was done to organize and mobilize the northern women to challenge this injustice, a clear-cut example of the male discriminatory attitude towards women that has been intricately woven into the socio-political fabric of the society.

To vote is a civic responsibility, and to deny any group in the society the right to vote is tantamount to deprivation of fundamental human rights. This era witnessed, rather belatedly, the emergence of women activists like Hajiya Gambo Sawaba of the NEPU, Malama Noanusa of the Action Group and Mrs Funmilayo Kuti. Those women had one thing in common: their commitment to improving the lot of Nigerian women, and educating them on their rights when and where they are deprived of such rights. Foremost among their aims was to bring about an awareness among women as to their very significant function in society, and how much power they could wield by initiating and influencing policy if they were organized.

As is to be expected, these pioneers had a difficult time awaiting them, mostly from unsympathetic men who believed they were just troublemakers. Hence Hajya Gambo Sawaba was jailed 16 times and finally had to move from Kano to Zaria to continue her arduous task of emancipating the northern women.

The Breakthrough
The third stage began with the lifting of the ban on politics by the military after 13 years of political inactivity. This third stage, which continues to date, can rightfully be called a breakthrough because it has pushed more women into the political limelight than at any other time. A number of women have emerged, what they have achieved is still disappointingly minimal, especially after 13 years that could have been fully utilized for embarking on a strategy that would launch Nigerian women into the fast-moving wheel of political activity. One would have expected the women to use that lull for planning their tactics and gathering momentum for a return to politics. However the rapidity with which certain women, who are newcomers in the Nigerian political scene, were drawn into politics marks this period. Within this period they have made a political career for themselves. They are people like Miss Feliz Mortune who made history with the launching of the National Democratic Action Party (NDAP), Mrs Abiola Babatope and Mrs Justina Eze (both are members of the House of Representatives), Mrs Janet Akinrinade who contested for deputy governorship of Oyo State, and Hajiya Gambo Sawaba, the GNPP National Deputy President. Their enthusiasm is fed by their urge to lift as far as they can the veils that have been allowed to shroud the colossal contribution that womenfolk could

make towards the political development and progress of this country. They are committed to the task of shedding the shackles that have kept women away from active politics at all levels, from the local governments to the Senate and State House. Nigeria cannot boast of a single woman in the Senate, and even the State Houses of Assembly are dominated by the men. Nothing much has been done to improve the lot of women, contrary to the election promises, and this disparity between word and deed should be a warning signal for women to double their effort in pursuit of their interest. If women want things done their way, they must get up and do it themselves. I believe the poster that says it loud is: "Women's place is in the home and in the Senate".

Remedial Measures

Having said all this some may want to ask, why is there a need to organize? As the last registration-of-voters exercise revealed, a sizeable number of this country's population is composed of women. Will women continue to be simply nose-led by the men? Will they allow themselves to be useful only during election campaigns when their male counterparts are canvassing for the first female President in Africa? What has the present situation revealed? Have we achieved much in changing jobs, career options and lifestyles? We have to trade in the traditional stereotype idea of women as docile voters for that of new challenging possibilities in the decision-making bodies. We should stop dancing backwards by voting for anti-feminists to represent us at those important places. Dancing backwards is allowing only the men to legislate on our problems, problems that are close to our hearts. Women wear the shoes, so they know where it pinches. Therefore dancing forward is electing women to legislative houses and executive posts. There are no ready-made solutions to many problems, let alone problems as complicated as this. It requires tireless effort and a voice and vision for change on the part of the women.

In politics, we have watched as women have slowly been transformed into deprived voters, and most have, without realizing it, taken it upon themselves to defend this lop-sided system which highlights women as a peripheral majority in the society. We have to rcognize that individual efforts will not make it. Therefore we must organize.

Viewed differently, the problem of women is linked with that facing the oppressed masses in this country, but beyond the dialectics of class struggle, we ought to start searching for those flaws in our socio-political structure that constitute an impediment to female participation. We must put an end to political escapism on the part of the men. We must make the men recognize the plain fact that they have to accept female participation in politics just as they have to accept their participation in other fields of human endeavour. More women must be encouraged to contest elections at various levels, at local government level, the state level and national assemblies, most especially the Senate. We must

215

organize our penetration into these male strongholds where the major decisions are made, and seek the means of influencing those decisions. What we should strive to develop is a reciprocal process instead of the one-sided one that presently prevails.

Conclusion

If Miss Mortune's party succeeds in mobilizing women and meeting the criteria for registration, then the future will be more promising than ever for Nigerian women. What women should fight is political passivity and inactivity. Waiting for the men to work wonders will not do! Such a goal is only a minimum objective, as this alone will not rally women to our common purpose, or help cope with the complex problems which face women in their roles as trainers of every generation of mankind. Neither will it solve the problem of the growing realization among women that they are not playing the role in the political and economic development of their country that is commensurate with their great human qualities.

Nigerian women must meet the challenge of these dynamic factors. Only then can we attain the voluntary association of all democratic-minded people, whether male or female, for the progressive development of the country. Only then can we achieve the degree of collective security and fraternal cooperation upon which our future existence as a force will be built, and will be reckoned with in our country's political arena.

Some Notes on the Image of "Woman" in Some African Poems

John Haynes

> These groups, [Blacks, women, youth,
> those on welfare] are defined by their lack
> of responsibility, and hence, they are at
> "zero point" of the code where their
> speech does not count. Thus, they are in a
> truly radical position because they must
> oppose not simply an inequality in the
> code, but the code itself.
> (Poster: 176)

> I have grown old,
> I have lived much,
> Many things I understand
> But four riddles I cannot solve.
> Ha-ya-ya-ya.

> The sun's origin,
> The moon's nature,
> The minds of women,
> And why people have so many lice.
> Ha-ya-ya-ya.
>
> (Finnegan: 254)

> A Khymer girl was proverbially
> compared to a piece of cotton wool; a
> boy, to a diamond. If a diamond is
> dropped in the mud, it can be picked up
> and washed as clean as before, but cotton
> wool, once it has fallen into mud,
> can never be restored to its original purity, no
> matter how much cleaning is done.
> (Boua: 46)

My own interest in women is not pure. These notes are, I hope, sincere, and as far as reasoning goes, valid. But a conscious, argued, "wanted" position is never more than part of the story. Deeper than these the past does indeed weigh like a nightmare with its bedrock of slogans, prejudices, and clichés. Poetry is usually thought of as a direct opposite to cliché. But really the two uses of language are intimately related. Poetry is based on, and in, cliché. It represents the relation of the poet to the clichés of his contemporary language; and the clichés in turn are the linguistic encoding of cultural and other prejudices — which we sometimes call "norms". Poetry, or poetic sayings, may be original, but when we notice this what we are noticing is how, and how far, they have strayed from the dully predictable — on which the semantics of a language relies.

One reason for studying the poetic use of language, whether in "literature" or in ordinary conversations, idioms, proverbs and so on, is that it throws light on prejudices. And in the end all knowledge is a matter of becoming slightly more aware of our prejudgements. In what follows, I shall be talking mainly about poetry in the sense of composed literary works of art, but in doing this I do not mean to get involved in narrowly literary critical questions. The works of poets are of fairly wide interest because in them, people of sensitivity and sympathy, and masters of language, we can get an idea of which clichés socially and linguistically self-conscious people take as a starting point for social questioning. Although, of course, women are a common subject for poems, as we shall see, on the whole they are looked at through very deep-seated presuppositions. And these presuppositions are not normally questioned. The fact that even the most imaginative among us take the stereotypes of "man" and "woman" for granted is itself significant. Generally speaking, in the oral tradition, the poet aims to highlight cultural norms with the intention of reinforcing them, and so of strengthening what are felt to be the bonds of meaning and value that hold the community together. Much poetry in the written tradition does this too. But some poetry has the more subversive aim of highlighting generally accepted notions in order to question them. For fairly clear historical reasons the poetry written in the former colonial languages by Africans has challenged prejudices to be found in the former colonialists' use of their language in relation to the colonized. This movement is reflected in our everyday speech, so that words like "native", "primitive", "tribe", "uncivilized" are used now, at least by people who are sensitive to the past, in a much more careful and defined way than was once so. But in modern African poetry, the questioning of clichés tends to be limited to those associated with colonialism; while on the whole the poets confirm — or reconfirm — traditional clichés, including those about women, though women are treated in a variety of ways.

For example, the Amharic poem "Love Song" takes a "romantic" view. The poet praises his beloved in the following way:

> You mistress of my body:
> More precious to me than my hand or my
> foot.
> Like the fruit of the valley, the water of
> paradise.

(Soyinka: Ed.)

More precious than his hand or foot? Does he really mean it? Nevertheless it seems, on the surface at least, as if the poet is elevating the woman, and he assumes that she has a good deal of personal liberty and power. After all, he is abasing himself and begging, and comparing her to "the water of paradise". Indeed, she seems to have some actual power over him.

> With muscular thigh she stepped on my
> heart.
> Her eternal heel trod me down
> and his admiration is quasi-religious.
> Saviour's image!
> And Jerusalem herself, sacred city,
> Shouts "Holy, holy!"

This is when she reveals her breast, or perhaps when he thinks of the prospect. But such praise, such avowals, and such "elevation" are only conventional. In this kind of love poetry, the emotional charge is lit by the fact that the woman is married (so he is safe), and of a higher social status than the poet. Her unattainableness is thus social and economic, as no doubt are her soft skin and enchancing clothes. Her rich beauty is a symbol of a style of life, a kind of status symbol, one more luxurious acquisition, even though her position is in a sense privileged. Whatever apparent power she has derives from her husband, and of course the source of the lover's lust comes from that; it is the lust of the thief, an acquisitive emotion, always presupposed in an ideology of possession. She is an idol rather than a person. The poet likens her breasts to pure gold, which reminds us more of a statue, than to a precious substance. The flattery and the masochism are, of course, of doubtful sincerity. The penniless poet has an ulterior motive, and may indeed succeed given that the lady may well be bored stiff with being beautiful and having nothing else to do. She exists in an enclave, away from the realities of life, from the men's world, and she is turned to as a kind of respite from and consolation for the economic and status struggle outside.

Nevertheless many African women would envy her and indeed mistake her position, as they may mistake that of many European women, for sexual liberation. Her situation is very much preferable to that of the butt of Na Mangi's "Song of the Slattern". The Amharic Lady is worshipped, the Hausa slattern reviled as even worse than an ugly and old wife.

> Her first vice is to use her right hand when
> she blows her nose;
> You'll eat her hair inside her *tuwo*.
> She scratches her head and crotch at once.
> Snot swings from her nostril. Her eyes are bleared.
> Her mouth's enlarged with sores.
> Look at her rat-like hair. She pisses the bed.
>
> (Na Mangi)

The Amharic lady is too good to be true, the Hausa slattern too bad. In both poems, the poet uses his licence to exaggerate. And each woman is confined in her role, the Amharic lady to beautiful irrelevance to real life, the slattern to domestic drudgery. The Hausa poet, Na Mangi, very clearly reinforces male requirements and this kind of passage has an obvious role in the social control of women, to buttress which the religious sanction is brought in:

> May Allah make our women clean
> and not punish us with slatterns

and their sensibilities on this subject are, it seems, taken account of in the afterlife:

> To spare the shame of husbands,
> no slattern lives in Paradise.

Hiskett points out that this cautionary writing is very common in Hausa poetry. The poet likes to have an excuse to exploit it. So, even in a poem about poverty, Darho takes disproportionate amounts of time delineating the way in which the poor man's daughter gets abused.

> However fine his daughter looks
> it's said she's short and ugly,
> her navel sticks out, her face is fat,
> she's as bald as *tumfafia*,
> bandy-legged, sunken eye,
> mouth big as a tree,
> sores on her buttocks, and she stinks
> like *rajiya* fish.
>
> (Darho)

Although the poet is sympathetic in seeing this abuse as coming from prejudice against poverty, he nevertheless makes the most of it artistically. And in fact the poem is not so very distant in attitude from the Amharic since in the end Darho's solution to the poor man's problems is that he should work harder at trading, travel more, and get rich! Then, we presume, his daughter will get more flattering comments passed about her. As with the Amharic poem, the daughter here and the slattern in Na Mangi's song, are generic. The sexual prejudice comes in with the freedom the poet assumes for himself to issue this kind of holier-than-thou criticism, and it is made in a brutal language in which graphic mention is made of the body such as to cause male listeners to turn up their noses in a specifically sexual disgust.

In "Song of Lawino" Okot p'Bitek makes use of a similar vein of abuse when he makes his chief character, the traditional Acoli wife (Lawino), attack the appearance of her husband's girlfriend, Clementine. Lawino's scorn concentrates on Clementine's inept use of Western-style cosmetics, her use of lipstick, powder, hair-straightening and her slimming:

> Her lips are red-hot
> Like glowing charcoal,
> She resembles the wild cat
> That has dipped its mouth in blood,
> Her mouth is like raw yaws,
> It looks like an open ulcer,
> Like the mouth of a fiend!

> (Okot)

And so on. This passage always appeals very much to men of a traditionalist persuasion. And of course Okot biases it heavily. He would have had more trouble had Tina been the more unusual African woman who makes very skilful use of make-up. On the other hand, part of Okot's attempt is to represent an element of "womanish" jealousy in Lawino.

On the surface it may seem that Lawino herself has gained a certain liberty in that she heaps a great deal of abuse, not just on "the other woman" but on a man, Okot, her husband. But she feels free to do this only because Okot has offended against traditional ways, especially ways of behaving towards members of the family. Okot expresses the view that black people are primitive and traditional cooking methods are dirty, and so on. She can therefore count on overwhelming support from all members of the community. In the end she is speaking in the name of the Acoli family. She accepts the double standard quite as a matter of fact (Okot: 69), and her rock-bottom assumption about life is

> If you are not married you are nothing.

But Okot never looks at the traditional marriage itself. He never questions the domestic role which he makes Lawino defend so strongly. He does not allow, it seems, that the use of modern make-up and Western fashions are in some ways symbolic of a relative emancipation, that the "free" women might have gained in liberty.

In his poem about a prostitute, "Song of Malaya" we get a corresponding sexual onesidedness. It is the prostitute seen from a male viewpoint. Everything is focussed on her sexually defined occupation, and she is represented as enjoying her work and as taking a defiant pride in it. She gains a cynical satisfaction in mocking her clients and accusers (often one and the same person). There is one reference to her being arrested, but no serious treatment of police harrassment and extortion, health risks to herself, bedroom humiliations, nor, above all, to insecurity as she grows older.

Lenin once raised the question as to whether prostitutes might be thought of as a revolutionary group, and it seems true to say that they do raise questions about the Western bourgeois family. But Okot never gets anywhere near this kind of thoughtfulness. He accepts the contrastive stereotypes of "wife" and "prostitute", and he treats the prostitute within the typical framework as the practitioner of seduction and "nine wiles", as is shown in the way she adjusts her style of smile to different clients.

> The hot devil smile
> For the priests and their kind,
> The cool confident smile
> For the faint-hearted and the unsure,
> The innocent infant smile
> For the fatherly and the senile

And so on for another page. Again the point here is that the woman is shown as having no other interests than her profession, which is full-time sex. But when we ask ourselves what this woman does when she is not working, we find our minds quite empty; we have no idea.

The image of the African woman has often been used to symbolize African cultures and human blackness. In Senghor's well known poem, "Naked Woman, Black Woman", the woman is intended to exemplify the qualities of black culture looked at from the conservative philosophical position of negritude. Negritude may have had some polemic value once but in the end its ideas are very suspect since they depict an African personality which is strong on the physical and the intuitive and emotional, but weak on reason. Such ideas derive from French philosophy as these came into European romanticism, a movement which in poetry aimed to emphasize the emotional aspects of man in reaction against the then still developing industrialized state (which African writers tend to identify with Western culture as a whole). The romantic poets took a special interest in the "primitive", in allegedly intuitive people such as children, madmen, and of course women. Still Senghor, who married a white and follows neo-colonial policies, can sing out loudly in praise of the physical African woman.

> Naked women, black woman,
> Clothed with your colour which is life,
> with your form which is beauty!
> In your shadows I have grown up; the
> gentleness of your hands was laid over
> my eyes;
> And now, high up on the sun-baked pass,
> at the heart of summer,
> at the heart of noon, I come upon you,
> my Promised Land,
> And your beauty strikes me to the heart
> like the flash of an eagle.

(as quoted by Peters)

In many ways this resembles the Amharic praise song. The woman herself is not described. We are told she is naked and beautiful but not how, whether slim or monumental. What kind of profile does she have? What shape are her breasts? It is all abstract and rhetorical, and a bit corny ("Your beauty strikes me to the heart"). She is another generalized tender of men with her hands, an aesthetic object, a quasi-religious symbol ("my promised land"). It is "woman" as the unreflecting male sees her, restricted to the service functions of mother and lover. Again, as with Okot's prostitute, we may ask what she does in her "spare" time — play ludo? gossip? go mad with boredom? Senghor, like so many poets, has not seen his own assumptions. More important in one sense, he has not thought through the implications of taking the second-class citizen as the epitome of blackness and black culture. His explanation makes things worse.

> Because the woman is "permanent" in the family and life-giver (*donneuse de vie*) she has been elevated as source of the life-force (*source de force vitale*) and guardian of the home, that is, the repository of the past and guarantor of the clan's future.

(Peters: 81)

So much bad second-hand philosophy and prejudice in one elegant sentence. Senghor the "socialist" sees this role of women as, it seems, biological and primordially unaffected by history and social relations. And there is nothing particularly African in those assumptions.

We find very similar prejudices in the very different poetry of Dennis Brutus. He talks of his dispossessed country, South Africa, like this:

Dear my land, open for my possessing,
ravaged and dumbly submissive to our
will, in curves and uplands my sensual
delight mounts, and mixed with fury is
amassing torrents tumescent with love and pain

(Brutus: 2)

Brutus arouses controversy as a poet because he takes a Christian liberal humanist stance, and his critics find that weak-kneed. His message is that through all the racism and torture in his country someone must retain some last grains of humanity, and this responsibility falls to the victims, the blacks, since there is no hope of the white oppressors retaining their humanity. Whatever we may think about this position it is deeply felt; yet the sexual imagery seems to belie the philosophy of gentleness. The land he sees as a woman is "dumbly submissive to our will", and he "mounts" her "with fury". Of course Brutus is not primarily concerned with the status of women here, and this is an early poem. In "Letters of Martha" he talks to Martha about political and ethical problems relating to his experience in prison, and here makes no sexist concessions to her being a woman. Yet the poem from which I have quoted, like the Senghor poem, is representative of a trend in African poetry which sees liberation in exclusively male terms.

The gist of these comments is clear enough. I should not want to be too categorical on the evidence of just these few poems, but it seems that generally African poets are less than radical in their views of women. They tend to leave the clichés unquestioned, and since their work is to question, or at least to highlight, clichés, this is a significant fact. The point as some relevance for the teacher of poetry, and the teacher of other topics through poems and songs. But the prejudices of African poets — if I am right — have a wider symptomatic significance. They show us how linguistically deep-seated these conceptions are, and they remind us of the role of such uses of language at a very early stage of our lives, and in the formation of our models of social and personal relations. And this comes down to the power relations within the family, and the implicit acceptance of attitudes there which have wider social significance, not least the idea that one person "belongs to" another, or that muscular might is right.

I am not claiming that a change in the metaphors of poets is going to help the women's cause very much. Nevertheless any speaking out of things which have hitherto been kept silent represents progress. Whether in poetry or in other kinds of utterance, to formulate something is to render it public, and hence socially real. I conclude with one example from poetry. This is a line from the Marxist poet and critic Omolara Ogundipe-Leslie. I have not been able to get the text of the poem and am quoting from my memory of a reading given by the poet in Ibadan two years ago. As I recall it was an account of the poet's daughter describing a dream. The girl had been dreaming about God, and in the poem she was answering the question, What was God doing? The reply is revealing:

> He was watching ballerinas.

So often sexism is defended in the name of religion and the family, but here is God (the father) as the primordial "dirty old man" and his heavenly angels are bare-legged dancing girls. No doubt such an image will offend the traditional — as we must risk. But it gets a bit near to the bottom of things, it seems to me.

Rapporteur's Report:

F.J.A. Kamara

Two positions were taken in the session. The first is that all women are oppressed. The second is that the majority of women are oppressed, but some women are members of the oppressing class. It was noted that the fact that middle-class women fight for social and economic equality along with men will *not* ensure equality for all women. The system has to be restrictured to ensure equality for all. Contrary to this view, a speaker warned the participants that they should not be deluded and confused by Marxist analysis of female oppression. However, several participants challenged this anti-Marxist advice. Instead women were advised not to vote for anti-feminist men to represent them politically, and they were encouraged to stand for election.

It was observed that although the Nigerian Constitution does not discriminate against women, civil service regulations do. Contributions relating to women in the media revealed that in Sweden the male-dominated media acted as a barrier in the fight for equality between men and women. In Nigeria, a similar accusation could be made. As a result, a recommendation was made that women should support their own world news agency to gather news and make their views known. In addition, Nigerian women should start media which are under their own control.

PART VII
What is to be done?

Organizing for the Future

Renée Pittin

"Woman was the first human being that tasted bondage, woman was a slave before the slave existed."
(A. Bebel, *Woman in the Past, Present and Future*, 1895, p.7, cited in J. Mitchell, p.80)

The origin of women's oppression is shrouded in the past. We shall not dwell on the various theories which have been formulated to explain the origin or the continuation of the oppression of women, except to note that it would seem that to comprehend adequately the nature of women's oppression, one must examine both class relations and sexual asymmetry; to reduce women's oppression to one or the other produces an all-too-limited and incomplete view which does an injustice to the complexity of this form of injustice. Given the universality of women's subordination, and its longevity, it would seem almost inevitable. Yet we know that nothing is immutable, and that "no condition is permanent". Through collective action, understanding, and strength, we can prevail against the deeply-rooted, millennia-old, and systematic oppression which all women have endured.

Organizing for Understanding

Women must meet, and speak with (not to, or at) each other. Women's oppression takes many forms, and we agree, I expect, that women are aware of at least some aspects of their oppression, although it is also true that "the most economically and socially underprivileged woman may be bound much tighter to her condition by a consensus which passes if off as 'natural' " (J. Mitchell, 1971, p.22).

In China, as Mao Tse-tung's army liberated areas of the country in the 1940s, cadres moved in to speak with women. Initially fearful and reluctant to speak, the women were urged by the cadres to meet together in small groups, and to tell the story of their lives. Encouraged to recall the pain, horrors, and indignities of their condition, women wept, and

231

became enraged, while other women sat listening, often with tears running down their cheeks, as they empathized with their fellow-women in the recognition of their common oppression. Through this technique, "speaking bitterness", Chinese women were transformed — person by person, group by group, experience by experience — from victims to activists, revolutionizing their own roles.

The value, the importance, of such a technique, is unquestionable. One can begin to deal with oppression by capturing the *experience* of oppression. Personal repression and dilemmas, experienced in the isolation of the family or marital home, turn out to be not "personal" at all, but rather are manifestations of the oppression experienced by all women. Individual experience leads to emerging group consciousness; from examination of the specificities of one's own and others' subordination, emerges understanding of the wider condition of oppression. Together, women may "speak the unspoken", pool their experiences and their knowledge, and understand with greater compassion and wisdom, each other's and the common condition.

There is room here too for the academics, provided we recognize that we have no monopoly on truth. We women have the knowledge of our own experience of oppression, gained within a particular class position and a specific social context. And we also have access to additional sources of knowledge, which can widen our perspectives, sharpen our perceptions, and permit us to construct (often times conflicting) models and theories concerning the nature of the oppression we suffer, for, ultimately, political relations cannot be defined solely in terms of the personal. In discussions with other women we can share our experiences, and the fruits of our knowledge and training. And, if there is proper communication, other women will share their experiences and perceptions with us. Communication should, must, operate in both directions; there must be dialogue. We can learn from each other — if we will but listen.

The prime arenas where such dialogue (polylogue?) could occur are the Women's Centres such as those established in Kano and proposed for Kaduna State. What lively discussion such topics could provide, while, say, women learn and practise new crafts! But *anywhere* that women meet, and talk, is an appropriate venue.

One major positive consequence of the quest for understanding and the sharing of experience, is the quantum leap in women's feelings of self-esteem. Sexual asymmetry is a feature of all societies: men, their activities, and their roles are treated as more important, more valuable, and more authoritative, than those of women. And to the extent that men remain the locus of social value, women are equally devalued. Maduewesi (1980, p.880) states that the source of the greatest damage to women's self-esteem is through "socially mediated experience using language", from the "millions of words (mothers expend) teaching their daughters their expected social roles", to the "loaded comments . . .

overheard by female children" such as "He has no child, only daughters . . ." and the contemptuous "She's only a woman, what do you expect . . ." This latter comment is an example of the most pernicious, pervasive, and systematic source of social devaluation of women: sex-role stereotyping.

From her earliest youth, a girl is subjected to a barrage of images, myths, and stereotypes portraying her as physically, mentally, and spiritually weak, limited in options and forced to seek a man to look after her. ABU students, writing of men's and women's roles, described men as "naturally endowed with better skills than (women)", and saw women as "biologically inferior to men in strength and courage", needing male protection, "less intelligent and less competent" than men, "impatient, uncontrolled", and "too talkative to be entrusted with secrets".

Stereotyping has been described as "an exaggerated belief associated with a category . . . to justify (rationalise) our conduct in relation to that category" (G.W. Allport, *The Nature of Prejudice,* cited in M.C. King, 1973, p.12). Thus, stereotyping has a political basis, and a political purpose, for it is designed to render less powerful, or powerless, the category in question. Paulo Freire was well aware of the effectiveness of stereotyping; he wrote that a subject people may be kept passive by

> . . . depositing myths indispensible to the status quo: for example . . . the myth of the industriousness of the oppressors, . . . as well as the myth of the natural inferiority of the (oppressed) and the superiority of the oppressor.

> (1970, pp.135-6).

Characteristics associated with sex-role stereotyping are

> . . . based on the needs and values of the dominant group and are dictated by what its members cherish in themselves and find convenient in subordinates: aggression, intelligence, force, and efficacy in the male: passivity, ignorance, docility, "virtue" and ineffectuality in the female.

> (K. Millet, 1972, p.26)

These "attributes" of women, created and reinforced by socialization, are uncannily echoed in another ABU student's essay:

> . . . girls are trained from the age of three or four to be ready for the kitchen, child-rearing, and to be obedient, careful, good and passive, for they follow in their mothers' footsteps.

It creates, as intended, a class of persons meant to serve, responsible to everybody except themselves. Women have been so thoroughly defined and devalued by stereotypes that they have been largely dispossessed of their self-hood, and self-assurance, and it is only through the recognition of the political nature of their condition and the falseness of the basic premises, that they can reaffirm their own, and their fellow-women's, worth. In China, where the government was positively and actively geared to promoting the full participation of women, a media barrage was used to aid women "to develop confidence, courage, self-respect, initiative, the attitude of overcoming all difficulties . . ." (C.B. Cohen, 1970, p.401). In Nigeria, women must work together to recognize the myths supporting their oppression, and fight together against that oppression; this government will not do it for them, for it maintains a vested interest in supporting the status quo.

Individual solutions are not the answer. Resort to manipulation, appeals to the benevolence of men, or to their guilt, simply maintain and reinforce the present system of oppression. And even if, in marriage or at work, your husband/boss/colleague is the "exception to the rule", it is imperative to remember that "where a system of oppression has become institutionalized, it is unnecessary for individuals to be oppressive" (F. Kennedy, 1970, p.439).

It is "the right of the oppressed to organize around their oppression *as they see and define it*" (S. Firestone, 1971, p.681) (emphasis in text).

According to Emma Goldman:

> History tells us that every oppressed class gained true liberation from its masters through its own efforts. It is necessary that woman . . . realize that her freedom will reach as far as her power to achieve her freedom reaches.
>
> ("Woman's Suffrage" in *Anarchism and Other Essays,* NY, 1910, cited in S. Rowbotham, 1972, p.78)

The task is daunting. We can take heart, perhaps, in Rowbotham's stern statement that:

> . . . the right to make your own mistakes . . . is an essential, if costly, part of the process of the emergence of the oppressed.
>
> (1972, p.168)

Nothing ventured, nothing gained. We can but try.

Organizing for Action: Rural Development

No one can fault the credentials of Nigerian women for organizing, and acting, when they see their interests as threatened: the actions of Yoruba market women, for example, and the conduct of the 1929 Women's War, attest to women's determination and solidarity. The structures and organizational framework still exist, and some women continue to "organize around their oppression as they see and define it".

We are well aware of the constraints acting against opportunities for women in the rural areas, including women's own multiple and time-consuming roles. Statistics and data-collection techniques themselves militate against an accurate appraisal of women's economic roles and needs. Research that measures women's work in "man-days", values women's agricultural labour as 75% of that of men, and labels a woman who toils in the fields equally with her husband, a "farmer's wife", is obviously riding rough-shod over the real extent and value of women's work.[1] The male-dominated banks, cooperatives, and government organizations are usually ignorant of or uninterested in the needs of women, nor do women necessarily have the necessary contacts, or lines of communication, to make their wishes known — if, in fact, they even recognize their right to participate in the high-powered development projects which are dropping upon men like manna from heaven.

Okonjo (1980, pp.1027-8) describes how male extension workers in Bendel State seek out male farmers to pass on new techniques, and new agricultural inputs such as improved seeds and fertilizers. Women were believed to be afraid of agricultural machinery, and unable to follow instructions. The actual situation was that they lacked capital and access to credit for even simple, low-cost machinery, and, yes, they didn't know how to run a tractor! Women have become more marginalized, and more invisible, as development passes them by.

Where women have organized, the process, and the results, bode well for the future. One such project is that initiated by women in the Isoya Rural Development Project area of Oyo State. The Isoya Rural Development Project, a pilot scheme introduced in 1969 by the University of Ife, concentrated its efforts in agriculture, and particularly upon the introduction of a new variety of yellow maize, which was perceived and marketed as a cash crop, controlled (as other cash crops) by men, and sold by men's cooperatives. The local white maize, a food crop, had been in the hands of women, who thereby benefited from the sale of the surplus. Within two years, land devoted to white maize, the women's crop, had been given over to yellow maize and, as men gained, women lost an important source of income, and were, in some cases, reduced to seeking capital from their husbands, a state of affairs women considered both "degrading and not very profitable" (Ladipo, 1981, p.124). While the Ife workers had concentrated on enhancing the men's agricultural productivity, they provided women with a home economics programme focussing on nutrition. The women sought out the project staff, and explained that they:

> . . . appreciated the goodwill of the staff . . (but that) they saw the maize programme as evidence of concrete achievement, while the home economics programme . . . (showed) concern for their welfare. They saw their basic

problem as one of money, and noted that the project had brought progress, literally "marching forward" to the men while they as wives had been "pulled backwards".

(Ibid.)

The women were fortunate in having the assistance of extension workers, including women,[2] who sympathized with their plight, and assisted them in organizing their own cooperatives.

The reactions of the men were interesting. Ladipo believes that men's experience of previous women's groups paved the way for their acceptance of the cooperatives, for other associations were either "non-economic, . . (posing) no threats to male interests" or "sub-units of male-dominated systems" or so distant that the men did not recognize their economic nature and independent orientation (p.131). The men were described as 'happy that something progressive might also reach their wives" (ibid), but that didn't stop them from giving the women of one group "land from which the top soil had been scraped for road construction" (p.128). Men also resented women's ownership of machinery which they felt should rightfully be theirs. Ladipo notes that "both the staff and the members learned that the men's approval was conditional and a continuing process" (p.131). The groups managed to get by, by adopting a low profile.

The most promising aspect of the Isoya women's cooperative programme, however, was the cohesion, trust, and increased self-esteem which built up in the smaller of the two cooperative groups.

> In addition to fostering collective confidence, group cohesion seems to have built up personal confidence . . . the group asked that the project organize literacy and numeracy lessons in the village . . . Optimism and cooperation pervaded the classes . . . participants who were slow to learn were encouraged . . . the prospect of helping the group seemed to be the main factor motivating class efforts.

(p.132)

From these beginnings, the women increased, together, their knowledge, abilities, confidence, and control over themselves and their future.

Counterpoint to the Isoya Rural Development Project is Project Answer, designed by Dr Felicia Ekejiuba of the University of Nigeria, Nsukka. Whereas the creation of the Isoya women's cooperatives was at the request of the women, who joined together for the cooperative scheme, Project Answer is a scheme devised in part to bring socio-economic opportunities to women in Anambra State, by capitalizing upon the networks and organizations available through existing women's groups and associations. According to Dr Ekejiuba, the project design and purpose were "developed on the basis of a dialogue with those left behind in the rural community — women of all ages, young and old men —

in an attempt to monitor and incorporate their aspirational experiences, values, and their definition of underdevelopment" (1980, p.388). She sees the initial emphasis to be "on mobilizing women, women's associations, and rural families for production, (but) the ultimate focus is on individual initiative, and membership in the production-oriented cooperative" (ibid).

The cooperative, based on the production of poultry, vegetables, rabbits and goats, is one of three components which make up Project Answer, the other two being the promotion of education and the carrying out of research. Education is intended to include, among other things, basic literacy and numeracy, nutrition, family planning, and economic organization and management, with emphasis on small-scale business. The research is meant to document "the experiences, processes and problems of transforming rural familes" (p.375) as well as the value of voluntary associations as adaptive mechanisms for non-formal education and rural transformation. A focus of the programme is the promotion of increased nutrition among women and children, through foodstuffs which will be relatively inexpensive, and controlled by women.

Project Answer had not yet taken off by late 1980; it may have done so now. It is an expensive, and extensive, project. It will be extremely interesting to learn of the effects of the project on the participants and, more interesting still, the influence of the participants on the running of the project, the effects within the community, and the wider ramifications and effects of this woman-oriented project in general.

Before leaving the issue of rural development, one more constraint militating against women's effective participation should be mentioned: this is the differential access of men and women to the ownership of land. Farming on one's husband's/father's/brother's land is all very well, but it is all too common for women to be given the poorest, most marginal (commensurate with their status?) land, while the men's and "family" plots occupy the most fertile areas. And, given women's lack of control over land allocation, and their automatic loss of (husband's) land in the event of divorce, their situation is one of considerable insecurity, rife with the likelihood of exploitation.

The alienation, or the possibility of alienation, of women from the land is becoming more, rather than less, of a problem. Raza and Famoriyo, for example, have pointed out that the current Land Use Decree "makes no mention of women in (relation) to access to rights in land" (1980, p.944), and that this oversight[?]/irregularity may be utilized to separate women from the land. A specific, considered, and organized effort which would effectively and legally divest women of landed property is the *Customary Law Manual* of Anambra and Imo States, published in 1977. The manual is said to be based on the work of 39 law panels, with a total membership of 463 persons; *two* of these were women! And this in an area with a far higher than average number of educated and professional, and politically aware, women.

The effect of the land provisions in the Manual, if followed, would be to prohibit *all* women in certain areas of Anambra and Imo States from owning land, to prohibit *married* women in other areas from owning land, and to prohibit all married women from divesting themselves of any land or landed property without their husbands' consent. According to Euna Amechi, herself a lawyer based in Enugu, the provisions run counter to actual Igbo practice, which the manual is supposed to be codifying. While traditionally, in some areas, women did not have the right to *inherit* land, they have full capacity to otherwise acquire and dispose of their property without restraint. An organized and strong response can be the only effective reply to this kind of wholesale removal of women's rights.

These problems represnt an infinitesimal proportion of the ways in which women may be discriminated against, and in which they may be oppressed. The Isoya case is particularly interesting, inasmuch as we can see, in microcosm, the kinds of decisions in development planning which tend to marginalize women all over the world; we can follow the women's changing fortunes, and we are privy to thir solutions, from the stop-gap and unwanted recourse to financial assistance from their husbands, to the joint presentation of their difficulties and their perceived needs to the Project staff. The Project staff, to their great credit, were able to recognize and accept their errors, and learn from the experience. They then proceeded, *with the women,* to design a programme which made use of staff expertise, increased the women's own expertise and abilities, and directly catered to what the women saw as their priorities. Not a very radical solution, maybe. Or maybe it is, for the women acted on their oppression as they saw it, and, in the continuing process, gained the confidence necessary to seek additional knowledge and opportunities, and the consciousness to expand their horizons further.

Nigerian women have a history of organizing against their oppression, and more and more women are becoming aware of the extent and the depth of their subordination. The personal response to the myriad manifestations of women's oppression must be discarded altogether; it was never satisfactory. To work effectively, we must work together. Beliefs and practices which contribute to women's oppression must be identified, exposed, and, ultimately, eradicated. We must meet, speak out, organize, and act, so that all Nigerians, women and men, may choose their own paths to their own destiny, as equal citizens with equal opportunities in an equitable and just society.

Notes

1. The problems surrounding the data concerning women's work in Nigeria are dealt with in Pittin (forthcoming). It should, at this point, go without saying that far more research is needed to understand the situation regarding labour allocation, and the actual participation of women in production and reproduction. A brief list of relevant considerations and possible research priorities is included in Pala, 1976, pp.28-35.

2. Okonjo (1980, p.1029), and Igben (1980, p.960), are among the relatively few Nigeriens who have pleaded for the hiring of more female extension workers, to relate more effectively with women farmers. The Nigerien government agency, Animation Feminine, not only depends primarily on women extension agents, but also trains local peasant women to become animators, as a matter of policy (N. Nelson, p.54).

References

Amechi, E.E.A.   1979   "The Legal Status of Nigerian Women, with Special Reference to Marriage", Ph.D. Dissertation, Faculty of Laws, SOAS, University of London.

Cohen, C.B.   1970   "Experiment in Freedom: Women of China", in R. Morgan (ed), *Sisterhood is Powerful,* Vintage Books, NY, pp.385-417.

Ekejiuba, F.I.   1980   "Project Answer: an Organizational Framework for Integrated Rural Development", in F.I.A. Omu, P.K. Makinwa, & A.O. Ozo (eds.), *Proceedings of the National Conference on Integrated Rural Development and Women in Development,* Vol.I, University of Benin, Benin City, pp.366-392.

Firestone, S.   1971   "On American Feminism" in V. Gornick & B.K. Moran (eds.), *Woman in Sexist Society,* New American Library, NY, pp.665-686.

Freire, P.   1970   *Pedagogy of the Oppressed,* The Seabury Press, NY.

Igben, M.S.   1980   "Socioeconomic Activities of Women in some Selected Nigerian Rural Communities: Implications for Integrated Rural Development in Nigeria", in F.I.A. Omu et al, *Proceedings . . .,* Vol.II, pp.950-962.

Kaduna State   1981   "Report of the Committee on Kaduna State Women's of Nigeria   Programme" (mimeo).

Kennedy, F.   1970   "Institutionalized Oppression vs. the Female", in R. Morgan (ed.), *Sisterhood is Powerful,* Vintage Books, NY, pp.438-446.

King M.C.   1973   "The Politics of Sexual Stereotypes", *The Black Scholar,* Vol.4, Nos. 6 & 7, pp.12-23.

Ladipo, P.   1981   "Developing Women's Co-operatives: an Experiment in Rural Nigeria", in N. Nelson (ed.), *African Women in the Development Process,* Frank Cass & Co., Ltd., London, pp.123-136.

Maduewesi, E.   1980   "Self-esteem: a Psychological Dimension of Female Socialization", in F.I.A. Omu et al, *Proceedings . . .,* Vol.II, pp.877-885.

Millett, K.   1972   *Sexual Politics,* Sphere Books Ltd., London.

Mitchell, J.   1971   *Woman's Estate,* Penguin Books, Harmondsworth.

Nelson, N.   1981   "Mobilizing Village Women: Some Organizational and Management Considerations", in N. Nelson (ed.), *African Women . . .,* pp.47-58.

Okonjo, K.   1980   "The Role of Igbo Women in Rural Economy in Bendel State of Nigeria", in F.I.A. Omu et al, *Proceedings . . .,* Vol.II, pp.1017-1034.

Pala, A.O.   1976   "African Women in Rural Development: Research Trends and Priorities", OLC Paper No.12, American Council on Education, Washington, DC.

Pittin, R.   forth- "Documentation of Women's Work in Nigeria: coming Problems and Solutions", in C. Oppong (ed.), *Sex Roles in West African Households,* ILO, Geneva.

Raza, M.R. &   1980   "Integrated Rural Development as a Framework for Famoriyo, S.   Women's Participation in Development", in F.I.A. Omu et al, *Proceedings . . .,* Vol.II, pp.933-949.

Rowbotham, S.   1974   *Women, Resistance and Revolution,* Vintage Books, NY.

Sidel, R.   1973   *Women and Child Care in China,* Penguin Books Inc., Baltimore, Md.

On Combating Women's Exploitation and Oppression in Nigeria

A.R. Mustapha

To say that women suffer an extra oppression and exploitation, as women, in Nigeria today, is to state the obvious. An illustration will suffice. The poverty, misery and squalor of our rural life is well-known. However, against this depressing background the womenfolk in the rural areas suffer additional subjugation. In some parts of rural Nigeria, it is common to see women doing back-breaking work on the farms, while their husbands, who are ostensibly out "hunting", spend their time in *burukutu* bars. In point of fact, these rural women are almost slaves to their husbands, for they not only farm their individual plots, but also collectively farm their husband's farm. And on their individual "days" with their husband, they not only warm his bed, but also cook for him from the proceeds of their own farms! Furthermore, these women invariably have almost exclusive responsibility for housekeeping and childcare.

So in a dependent capitalist society such as Nigeria, where exploitation, political oppression, want and misery are the order of the day for the ordinary people, the bulk of our womenfolk carry the additional burden of being subjugated as women — i.e. the oppressed even amongst the oppressed. As I see it, this subjugation of women expresses itself in a number of specific dimensions. These are mainly the ideological and the economic as well as through the application of force, physical or psychological. However, it should be stressed from the onset that all these dimensions are actually closely related in real life.

Every ruling class maintains its control over society through military force, ideological manipulation or a combination of both, depending on the specific circumstances. In relation to women, the ideological offensive is particularly intense, deep-rooted and effective. To be a "lady", or better still a "respectable lady", there are prescribed modes of dressing, speech, walking, eating, etc. which the woman in question must conform to. It needs to be pointed out that the yardstick for arriving at these prescribed models are often hypocritical and without regard to the comfort, interests, or even wishes of the "ladies" in question. Furthermore, it is a common practice to hear lengthy sermons dealing with the fact that the gates of heaven are only open to obedient daughters and faithful wives etc. The sum effect of this ideological barrage which is often moralist — in the sense that it prescribes modes of behaviour, without taking into account the objective conditions — is to control the lives of most women, be it in the personal or social spheres. Additionally, most women, especially girls, are brainwashed into seeing society basically through the prism of ruling class values and views on women. So it is not too difficult to hear women saying such things as: "you know how childish, kindhearted, etc., we women can be sometimes."

Once this stereotype of the woman is established and enforced, it then serves as a tool for the perpetuation of exploitation and oppression of not only women, but often the whole of society. For example, it is on record that "Governor Aku (of Benue State) frowned at the exotic taste of some women which, he said, was responsible for the high crime rate and smuggling in the country".[1] While it is true that some cultural trends amongst our womenfolk need to be condemned, the truth is that cultural and moral bankruptcy is not the sole preserve of women. What of our politicians and our contractors? Furthermore, the naiveté apparent in ascribing the criminality in our society to the "exotic tastes" of "some women" is so glaring that it needs no further comment. Through this idological manipulation, our women become willing victims of all sorts of chauvinist prejudices. Whether a girl is slim or a bit fat is no longer dictated by natural genetical and nutritional factors. The current "fad" is the determinant factor. And no costs are spared to be in the race. And the society which created these demented and pathetic women, can then turn round and use their "exotic tastes" as excuses for all sorts of crimes committed by others.

The impact of bourgeois ideology on women is not limited to their personal lives alone. It has ramifications also in their social and political perspectives.

Politics, agitation for democratic rigbhts, and other such public-spirited endeavours are classified for the "men's world", despite the fact that the Nigerian world is about 50% female. For example, it is common knowledge that the NPN zoning system for the 1979 Presidential elections conceded the Vice-Presidential position to the eastern states of the country. Well-known political heavyweights in the NPN, people like Dr K.O. Mbadiwe and Dr Joseph Wayas, fought tooth and nail for the position. As a result, it was impossible to choose any of the well-known candidates without risking a party split.

It is alleged that against the above background, Alhaji Shehu Shagari had chosen "an Ibo lady, a much respected educationalist, to join his ticket".[2] It is also alleged that the lady, "with great *common-sense* and *modesty* [emphasis mine], told him that a woman was no greater an electoral asset in her part of Nigerian than in his . . ."[3]

If the above incident did take place, then we can safely conclude that not only does the lady "know her place", she is also not sparing any efforts to behave strictly as expected. However, given the nature of bourgeois politics in Nigeria today, she would have to wait till hell turns to heaven before she becomes an "electoral asset". Yet the Constitution says we are all equal regardless of sex!

Many women have been conditioned to accept and even propagate such "devalued" estimations of themselves. Where some women refuse to be subjected to this type of stereotyping and manipulation, they become subjected to psychological and physical force. Some religions specifically permit the caning of daughters and wives! Furthermore, forced sexual intercourse, within wedlock, is not defined as rape, while some outright rape cases are blamed on the raped, who is guilty of "unwarranted provocation" either because of her dress, or some other personal thing!

The last dimension of the subjugation of women I listed is the economic. The pathetic position of the rural womenfolk has been mentioned earlier. But the female worker in the urban centre has not escaped from this type of subjugation. The "ordinary" female worker, basically ill-educated, bogged down in family problems and of peasant background, often finds jobs in labour-intensive factories, mostly making sweets, textiles etc. These women invariably have no written conditions of service since they are daily-paid. This means no health care, no pensions, loss of jobs during pregnancy, and a wage below that paid to her exploited male colleague. Some of these "ordinary" women, who do not find work in factories, can be seen sometimes with babies strapped to their backs, carrying cement blocks at building sites for 10 hours a day for a wage of between N2.00 and N3.00!

The "elite" female worker has not escaped the "curse" of womanhood. These women, basically educated — a healthy fraction with university degrees, with a secure job and mainly of a petty-bourgeois perspective — find themselves victims of ". . . a discriminatory attitude that is most repugnant to civilization and human conscience".[4] They complain, and quite correctly too, that despite the fact that the qualification requirements for posts in the Civil Service and private firms are the same for men and women without distinction; and despite the fact that "no circular has ever exempted the female worker from paying any revenue to the employer because she is a weakling",[5] they are victims of blatant and shocking discrimination when it comes to issues of remunerations and fringe benefits to which they are entitled. Another woman complained that "a woman's success in life is judged by her success at home and not by her accomplishments and achievements outside the home".[6]

Causes of Women's Subjugation

How do we explain the exploitation and oppression of women in Nigeria? This question is of crucial importance in combating the evil of women's subjugation. Many answers have been posited over the years. Some scholars tell us that women are biologically weaker than men, and therein lies the reason for their subjugation. This is the theory of the "weaker sex". Some other scholars have posited religious explanations. Copious quotations from all sorts of religious books are cited to prove that after all is said and done, a woman is nothing but a man's extra and disposable rib-bone. The above points of view are not only unscientific and mythical, they are clearly designed to justify the oppression of womenfolk.

Based on available anthropological and historical evidence,[7] it is my firm conviction that women are exploited and oppressed in society because of the way the resources of that society are produced, controlled and distributed. That is to say that, historically speaking, we can broadly conclude that the *need* to subjugate women arose with the need to maintain the institution of private property. However, it should be noted that the institution of private property has taken various differing specific forms over the ages. Each historically determined and specific form of ownership and type of private property also brings into being its own specific form of the subjugation of women. For example, under feudalism, women are subjected to the humiliations of the "right of the first night", while under capitalism, they are either forced into prostitution, or are subjected to the most brutal exploitation or the most glaring discrimination.[8] It is thus my considered opinion that the woes of womanhood in Nigerian today are largely a direct consequence of the dependent capitalist system which we operate.[9]

Combating Women's Exploitation and Oppression

What have women done to combat their subjugation in Nigeria? Regrettably, not much. A great percentage of our women, due to their lack of education, poverty and acute want, find solace in either religious teachings, or in their children. The more educated and articulate woman does not fight the injustice done her through discrimination, neither does she reach out to claim her rights. Instead she conforms, bemoans her fate and waits for someone else to do her battle for her".[10] This apathy on the part of our women is clearly tied to objective factors of their subjugation, for as Lenin pointed out, "in all countries women have been the slowest to stir".[11] But while the low level of organization of women for their rights is quite understandable, we cannot allow it to persist or the interest of women and of society as a whole will be jeopardizd. It is thus necessary for women to fight for their rights. Moaning about it, or waiting for society to mend its evil ways, are tantamount to waiting for manna from heaven. They are basically ways of conforming to subjugation.

From my personal experience as counsellor to sisters and female friends, and my general understanding of the dynamics of our society, I tend to imagine that there are a number of ways open to our womenfolk. Many women, *as individuals,* fear to fight for their rights. It is either that they pay far too much attention to what society expects of them, or they are unwilling or unable to pay the price of defying society's prejudiced values and asserting their rights as women and as persons. The point must be made, however, that all personal and social freedoms in history have had to be fought for. Past generations have paid dearly for quite a number of rights which we take for granted today. If the democratic and personal rights of our womenfolk are to be advanced, and those few they now have protected from erosion, then they must show a willingness to fight and sacrifice. They could also intensify efforts to study the conditions of the ordinary women in our society, and the dynamics of the society as a whole.

However, the personal dimension to combating women's oppression is of limited effect. The more effective approach is that of an organization of women to fight for their democratic rights and to defend individual women from abuse. Such an organization will have the duty of educating and mobilizing women. It will also have the task of bringing more women into the social and political life of the country, and through this process help to build the foundations of a democratic culture. The type of organization which I have in mind is a patriotic one, alive to its responsibilities to the masses of this country. I do not know very much about the National Council of Women's Societies, but I have serious doubts about the ability of the NCWS to undertake the arduous task of liberating Nigerian womahood.

For example, while the recently announced austerity measures by the Federal Government are fuelling inflation, with sharp increases in what the mass of our womenfolk have to pay for virtually everything, the patron of the NCWS is calling on our womenfolk "to demonstrate their solidarity with the government . . . by supporting all the regulations and measures adopted by the government . . .".[12] Our womenfolk are also called upon, in these trying economic times, to ". . . do something about the filthy conditions of our cities".[13] It would appear as if the NCWS is interested more in uncritically supporting the powers that be than in articulating and promoting the interests of Nigerian women. In the final analysis, only women, organized for the fight for their democratic right, can effectively contribute to combating the exploitation and oppression of women. They can best do this in alliance with other democratic forces in society.

Notes

1. *National Concord,* 24 May 1982, p.21.
2. From David Williams book on President Shagari, excerpts of which were published in the *New Nigerian,* 20 May 1982, p.3.
3. Williams.

4. Association of Female Civil Servants, in *Africa Woman*, No.38, March/April 1982, p.20.

5. *African Woman.*

6. Mrs F.Y. Emmanuel, Permanent Secretary, Federal Ministrry of Health, Ibid.

7. Engels' *The Origin of the Family, Private Property, and the State; Condition of the Working Class in England in 1844*, and Marx's *Capital*, Vol.I.

8. Some people argue that women are also oppressed by men under socialism. They thus try to refute the thesis that the subjugation of women is tied to the institution of private property. However, this is an erroneous view, based on a misconception of the problem of socialist construction.

There is no doubt that in destroying the institution of private property, socialism attacks the material foundations of women's subjugation. But commensurate developments on the ideological plane, espcially amongst the masses of the male population, often take time. Lenin pointed out that the task of ideological re-orientation was "far from easy", and the stiff opposition which the Family Code, which gave women extensive social and democratic rights, met in Cuba tends to illustrate Lenin's contention.

However, the fact still remains that it is only under socialism that women's rights can be fully achieved. A comparison of the relevant articles of the USSR Constitution of 1936, and the Nigerian Constitution of 1979 clearly shows the different approaches of the two systems: "Women in the USSR are accorded equal rights with men in all spheres of economic, state, cultural, social and political life." "The possibility of exercising these rights is ensured to women by granting them an equal right with men to work, payment for work, rest and leisure, social insurance, and education, by State protection of the interest of mother and child, by State aid to mothers of large families and unmarried mothers, pre-maternity and maternity leave with full pay, and the provision of a wide network of maternity homes, nurseries, and kindergartens". Article 122, Const. of the USSR, 1936.

"A citizen of Nigeria, of a particular community, ethnic group, place of origin, sex, religion or political opinion shall not by reason only that he is such a person (a) be subjected either expressly by or in the practical application of any law in force in Nigeria or any administrative or any executive action of the government to disabilities or restrictions to which citizens of Nigeria of other communities, ethnic groups, place of origin, sex, religion or political opinion are not made subject . . ." Chapter IV, (Section 39), Sub-section 1a of the Constitution of Federal Republic of Nigeria, 1979.

9. There are also remnant aspects of patriarchal and feudal oppression. These are sometimes the decisive forms.

10. Mrs Emmanuel.

11. V.I. Lenin in "Women and Society", quoted in *The Woman Question*, International Publishers, New York, 1977, p.42.

12. Mrs Beatrice Ekwueme in *National Concord*, 24 May 1982, p.21.

13. Ekwueme.

Rapporteur's Report:

Jibo Ibrahim

Two papers were presented in this concluding session. One was by R. Pittin, on "Organizing for the Future", and the other on "Combating Women's Exploitation and Oppression in Nigeria", by A.R. Mustapha. The papers set the tone for the session by stressing the necessity for practical suggestions to fight for the emancipation of women in Nigeria.

The major suggestion that arose was the necessity for the formation of an organization to engage in research, policy-making, and action aimed at improving the conditions of women. The session resolved that existing women's organizations such as the National Council of Women's Societies are not adequately committed to fighting the cause of the majority of Nigerian women. As a result of the enthusiastic mood of the session, there and then it was resolved to form the said organization, and a steering committee was formed to work towards its takeoff.

Other suggestions were made on how the struggle for the emancipation of women could be pursued. These included the organization of small groups of women to sharpen their consciousness. Another means of combating oppression is through the use of media, literature, and other forms of communication to fight sexual stereotypes. The point is to highlight the capacities of women, expose stereotypes, and present alternative conceptions of humankind to society. Other suggestions proposed include exposing the oppression of women which is effected through the use of religion.

Finally, the session highlighted the importance of the sensitization and politicization of women into realizing that their exploitation and oppression has a political objective and can, in the last instance, only be resolved politically.

Notes on Contributors

Rachael Agheyisi is a labour economist in the Department of Economics, ABU. She is presently working for her Ph.D. abroad.

Mary Alfa is a graduate of the Department of Sociology, ABU. She is presently carrying out her National Youth Service.

Mairo Alti-Muazu is an employee of the Kaduna State Ministry of Education, currently on in-service training. She is working for an M.Sc. in Sociology, and is doing research on the training of traditional birth attendants in Nigeria. She is an addict where reading novels is concerned. She is married with three children.

Bukola Aluko is now in the National Youth Service Corps, after graduating from the Department of Sociology, ABU.

Sule Bello lectures in the Department of History, ABU. He has just finished his Ph.D. thesis on the colonial economy of Kano in the twentieth century. His hobbies are playing chess and debating.

Arlene Enabulele is a research fellow with the Centre for Social, Cultural, and Environmental Research at the University of Benin. She is currently completing work on an exploratory study of Child Rearing Practices Among Working Mothers in Rural and Urban Areas, Bendel State. She is married and the mother of two children.

John Haynes was born in England, but has been working with ABU Zaria since 1970, and is at present Acting Head of the Department of English. He has published a volume of poems, *Sabon Gari* (London, 1974), and a number of poems shortly to be collected in a second volume have appeared in periodicals in Europe and Africa. He is now preparing a volume of essays on the relation of style and meaning in modern African poetry. He is an editor of the journal *Saiwa*. He is married to a Nigerian, and has a son by a former marriage.

Ayesha Mei-Tje Imam works in the Department of Sociology, ABU. She is currently doing research on women and the mass media and national development for an M.Sc. She was the co-ordinator of the seminar on "Women in Nigeria". She is also a member of the Nigerian Association of Media Women, and Deputy Editor of the *New Dimension* newspaper. She likes playing badminton and scrabble and reading.

Ifeyinwa Iweriebor now works as the Public Relations Officer for ARMTI, after being a Senior Staff feature writer for the News Agency of Nigeria. She has two children and is married. She is also the President of the Kwara State Chapter of the Nigerian Association of Media Women.

Caroline Knowles teaches in the Department of Anthropology and Sociology at the University of Maiduguri. She is doing research on the impact of irrigation projects in Borno State.

Bene Madunagu is a biologist, specializing in physiopathology and mushroom science, working in the Department of Biological Sciences, University of Calabar. She is also the Secretary of the Academic Staff Union of Universities, Calabar Chapter. She and her husband Edwin are radical political activists in Nigeria.

Edwin Madunagu is a mathematician who works at the University of Calabar. His third book, *Problems of Socialism: Nigerian Challenge* has recently been published by Zed Press. Both he and Bene were dismissed from their university teaching jobs as a result of the Mohammed Commission of Inquiry into the 1978 crisis in the universities, but were reinstated in 1980 after successful strike action by the Academic Staff Union of Universities.

Halima Mohammed is a third-year student in the Department of History, ABU. Her hobbies are reading and playing hockey. She is a member of the Steering Committee of "Women in Nigeria".

Abdul Rauf Mustapha is a member of the Department of Political Science, ABU. He is researching the nature of capital formation in Kano. He has been, for two years, the branch secretary of the Academic Staff Union of Universities at ABU. He is also part of a research team on Women and Industry in Kano.

Therese Nweke is a member of the editorial staff at the News Agency of Nigeria, and is Nigeria's representative in the Women's News International. She has three children.

Elizabeth Obadina is a columnist with the *Punch* newspaper, and the acting editor of *Happy Home* magazine as well. She has worked as a geologist, and also as a teacher. She has two children.

'Molara Ogundipe-Leslie is a senior lecturer in the Department of English at University of Ibadan, and a Marxist literary critic. A volume of her poems, *Sew the Old Days and Other Poems* has been published by Evans Bros. She has been active in women's organizations, and has been writing and lecturing on women since the mid-sixties. She is a founding member of the Association of African Women for Research and Development. Her hobbies are jogging, cycling, swimming, dancing, gardening and listening to music. She has two daughters.

Norma Perchonock has been lecturing in the Department of Sociology, ABU, since 1970. She has carried out research on urbanism in Jos and Kano. She enjoys reading, cooking, and gardening.

Renée Pittin is a member of the Department of Sociology, ABU, where she established and teaches the first course on women in Nigerian universities. She is presently engaged in research on women and work in Nigeria, and on women's organizations in Kaduna State. Her hobbies are reading and astronomy.

Hauwa Sani Dangogo is a senior editor with the Federal Radio Corporation of Nigeria, Kaduna. She likes reading novels, singing, and discussing topics like politics, health and family affairs. She has three children.

Gloria Thomas Emeagwali is a Trinidadian national who has been lecturing in the Department of History, ABU, for the past three years. She is a graduate of the University of the West Indies, and Toronto University. She has published papers on Nigerian historiography, and is currently engaged in further research in that area.

Bilkisu Yusuf is a journalist. She studied political science at Ahmadu Bello University, Zaria, and at the University of Wisconsin, USA. After graduation, she worked at the Ministry of Information, Kano, as a feature writer, and briefly at the Kano State Broadcasting Corporation as a producer. She was then posted to the editorial department of the Triumph Publishing Co., Kano. Bilkisu is interested in international relations with special emphasis on developing countries. Her other hobbies include reading and travelling. She has two children.

Alfred B. Zack-Williams is a lecturer in Sociology at the University of Jos. A student of underdevelopment in West Africa, he is the author of numerous articles and reviews on Third World underdevelopment. He has carried out research on "Underdevelopment and Economic Planning in West Africa"; "Underdevelopment and the Diamond Industry in Sierra Leone" and is currently working on "The Urban Poor in Jos: the Case of the Garbage Pickers". He is married with children.

Index

AAWORD: development of class perspective in 121-2
Aba Riots *see* War of the Women
abortion: campaign in West 139; emphasis on rights of children and society 166-7; issue in Nigeria 33, 125-6
Action Group 213-14
Ahmadu Bello University: differential participation of women, by faculty 153; female student enrolment in 150-3
Akinrinade, Janet 139, 214
Amechi, Euna 238
Amina, Queen of Zazzau 45-6, 50, 53
Amon-Nikoi, Gloria 154
associations *see* organisations
Awe, Bolanwe 128-9
Ayoola, Adeola 130

Babatope, Abiola 214
barrenness *see* childlessness
bigamy 124
Borno: irrigation project in 68, 71-80; women in aristocracy in 45-6, 78-9
Brutus, Dennis 223-4

capitalism: in contemporary Nigeria 132-3; and rural development 72-4; and oppression of women *see* oppression of women; *see also* economy; employment; labour, domestic; labour, market
Chabaud, Jacqueline 154
chauvinism, male 141
childbirth: Hausa genital cutting 6, 180, 195; Hausa medicines to ease delivery 178; Hausa practices 178-86; home delivery 179, 196; influence of Islam on 179; need for educational campaign 186; objections to home delivery 196;

objections to hospital delivery 179; post-natal practices among the Hausa 180-3; treatment of new-born children among the Hausa 183-5
childlessness, stigma of 125
children: male ownership of 176-7, 195; recognition of paternity of 176; treatment of new-born among Hausa 183-5
circumcision, female 126, 158
class: basis of differentiation of women 123; interrelation with race 121; and neglect of women 56; oppression and land alienation 88-99; oppression interrelated with gender oppression 1, 4-5, 7-8, 15, 20-1, 24, 28-9, 33, 69, 79, 82, 90, 100-2, 114-15, 132, 136-7, 157-8, 210, 226, 231; perspective in AAWORD 121-2; in relation to gender 32; relations in construction industry 111; relations in contemporary Nigeria 133; relations in First Republic 89; relations in Sokoto Caliphate 86; as sole basis of women's oppression 3-4, 5, 15, 19-20, 24-7; women as separate class 19; *see also* ruling class; women, ruling class; working class
colonial period in Nigeria: control of land during 88-9; erosion of women's economic opportunity 122; feudal relations in 88-9; and oppression of women 19; political participation of women during 49-50, 213; production during 88; and rural development 71-2
consciousness-raising: in China 231-2, 234; importance of 232, 247; and nature of oppression 232; role of academics in 232, 247
Constitution: Nigerian 226, 246; Russian 246

THIRD WORLD WOMEN TITLES FROM ZED

Bobby Siu
WOMEN OF CHINA:
Imperialism and Women's
Resistance, 1900-1949
Hb and Pb

Ingela Bendt and James Downing
WE SHALL RETURN:
Women of Palestine
Hb and Pb

Miranda Davies (editor)
THIRD WORLD — SECOND
SEX:
Women's Struggles and National
Liberation
Hb and Pb

Juliette Minces
THE HOUSE OF OBEDIENCE:
Women in Arab Society
Hb and Pb

Margaret Randall
SANDINO'S DAUGHTERS:
Testimonies of Nicaraguan Women
in Struggle
Pb

Maria Mies
THE LACEMAKERS OF
NARSAPUR:
Indian Housewives Produce for the
World Market
Pb

Asma el Dareer
WOMAN, WHY DO YOU WEEP?
Circumcision and Its Consequences
Hb and Pb

Raqiya Haji Dualeh Abdalla
SISTERS IN AFFLICTION:
Circumcision and Infibulation of
Women in Africa
Hb and Pb

Maria Rose Cutrufelli
WOMEN OF AFRICA:
Roots of Oppression
Hb and Pb

Atar Tabari and Nahid Yeganeh
IN THE SHADOW OF ISLAM:
The Women's Movement in Iran
Hb and Pb

Bonnie Mass
POPULATION TARGET:
The Political Economy of
Population Control in Latin
America
Pb

Nawal el Saadawi
THE HIDDEN FACE OF EVE:
Women in the Arab World
Hb and Pb

Else Skjonsberg
A SPECIAL CASTE?
Tamil Women in Sri Lanka
Pb

Patricia Jeffrey
FROGS IN A WELL:
Indian Women in Purdah
Hb and Pb

June Nash and Helen Icken Safa
(editors)
SEX AND CLASS IN LATIN
AMERICA:
Women's Perspectives on Politics,
Economics and the Family in the
Third World
Pb

Latin American and Caribbean
Women's Collective
SLAVES OF SLAVES:
The Challenge of Latin American
Women
Hb and Pb

Christine Obbo
AFRICAN WOMEN:
Their Struggle for Economic
Independence
Pb

Gail Omvedt
WE WILL SMASH THIS
PRISON!
Indian Women in Struggle
Hb and Pb

Agnes Smedley
PORTRAITS OF CHINESE
WOMEN IN REVOLUTION
Pb

Raymonda Tawil
MY HOME, MY PRISON
Pb

Nawal el Saadawi
WOMAN AT ZERO POINT
Hb and Pb

Elisabeth Croll
CHINESE WOMEN
Hb and Pb

M. Thomson and N. Wintour
WOMEN OF EL SALVADOR
Hb and Pb

Jenefer Sebstad
WOMEN AND SELF-RELIANCE IN
INDIA:
The Sewa Story
Hb and Pb

J. Liddle and B. Joshi
DAUGHTERS OF
INDEPENDENCE
Gender, Caste and Class in India

Arlene Eisen
WOMEN AND REVOLUTION IN
VIETNAM
Hb and Pb

Mi Mi Khaing
THE WORLD OF BURMESE
WOMEN
Hb and Pb

ANGOLAN WOMEN BUILDING
THE FUTURE
From National Liberation to
Women's Emancipation
Hb and Pb

Madhu Kishwar and Ruth Vanita
(editors)
IN SEARCH OF ANSWERS
Indian Women's Voices
Hb and Pb

Kumari Jayawardena
FEMINISM AND NATIONALISM
IN THE THIRD WORLD
Hb and Pb

Nawal el Saadawi
GOD DIES BY THE NILE
Hb and Pb

WOMEN IN NIGERIA TODAY
Hb and Pb

Maria Mies
PATRIARCHY AND
ACCUMULATION ON A WORLD
SCALE
Hb and Pb

AFRICA TITLES FROM ZED

Dan Nabudere
IMPERIALISM IN EAST AFRICA
Vol. I: Imperialism and Exploitation
Vol. II: Imperialism and Integration
Hb

Elenga M'Buyinga
PAN AFRICANISM OR NEO
COLONIALISM?
The Bankruptcy of the OAU
Hb and Pb

Bade Onimode
IMPERIALISM AND
UNDERDEVELOPMENT IN
NIGERIA
The Dialectics of Mass Poverty
Hb and Pb'

Michael Wolfers and Jane Bergerol
ANGOLA IN THE FRONTLINE
Hb and Pb

Mohamed Babu
AFRICAN SOCIALISM OR
SOCIALIST AFRICA?
Hb and Pb

Anonymous
INDEPENDENT KENYA
Hb and Pb

Yolamu Barongo (Editor)
POLITICAL SCIENCE IN AFRICA:
A RADICAL CRITIQUE
Hb and Pb

Okwudiba Nnoli (Editor)
PATH TO NIGERIAN
DEVELOPMENT
Pb

Emile Vercruijsse
THE PENETRATION OF
CAPITALISM
A West African Case Study
Hb

Fatima Babikir Mahmoud
THE SUDANESE BOURGEOISIE
— Vanguard of Development?
Hb and Pb

No Sizwe
ONE AZANIA, ONE NATION
The National Question in South
Africa
Hb and Pb

Ben Turok (Editor)
DEVELOPMENT IN ZAMBIA
A Reader
Pb

J. F Rweyemamu (Editor)
INDUSTRIALIZATION AND
INCOME DISTRIBUTION IN
AFRICA
Hb and Pb

Claude Ake
REVOLUTIONARY PRESSURES
IN AFRICA
Hb and Pb

Anne Seidman and Neva Makgetla
OUTPOSTS OF MONOPOLY
CAPITALISM
Southern Africa in the Changing
Global Economy
Hb and Pb

Peter Rigby
PERSISTENT PASTORALISTS
Nomadic Societies in Transition
Hb and Pb

Edwin Madunagu
PROBLEMS OF SOCIALISM: THE
NIGERIAN CHALLENGE
Pb

Mai Palmberg
THE STRUGGLE FOR AFRICA
Hb and Pb

Chris Searle
WE'RE BUILDING THE NEW SCHOOL!
Diary of a Teacher in Mozambique
Hb (at Pb price)

Cedric Robinson
BLACK MARXISM
The Making of the Black Radical Tradition
Hb and Pb

Eduardo Mondlane
THE STRUGGLE FOR MOZAMBIQUE
Pb

Basil Davidson
NO FIST IS BIG ENOUGH TO HIDE THE SKY
The Liberation of Guinea Bissau and Cape Verde:
Aspects of the African Revolution
Hb and Pb

Baruch Hirson
YEAR OF FIRE, YEAR OF ASH
The Soweto Revolt: Roots of a Revolution?
Hb and Pb

SWAPO Department of Information and Publicity
TO BE BORN A NATION
The Liberation Struggle for Namibia
Pb

Peder Gouwenius
POWER OF THE PEOPLE
South Africa in Struggle: A Pictorial History
Pb

Gillian Walt and Angela Melamed (Editors)
MOZAMBIQUE: TOWARDS A PEOPLE'S HEALTH SERVICE
Pb

Horst Drechsler
LET US DIE FIGHTING
The Struggle of the Herero and Nama Against German Imperialism (1884-1915)
Hb and Pb

Andre Astrow
ZIMBABWE: A REVOLUTION THAT LOST ITS WAY?
Hb and Pb

Rene Lefort
ETHIOPIA: AN HERETICAL REVOLUTION?
Hb and Pb

Robert H. Davies, Dan O'Meara and Sipho Dlamini
THE STRUGGLE FOR SOUTH AFRICA
A Reference Guide to Movements, Organizations and Institutions
Hb and Pb

Joseph Hanlon
MOZAMBIQUE: THE REVOLUTION UNDER FIRE
Hb and Pb

Henry Isaacs
LIBERATION MOVEMENTS IN CRISIS
The PAC of South Africa
Hb and Pb

Toyin Falola and Julius Ihonvbere
THE RISE AND FALL OF NIGERIA'S SECOND REPUBLIC, 1979-83
Hb and Pb

Dianne Bolton
NATIONALIZATION: A ROAD TO SOCIALISM?
The Case of Tanzania
Pb

Zed Books' titles cover Africa, Asia, Latin America and the Middle East, as well as general issues affecting the Third World's relations with the rest of the world. Our Series embrace: Imperialism, Women, Political Economy, History, Labour, Voices of Struggle, Human Rights and other areas pertinent to the Third World.

You can order Zed titles direct from Zed Books Ltd., 57 Caledonian Road, London N1 9BU, UK.